I0323287

Olive Growing in Palestine

SERIES EDITORS

David L. Brunsma

David G. Embrick

SERIES ADVISORY BOARD

Margaret Abraham

Elijah Anderson

Eduardo Bonilla-Silva

Philomena Essed

James Fenelon

Evelyn Nakano Glenn

Tanya Golash-Boza

David Theo Goldberg

Patricia Hill Collins

José Itzigsohn

Amanda Lewis

Michael Omi

Victor Rios

Mary Romero

Olive Growing in Palestine

Stories of Everyday Forms
of Resistance

Juman Simaan

The University of Georgia Press
ATHENS

Sociology of Race and
Ethnicity web page

© 2026 by the University of Georgia Press
Athens, Georgia 30602
www.ugapress.org
All rights reserved
Set in by 10.5/13.5 Garamond Premier Pro Regular

Use of any part of this book in training for any artificial
intelligence (AI), large language model (LLM), machine learning
technologies, or similar generative language system without license
is expressly prohibited.

Printed digitally

EU Authorized Representative
Easy Access System Europe—Mustamäe tee 50, 10621 Tallinn,
Estonia, gpsr.requests@easproject.com

Library of Congress Cataloging-in-Publication Data
Names: Simaan, Juman, 1977– author
Title: Olive growing in Palestine : stories of everyday forms of
    resistance / Juman Simaan.
Other titles: Sociology of race and ethnicity
Description: Athens : The University of Georgia Press, [2026] |
    Series: Sociology of race and ethnicity | Includes bibliographical
    references and index.
Identifiers: LCCN 2025023507 | ISBN 9780820374864 hardback |
    ISBN 9780820374871 paperback | ISBN 9780820374888 epub |
    ISBN 9780820374895 pdf
Subjects: LCSH: Farmers—West Bank—Social conditions |
    Olive—West Bank | Palestinian Arabs—Agriculture—West
    Bank | Palestinian Arabs—West Bank—Social conditions |
    Settler colonialism—West Bank | Arab-Israeli conflict—1993–
Classification: LCC HD8039.F32 W477 2026 | DDC 338.1095694—
    dc23/eng/20250801
LC record available at https://lccn.loc.gov/2025023507

The image on the cover is the painting *Lunch Break* (2016) by Ayed Arafah.
Based on a family photograph of the artist who lives in the refugee camp Dheisha near Bethlehem. Ayed's
family were forced to leave their village and land in the Nakba of 1948, but continued to be attached to
land, trees and nature. During the olive harvest season, landless families glean surplus olives from other
families' groves. Groves and plots of land were commonly owned by all villagers before the privatisation of
land during the Ottoman Empire in 1858.

To Yousef Sager and all the fallahin guarding the land

CONTENTS

LIST OF ILLUSTRATIONS IX

Prologue: Honey of Resistances 1

CHAPTER 1. Studying Olive Growing in Palestine as an Everyday Form of Resistance 5

CHAPTER 2. Olive Growing for *Sutra* سترة 35

CHAPTER 3. Olive Growing for *'Awna* عونة 60

CHAPTER 4. Olive Growing for *Sumud* صمود 91

CHAPTER 5. Everyday Forms of Resistance مقاومة يومية 123

Conclusion 134

Postscript: Ongoing Daily Resistance 143

ACKNOWLEDGMENTS 147

NOTES 149

BIBLIOGRAPHY 153

INDEX 163

ILLUSTRATIONS

Painting by Ayed Arafah   x

The Israeli separation wall and an Israeli-only highway divides Palestinian communties from their groves   4

A map of the West Bank   10

An Israeli settlement encroaching on Palestinian olive groves   33

A gate blocking an entrance to a Palestinian community   59

Ancient olive terraces in the West Bank of Palestine   90

A site of an uprooted olive grove   122

Painting by Ayed Arafah.

Olive Growing in Palestine

PROLOGUE

Honey of Resistances

It is an unusually hot day for October and the car thermometer shows the temperature to be 35 degrees Celsius outside. It will vary from 35 to 38 during the journey from my hometown of An-Nasserah (Nazareth) southward to Beit Lahem (Bethlehem), where I plan to stay for the next four weeks for my first information-gathering trip. According to the New Testament this was a journey made more than two thousand years ago by Joseph and heavily pregnant Mary, taking three days. Today it takes less than three hours by car. It would take me even less if I had decided to take the coastal route or the newly constructed six-lane highway that crosses historical Palestine, swallowing big chunks of nature and cutting Palestinian Arab towns through the middle. I prefer this old and narrow road and its views through the Jordan Valley. Early in my journey before reaching the West Bank, the roads had been busy with day-trippers returning from a day out in nature, and a few hikers were on the edges of the road. It's *Sokot*, the Jewish holiday when people go out for picnics. The skies are busy with cranes and other migrating birds making their way from the northern hemisphere to the south to spend the winter.

I drive through the first checkpoint with no problems. The Fako'a hills are to my right, the Jordanian part of the valley to my left. I notice barbed wire and single-track patrol roads, and signs warning of mines and the dangers of trespassing, along the borders between the Jordanian and the Israeli controlled parts of the valley. As I drive southward the view changes to rocky canyons dotted with dry vegetation. I drive past an Israeli settlement with modern agricultural structures and equipment, next to small Palestinian villages with one-story houses and fields with narrow plastic polytunnels. Families are picking vegetables with their hands, and shepherds are herding their sheep and goats on their donkeys. An hour or so later I approach a sign that reads "Jericho, the oldest city on earth, situated more than 300 metres below sea level." I pass near the border crossing between the West Bank and Jordan on my left, then turn right to begin a more than one-thousand-meter ascent to Al-Quds (the Palestinian name for Jerusalem). To the east is the way leading to the Dead Sea. Driving up toward Al-Quds I see on both sides of the road Bedouin settlements consisting of tin structures and goatskin tents, surrounded with some vegetation. I can already see church towers on top of the hills ahead of me, and the large Israeli colony of Ma'ale Adumim on the lower hills. On my right I drive past a field of what seems to me to be the trunks of felled olive trees.

I take a wrong turn, as I would normally go through the city center and pass the walls of the old city toward Beit Lahem, but this time I go to what the sign calls "south Ma'ale Adumim." I enter an Arab suburb of Al-Quds, and the first thing I see is a junk market on both sides of the road. I drive through crowded streets with many cars parked on both sides of the streets. Houses and other buildings are in close proximity to each other. I look for signs directing me to Beit Lahem, but I can't find any. I ask pedestrians and shopkeepers, and they give me directions to the next checkpoint leading out of Al-Quds to the West Bank. I drive alongside the separation wall, a several-meters-high concrete barrier with anti-occupation slogans, peace messages, and other graffiti painted on it. I reach the checkpoint and pass it with no questions from the three soldiers who are sitting and chatting outside of the checkpoint post to my right, machine guns laid on their laps. I begin a steep ascent through Wadi Alnar (valley of fire), which I have heard was dangerously steep and narrow to drive through. Signs indicate that Beit Sahour is seven kilometers away, a few kilometers east of Manger Square, where I am meeting Moneer, who will be taking me to the apartment I am renting in the old city of Beit Lahem.

During my yearly visits to the region, I frequent a café in the old town of Beit Sahour, where I normally meet local and international activists living and working in the West Bank. It is a cold February afternoon, when I meet Jolene sitting at the bar. Jolene looks troubled. She had an accident in the rented car a few days ago, and needs to pay a heavy fine for the damage. A day before the accident she had been held for three hours with a Palestinian friend while they were taking photographs of the landscape near the apartheid barrier. Jolene is a young French artist who tells me she is sure she will be banned from entering the country again, as the soldiers had taken down all of her details. They had also joked in a macho way, asking if she had a date for Valentine's Day.

She wants to travel south of Al-Khalil (Hebron) to take a picture she plans to publish at the end of a book she is working on about the apartheid barrier. Her plan is to take a series of photographs of the landscape with the barrier in the

Prologue

background along its entire route from the north of the West Bank to the most southerly point. She invites me to travel with her.

We drive south of Beit Lahem onto Road 60, which connects the illegal Israeli colonies to occupied Al-Quds. It is starting to rain, and "Jana," the anticipated storm, is approaching from the north and west. Dark clouds and thick fog gather on top of the hills. From time to time the clouds break and allow a ray of sun and a hint of blue skies. The sun rays make the recently pruned vineyards and fruit trees look golden. The lush grass is splashed with yellow, purple, and white wildflowers. Almond trees are dressed in glorious pink and white blossom.

We eventually arrive at the top of a hill we think leads to the checkpoint we can see on the horizon, which is near the end of the part of the barrier Jolene wants to photograph. She parks the car at the side of the road near an entrance to a Bedouin encampment, and we walk in muddy, rugged terrain a few hundred meters, the icy wind in our faces. A dog barks at us, and from one of the three structures making up the encampment two women emerge. A man covered from head to toe in an *a 'baya*—a traditional Bedouin gown—follows the women and approaches us to ask what it is that we need. We tell him our purpose and ask him if there's a way to get to the barrier—which at this point of its route is made up of a patrol road with metal fencing—without having to pass near to the checkpoint and its watchtower. He tells us the only way to see the barrier is from where we are standing, so Jolene takes her photographs there, and the man invites us for tea.

We enter the structure, which is built from low stone walls and a tarpaulin roof, covered on the outside with black goatskin. Inside it is warm and cozy. Two wide-open eyes stare at me from the floor of the home where Nour—a one-year-old toddler—sits. Nour means "light of the prophets," 'Amer, her father, tells us. There are two single beds, and a stove in the middle of the small room, the floor is covered with rugs. 'Amer tells us they have been on this land for sixty years, and that their grazing grounds are shrinking because of the closed military zones the Israeli Army keeps extending. He tells us that the army destroys most of the structures the family tries to build.

We walk back to the car feeling pleased that we made it without facing any trouble from settlers or soldiers, as we know some of the most extremist colonies are situated on these ancient hills. Just before we reach the car, a hooded man asks us if we can give him a lift to his village near Al-Khalil. Salem is returning home early from a working day in construction on the other side of the barrier, which—not having a permit—he crosses every day through gaps, away from the eyes of the soldiers. He is returning home because of the coming snowstorm, and he wants to help his wife look after one of their daughters, who has just been through an operation.

The Israeli separation wall and an Israeli-only highway divide Palestinian communities from their groves. Photo taken by Ahmad Al-Bazz.

Salem has a beehive in the village, and he made one tonne of honey last year. He tells me proudly that his bees fly across the barrier to Israel to suck the nectar from the blossom there, an act of resistance by the bees in defiance of the barrier that doesn't allow humans to cross it unless they have a permit. Salem asks me what I do here, and tells me about a family he knows whose land "has been eaten away by the barrier"; they are now separated from their olive trees and unable to access their land.

After we drop Salem off, my thoughts keep turning back to the bees, returning with their nectar from across the barrier, from flowers planted by the occupiers, enjoying a freedom not possible for their human keepers, to make the honey of resistance to benefit the occupied. I regret not exchanging numbers with Salem so we can later take up his invitation to visit his house, meet his family, and taste his honey, but we are in a hurry to reach home before the weather worsens. I think of the other communities in Palestine whose everyday lives are worth highlighting, such as olive farmers, wage laborers, and Bedouins. I wonder perhaps if in the future I or others can tell the stories of these groups' forms of daily resistance, which I am seeing everywhere, even in the way of life of Salem's bees and the honey they make.

CHAPTER 1

Studying Olive Growing in Palestine as an Everyday Form of Resistance

> For the Palestinian, olive oil is the gift of the traveller, the comfort of the bride, the reward of the autumn, the boast of the storeroom and the wealth of the family across centuries.
>
> —Mourid Barghouti 2000, 58

These are the words of the Palestinian author Mourid Barghouti, which describe the multilayered meanings of olive growing and its main product (olive oil) for Palestinians. Olive growing is a key daily activity for hundreds of thousands of Palestinians. In addition to being a cornerstone for food sovereignty, growing olives has historical, social, political, and spiritual meanings for native communities in Palestine. This significance provided a motive for me to study the daily lives of olive growers, which this book is about.

In this chapter, I introduce myself, my positionality and motivations for carrying out this study that this book is about. I discuss olive growing as a daily activity in Palestine and contextualize this practice by sketching a brief history of Palestine and considering the concepts and practices of settler-colonialism and collective everyday forms of resistance. These introductions are followed by exploration of the terms "occupation," "health and well-being," and "occupational justice," after which the book's methodological and theoretical underpinnings are discussed. The book's motivations and questions will be explored, followed by an outline of the chapters to come. Finally, an overview of members of the participant families is provided.

I am a Palestinian citizen of Israel and the United Kingdom. My ancestors were fallahin (small-scale farmers) like most Palestinians were prior to the *Nakba* (catastrophe), when the majority of Palestinian communities were displaced to make way for the foundation of the state of Israel in 1948. After 1948 my grand-parents moved from their ancestral village of Tur'an to a An-Nasserah (Nazareth) and worked in menial jobs—a pattern of change that typified a process many Palestinians went through: the transition from being self-sufficient family-based workers of land to being landless laborers (Said 1999; Sayigh 1979). As someone whose ancestors came from the village but was raised in the town, and as a Pales-tinian living in Israel, I have always straddled what seem to be opposing world-views and identities: Palestinian versus Israeli; town versus village; and East, or Global South versus West, or Global North. This has brought with it some disad-vantages, but also some advantages. Some of the disadvantages I relate to being part of a Palestinian minority within what became a majority Jewish state that has systemically discriminated against Palestinians and segregated our communities. We were also restricted from knowing about our history and heritage in the edu-cation system. Even our language (Arabic) and place names have been colonized by modern Hebrew, which became the official language of the state of Israel. However, my liminal positionalities between what seem to be dichotomous worlds have allowed me to learn how to bridge between these worldviews in re-gard to the knowledge I acquired, and the way of life and praxis I have developed throughout my life so far.

In my early adulthood I migrated to the United Kingdom, where two things occurred: I struggled to conform to the individualized Western way of life, and I faced ethnicity-based discrimination on a microaggression level, directly and indirectly, and on a more systemic level. As I moved away from my country of birth, I became more interested in my roots and my Palestinian heritage and identity. Recently, as I established myself as an academic based in a Western higher education institution, I wished to use this privileged position to study my commu-nity and contribute to it in some way. I wished to go back to my peasant roots and learn what it must have been like for my ancestors to live this way of life. I also wanted to tell the world about a community in Palestine and their daily life to counter stereotypical and mistaken notions, and knowledge, about Palestine and Palestinians in Western media and academia. I wanted to show the world that learning about the daily lives of Palestinian communities can enrich a body of knowledge about social and political transformation of communities who are struggling for their sovereignty anywhere in the world, whether they are strug-gling for their land rights, food sovereignty, or for self-determination and their destiny as self-defined groups.

As part of my PhD study, I embedded myself with olive-growing families in the area of Beit Lahem (Bethlehem) in the occupied Palestinian territories (oPt), be-tween 2013 and 2018, to learn about their daily struggles, ways of life, and resistance.

Studying Olive Growing as Resistance

Since 2018, I have continued to travel to the region on a yearly basis to revisit the families I worked with, and to expand my research to study the daily lives of shepherding communities in the opt. *Olive Growing in Palestine: Stories of Everyday Forms of Resistance* is based on this study. It is a book about olive growing as daily resistance in Palestine, in the context of what Jasbir Puar (n.d.) calls Israel's "settler colonial occupation." The book highlights how olive growers resist "occupational apartheid," which refers to systemic segregation of communities—in this case based on their ethnicity—and restricting the essential daily activities they wish, or need, to participate in (Kronenberg and Pollard 2005). The book will describe and analyze how olive farmers resist this form of systemic ethnic-based oppression on practical and epistemological levels (through ways of knowing and producing knowledge and skills). Readers belonging to communities of activists, other marginalized communities, and social science scholars will witness olive farmers' lives, and will learn that despite the violence of systemic ethnic-based oppression, communities fight back in collective and historical ways that are adapted to the current interconnected world we live in; and that these ways not only combat settler-colonialism, but also neoliberal capitalism and the climate crisis.

I spent a long time worrying about whom I wish to speak to through this book: Are the readers going to be occupational therapists and occupational scientists (disciplines I am trained in) interested in Global South representations of daily lives and its links to health and well-being? Are they going to be other social and political scientists who are concerned with the social and political aspects of daily life under military occupation and settler-colonialism? Or, perhaps, am I wishing to write to activists who are seeking alternative, liberatory daily living and forms of mutual aid to construct more equal and just societies? I am also wishing to speak to other Global South and marginalized communities. Moreover, I am motivated to write for olive farmers, shepherds, and other Palestinians who, through reading this book, might see themselves and their daily lives in a new light. The aim, I concluded, is to speak to all these readers at once, but how do I manage this? How do I keep the conversational tone while maintaining the methodological rigor? How do I ensure the theoretical anchoring and keep academics and professionals interested without overwhelming the other readers with academic jargon? Only you, as the reader, will be able to judge how well I managed these conflicting aspirations.

The book will focus on four families who live in the southern hills of Palestine—the area between the city of Beit Lahem in the north and Al-Khalil (Hebron) in the south. During my visits to the families, lasting between two to four weeks each, I took part in their daily activities, such as harvesting, planting, and having meals and went on trips with them to the oil presses and to visit family and friends. I engaged in unstructured conversations with members of the families, and conducted semistructured and in-depth interviews. I kept detailed field notes and recorded my reflections on how I reacted to what I observed. The motivation to carry out such a study and write this book originated from my own family history and personal experiences detailed above. Moreover, my positionality in relation to the families of olive growers has played an important role in the process of the study and the writing of this book.

Writing Myself into This Book

As a Palestinian with Israeli citizenship, I had access to Israeli higher education and studied occupational therapy in an Israeli university. I wished to become an occupational therapist because I wanted to support people in my own community to do the things they want, or need to do, which have been restricted due to a medical condition or a disability, or factors in their environment. However, what I studied in the textbooks, in the classroom, and in practical placements was often not relevant to me or to my community. I studied in Hebrew and read books in English that were predominantly written by North American scholars and practitioners. The focus of the theories and models of practice was on the individual and their body structures and functions, and the aim was to help them become independent. When I graduated and worked with children and young people in the north of historic Palestine, I felt that the theories, models of practice, and methods and tools of assessment and interventions did not speak to the communal needs of the people I was supposed to support—people whose daily activities and health and well-being were affected by sociopolitical, historical, and spiritual factors. This dilemma persevered when I later moved to the United Kingdom and worked with adults, and children and their families. I didn't feel that what I was taught in the occupational therapy books equipped me to meet people's needs to do the things they want to do to give them purpose, meaning, and well-being. I felt that surely there should be other ways and means to enable individuals and communities to take part in their daily lives despite the barriers they experience in their bodies but also in their environment, which includes the sociopolitical, human, and more-than-human surroundings.

I felt that communities and scholars from the Global South could offer insights as to how to enable a better understanding of people's meaningful daily actions; why they do what they do, and how they respond to adversities—insights that might challenge and compliment Global North understandings. As a Palestinian who lived in Israel, and later in the United Kingdom, and who speaks Arabic, Hebrew, and English, I felt that I can offer a translation of olive farmers' meaningful daily activities to disrupt occupational therapy, and other Eurocentric disciplines concerned with people's daily lives and their health and well-being. And what better place to start this enquiry than the activity of olive growing, which is considered a key daily activity for many Palestinians and has been for thousands of years; and where else to begin than in the West Bank of Palestine, where people have been facing extreme restrictions on their lives based on their ethnicity, but despite that they persevered and continued this historical activity. As a U.K. and an Israeli citizen, I was able to travel freely between the United Kingdom and Israel, and between Israeli and occupied Palestinian areas, though with precautions and sometimes hair-raising experiences when facing the Israeli Army and Israeli colonizers. However, my experiences didn't compare to the daily misery the army and colonizers impose on Palestinian communities living within the West Bank.

This book is part of my own resistive acts and mission to "come and see and go and tell," as many of the olive farmers I met wanted me to do. The book highlights the daily forms of resistance olive farmers practice to counter the structures of the military occupation, apartheid, and settler-colonialism that affect their daily activities related to olive growing. My position in that liminal space, between Global South and Global North communities and knowledges, enabled me to carry out an intercultural translation of these forms of daily resistance that have not been highlighted to Western audiences before. The information in this book was gathered via decolonial ethnographic methods with the intention of contributing to efforts to combat the social and occupational injustices that many communities in the Global South and North experience (Simaan 2017, 2018). To that end, I hope to disrupt Eurocentric understandings of the concepts of "occupation," "social justice," and "occupational justice,"[1] and the individualized practices associated with them that do not apply to the majority of the world's population.

Olive Growing in Palestine

Olive growing, as described in this book, is an activity undertaken by native[2] communities of Palestine, and refers to the sum of all, or each, of the activities and tasks carried out by individuals, families, or groups of people that contribute to the growing and producing of olives and their products. These activities and tasks include planting olive saplings, ploughing the groves, harvesting the olives, pruning the trees, fertilizing the soil, using herbicides and pesticides, watering the trees, pressing the olives to produce oil, selling the oil, and pickling and preserving the olives for eating. Other tasks that relate to olive farming include traveling to and from the groves; accessing the land; traveling to and from the oil presses; and all the human communication, interactions, and relations that enable such activities. Traditionally, olives in Palestine have been pressed for oil and preserved for eating,

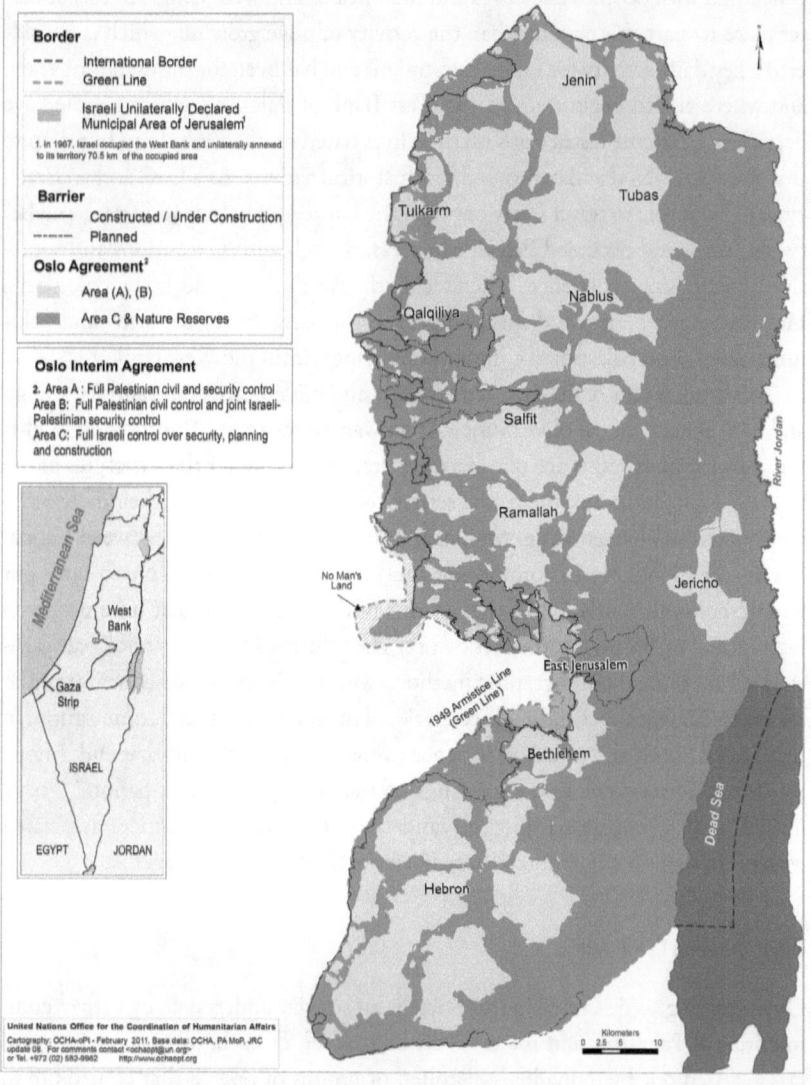

A map of the West Bank. Map created by UNOCHAoPt 2011, https://www.ochaopt.org /sites/default/files/ocha_opt_area_c_map_2011_02_22.pdf.

and the pips and waste products from pressing are made into fuel, fertilizers, and soap. The dead wood of the olive tree is used to make crafts and tools, and the leaves are brewed to treat human and animal ailments. The olive tree is a national, political, spiritual, and religious symbol that is ubiquitous in Palestinian culture (Al-Batma 2012).

Olive growers, like other communities in Palestine, have been living under ongoing oppressive circumstances that have influenced their daily lives. Since the earliest recorded history, Indigenous Palestinian communities including olive farmers have experienced wars, uprisings, and military invasions, leading to violence, segregation, and displacement (Khalidi 2021; Masalha 2012; Said 1992; Wolfe 2006). Despite these forces having led to large displacements from rural areas, olive growing has been a significant part of the "Mediterranean economy" pioneered in the Fertile Crescent since the Bronze Age, as a response to specific topographical and climatic circumstances (Thompson 2000). Olive growing remains an important part of everyday life for many: about half of farmed land is planted with ten million olive trees in the oPt (Oxfam 2010).

The Occupied Palestinian Territories

The oPt refers to the territory invaded by Israel in 1967, containing East Jerusalem, the West Bank, and the Gaza Strip. The term "Palestine," as used in this book, refers to the historic land of Palestine lying between the Mediterranean coast in the west and the Jordan Rift Valley in the east, including the modern-day state of Israel, the military-occupied West Bank, and the besieged Gaza Strip (see map above). The West Bank is a term created by Israel (Pappe 2017) to refer to the formerly (prior to the Israeli invasion) Jordanian-administered area that is located on the western bank of the River Jordan (see map above). Historically, *"Palaestina Prima"* was the designation the Byzantines—who ruled here between 325 C.E. and 637 C.E.—chose for the area between the River Jordan in the east and the Mediterranean Sea in the west, and from Mount Carmel in the north to the desert in the South (Khalidi 2010). *Filastin* is the name that was given to describe a military administrative region by the Arabs who captured Jerusalem from the Byzantines in 637 C.E. (Khalidi 2010). Palestine's history, dominated by invasions and colonizations by outside forces, is also a history of interdependent communities being influenced by the geography and sociopolitical conditions they live in; their way of life has mostly been land-based, and they believed in many gods before such pantheistic traditions were superseded by the monotheistic religions: Judaism, Christianity, and Islam (Thompson 2000). The Romans came and went, then the Byzantines, then came Islamic rule, then the crusaders, and the Ottomans. The Ottoman Turks ruled Palestine from the sixteenth century until the First World War, when the British took over the administration of Palestine. Their colonial project culminated in the creation of the state of Israel in 1948, upon most of what used to be known as historical Palestine (Khalidi 2010, 2021; Masalha 2018).

Modern Palestine's history has been characterized by the ongoing *Nakba*, which refers to the dispossession of the majority of the native population—between 780,000 and one million people—who became refugees in 1948, when the state of Israel was established on their lands (Said 1992). Coined by Constantine Zurayk in his 1956 book *The Meaning of the Catastrophe*, the *Nakba* came to be a key turning point for Palestinian identity, which was reconstructed around this event (Masalha 2012). The *Nakba* ushered in the foundation of a settler-colonialist state on approximately 80 percent of what was then British administered Palestine, the destruction of historic Palestine—as a distinct culture—and the ethnic cleansing of its people (ibid.; Pappe 2006; Wolfe 2006). Until 1967, Israel controlled the area within what came to be known as the Green Line—the declared Armistice border after the war of 1948 (Pappe 2017). Jordan was given the administration of the West Bank and East Jerusalem, and Egypt ruled in Gaza (ibid.). In 1967 Israeli forces invaded the West Bank and the Gaza Strip, the Egyptian Sinai Peninsula, and the Syrian Golan Heights, causing further civilian deaths, ethnic cleansing, and refugees (ibid.). In the oPt, Israel appointed a governing body called the civil administration, which managed the daily lives of the local society (Rosenfeld 2004).

The military-occupied populace in the oPt suffered a lack of services and welfare, lack of infrastructure, and a lack of self-determination. Most importantly, this was the start of a new era of colony building within the oPt (ibid.). The military occupation, land colonization, human rights abuses, and the poor living conditions in the oPt led to two major Intifadas (uprisings) in the 1980s and early 2000s, in turn leading to further oppression by Israel's occupying forces (IDF), land segregation, and restrictions on movement (Zureik 2016). Moreover, Israeli authorities have been constructing an illegal segregation wall that is annexing more land and separating families from their olive groves (ICJ 2004). The first Intifada—between 1987 and 1993—began as a civil disobedience movement and later came to represent in the literature and among activists a model for grassroots organization and community work (Qumsiyeh 2011). The first Intifada led to the Oslo Accords signed in 1993, a controversial deal that many experts believed disproportionately favored Israel's interests and objectives (Said 1995). The Accords created the Palestinian National Authority (PA) (Rosenfeld 2004), which has been criticized as not being supportive of farming communities, and which many consider to be a proxy tool of Israeli oppression, as when the PA arrests people and tortures prisoners in coordination with the Israeli authorities (Qumsiyeh 2011). The Oslo Accords created a territorial zoning of the West Bank that ensured Israel's control over 60 percent of land in the oPt. Area A is controlled by the PA (though ultimately remaining under occupation) and is made up mostly of urban areas. Area B is jointly administered: by the PA for civil matters, and by the IDF for security matters. Area C is under the full control of Israel and includes the most fertile land and the West Bank's major water resources (see map above). There are currently hundreds of illegal Jewish-only colonies in the oPt, with over half a million Jewish settlers residing in them, many of whom migrated from Jewish communities in the West (Pappe 2017).

Palestinian scholars, civil society, and human rights organizations have described the situation for Palestinians living between the Mediterranean Sea and the River Jordan as an apartheid regime (Said 1992; Sayigh 1979). However, it wasn't until recently that this concept has caught the world's attention after the United Nations, and Israeli and Western-based human rights organizations published reports highlighting the situation as an apartheid regime (Amnesty International 2022; B'Tselem 2021; Human Rights Watch 2021). These human rights reports ignored the fact that this apartheid is a tool of settler-colonialism, whose main focus is an ideology and practice that aims to capture as much land as possible with as few Indigenous Palestinian inhabitants as possible.

As this book goes to press, Israel has been accused of committing the crime of genocide against the Palestinian people.[3] On October 7, 2023, Palestinian armed groups broke into the other side of the fence enclosing the Gaza Strip to areas where Palestinian villages stood prior to 1948, attacking Israeli military bases and settlements. Over a thousand settlers were killed, including soldiers and civilians, and hundreds more taken as captives. On that same day, Israel began a military assault on the Gaza Strip, which, as of mid-September 2024, has led to more than forty-one thousand Palestinian casualties and more than ninety-four thousand wounded; destruction of homes, institutions, and infrastructure; and the displacement of most of Gaza's two million people.[4] While the world's attention has been on Gaza since October 2023, a further eighteen Palestinian communities have been forcefully displaced in the West Bank, according to Israeli human rights organization B'Tselem (2024).

Settler-Colonialism

Settler-colonialism, as defined by Patrick Wolfe (2006), refers to an ongoing structure (rather than a temporary event) that aims to replace a native community with foreign settlers, and to eliminate that community and its way of life. The main contest is for access to territory, but the practice employs discriminatory discourses and practices related to racial and religious differences. Wolfe (ibid.) distinguished settler-colonialism—as it exists in Australia, New Zealand, North America, and South Africa, whereby a European community aimed to settle on a land that was already lived on and worked by native communities—from the classical case of colonialism, as when the British state occupied and ruled India and its people but without seeking to replace those people with citizens sent from the "mother" country. Israeli settler-colonialism shares with other settler-colonial projects the motive of racial exclusivity, which is supported by myths such as colonized territory constituting "land without people for people without land" (a narrative that ignores the presence of native people); or European genius and industriousness being able to "make the desert bloom" (thus saving the land from the neglect, backwardness, and wastefulness of native people); and the notion of importing Western "civilisation" to the "inferior" and "uncivilised" Orient (Masalha 2012; Said 1992).

At the core of settler-colonialism there is the "logic of elimination," which might not necessarily mean "the summary liquidation of Indigenous people" but always "strives for the dissolution of native societies" by erecting "a new colonial society on the expropriated land base" (Wolfe 2006, 388). Wolfe cited Zionism's[5] colonization of Palestine as a specific type of European settler-colonialism, which he defined as "an inclusive, land-centred project that coordinates a comprehensive range of agencies, from the metropolitan centre to the frontier encampment," and which operates with state-based and other less formal agencies (ibid., 393). In the West Bank these include the military occupation's armed forces and fundamentalist settler organizations—all of which have maintained the "Zionist strategy" enforced from earlier colonization efforts before 1948 (ibid., 393). Therefore, the policies and strategies of the Israeli military occupation are seen in this book as an arm of the ongoing settler-colonialism that began in the 1880s with the first European Zionist settlements, and culminated in the establishment of the state of Israel in 1948, and the invasion of the oPt in 1967.

Baruch Kimmerling, an Israeli sociologist, described the Israeli regime's practices toward the Palestinians and its military occupation as a process of "politicide," the ultimate aim of which was to annihilate Palestinian society. He wrote:

> By *politicide* [italics in original] I mean a process that has, as its ultimate goal, the dissolution of the Palestinian people's existence as a legitimate social, political, and economic entity. This process may also but not necessarily include their partial or complete ethnic cleansing from the territory known as the Land of Israel. . . . Politicide is a process that covers a wide range of social, political, and military activities whose goal is to destroy the political and national existence of a whole community of people and thus deny it the possibility of self-determination (Kimmerling 2003, 3–4).

The ideology and practices of Zionism have led to demographic changes in the native communities in Palestine. Traditionally, and until the end of the British

Mandate in 1948, the diversity of climates, crops, crafts, and trades in historical Palestine had supported three main communities: the urban residents, the semi-nomadic Bedouins, and the rural land-based peasants, or fallahin. The land-based peasants living in the country traditionally constituted 70 to 80 percent of the Palestinian population. They currently number between 50 to 60 percent of Arab Palestinian society in the oPt (Qumsiyeh 2004; Rosenfeld 2004; Said 1999; Sayigh 1979).[6] Settler-colonialism, along with other external factors, such as changes in the global and local economy and climatic changes, have led many to shift from land-based and self-reliant fallahi (peasantry) lives to being wage-laborers dependent on permits, subject to movement restrictions, and with little social security (ICJ 2004; Rosenfeld 2004; UNHRC 2013). However, fallahi ways of life have not disappeared, as shown elsewhere in this book, and olive growing has been a key practice that helped in maintaining this way of life.

From a Palestinian perspective on settler-colonialism, Ghanim and Mustafa (2009) distinguished between three types of settler-colonialism, according to the desired outcome of what is to be done with the native communities. The first type aims to eradicate the local society and to control the space, such as what happened in the United States; the second type aims to integrate the native community with the invaders and to form one society, such as what occurred in South America; the third type aims to form a settler society side by side with the Indigenous society. This latter type is enabled by the segregation and the limitation of space for the Indigenous peoples at a gradual pace. According to Ghanim and Mustafa (ibid.), this third type is what has been occurring in Palestine-Israel. It is this specific form of control over land and the restrictions of the spatial environment that has the most negative effects on olive farmers' daily lives, which they respond to by employing collective everyday forms of resistance (Simaan 2017, 2018).

Collective Everyday Forms of Resistance and the Study of Occupation

Olive growing is defined in this book as a collective everyday activity, which is undertaken by families and groups, similar to other activities carried out by Global South communities elsewhere in the world, such as in Latin America, South East Asia, and South Africa (Ramugondo and Kronenberg 2015; Santos 2014; Scott 1985). Global South groups are not defined geographically here, but symbolically, to refer to groups anywhere in the world—in the "East" and "West"—who are experiencing and struggling against a variety of oppressive political, economic, and social forces such as patriarchy, capitalism, and colonialism (Santos 2014). Collective occupations are enacted in both organized and nonorganized forms, covertly and overtly, as means of confronting socioeconomic and political forces that restrict these groups' ways of life (Scott 1985). These communal acts are shaped by ways of being and knowing, values, and beliefs that include an awareness of injustice and an engagement in everyday forms of resistance against it to enable the continuation of communities' daily lives and their collective well-being (Ramugondo 2015; Scott 1985). In the case of Palestinian olive-growing families discussed in this book, the main force of oppression they struggle against is Israeli settler-colonialism and the military occupation of their land and communities.

In the disciplines of occupational therapy and occupational science, as in this book, "occupation"[7] signifies the things people do in their everyday life to maintain their health, well-being, and way of life (Wilcock 2006). Examples include self-caring tasks done at home such as washing and dressing, recreational activities such as play, and voluntary or paid vocations done for the economic or social benefit of the individual or groups. Occupation is not meant to refer solely to paid jobs, as it is often used to mean in the English language. Rather, it encompasses everyday actions and processes that provide purpose and meanings to the individual or groups, and that are sanctioned by the contextual factors within which humans live, such as culture, geography, gender, age, and political and economic structures (Wilcock 2006).

Occupational therapy is the practice that utilizes daily occupations as means and end goals for people who seek help as a result of experiencing restrictions from participating in their wanted or needed daily activities (Wilcock 2006). Occupational science is an interdisciplinary empirical and theoretical field of study that aims to inform the practice of occupational therapy and other academic and professional practices concerned with human everyday doing (Yerxa et al. 1989). Occupational science research employs diverse approaches to its research and theory, and has been increasingly interested in critical and transformative methodologies to challenge mainstream Eurocentric and anthropocentric perspectives; these approaches have included critical ethnographic methods and postcolonial theories aiming to broaden occupational science's scope and make it more inclusive and relevant to the majority of the world population (Frank 1996, 2012; Laliberte Rudman 2014; Whiteford and Hocking 2012).

Health and Well-Being

Both terms—health and well-being—will be used interchangeably in this book to refer to similar phenomena. Health and well-being in occupational therapy and occupational science approaches to public health, as in this book, do not refer only to the biology, structures, and functions of the human body (Wilcock and Hocking 2015). They relate to the environmental aspects of human wellness, and how social and political contexts can impact individuals' and populations' quality of life (Marmot 2005). Social and political factors lead to socioeconomic inequality between countries and within countries that affect the health of individuals and communities; factors that have been defined as the social determinants of health consist of the social gradient, stress, early life development, social exclusion, work, unemployment, social support, addiction, food and transport (Marmot 2005; CSDH 2008). It has been suggested that the social settings in which people are born, live, grow, work, and age—rather than their biological and physiological functions—lead to these inequalities and to ill health. The WHO's Commission on Social Determinants of Health (2008) considered health a social justice issue that needed to be tackled by improving the daily living conditions of the disadvantaged and by equitable distribution of resources, power, and money.

In Palestine, key determinants of health were found to lie in the structural and political conditions, and more specifically, the domains that influence adult Palestinians' well-being were identified as economy, education, employment, family relations, personal characteristics, social relations, physical and mental health, and religion (Barber et al. 2014; Giacaman et al. 2009; McNeely et al. 2014). Studies have demonstrated that the majority of Palestinians constantly live in varying degrees of emotional and psychological distress as a result of present life events related to the military occupation, but also because of the historic collective trauma of the *Nakba*. As a result, the assessment of the health of Palestinians was extended to include culturally specific derived measures of health related to the context they live in, in addition to the mainstream focus on trauma-related stress when studying communities living in political conflict. These studies of the Palestinian population's health were important in acknowledging the centrality of the economic, social, and political context for the daily lives of Indigenous communities, their health needs and their unique perception of their well-being (Barber et al. 2014; Giacaman et al. 2009; McNeely et al. 2014). In the following chapters I will show, through empirical examples, how olive-farming communities have their own unique conceptualization of wellness that is holistic and multidimensional. *Al-'afya*, which will be expanded on later in this book, is a concept rooted in the daily lives of communities, and its meanings signify a special way of considering wellness through the doing of daily activities.

Occupational Justice

Social justice approaches to health and well-being in occupational science have proposed the concept of occupational justice, which is a term complementary to social justice, and which addresses the inequalities between groups in society in accessing opportunities for wanted and needed daily activities; it describes how these inequalities are created by factors outside of the control of individuals (Pierce 2012; Wilcock and Townsend 2000). Occupational justice approaches to humans' daily activity are concerned with social change through exploring injustices and the lessons learned from communities about how they adapt, resist, and cope (Laliberte Rudman 2014). More empirical work is needed to provide specific examples of these concepts, and there is a need to explore theories that place collective occupations, communities, and their contexts within an inclusive frame (Hitch, Pépin, and Stagnitti 2014a, 2014b; Whalley Hammell 2015). It is hoped that this book contributes to reducing such a gap in knowledge.

Global South scholars have questioned the utility of the constructs of social justice, social inclusion, and occupational justice as tools within the system that produces exclusion and unfairness. Structural and political transformations need to occur in order for us to achieve social justice, and concepts such as occupation, social and occupational justice should be politicized to address power relationships created by colonialism, patriarchy, and capitalism (Guajardo Córdoba 2020). Guajardo Córdoba (ibid.) suggested taking things back to basics and asks what these concepts and practices mean in the Global South, and what other possible ways there are that can help us understand and help achieve fair daily life that can be amplified and highlighted. In my work in Palestine, I learned about forms of daily resistance and values of communal and cooperative living based on family, village, local, and international solidarities that shed light on what social and occupational justice may look like for these communities. Moreover, the concepts of social and occupational justice might not apply to such communities. Instead, as communities in the Global South such as Indigenous communities in the Americas have valued and practiced for thousands of years, the concept of "Good Living" might be a more appropriate term to use (Guajardo Córdoba, 2020, Santos 2014).

> The idea of Good Living/Living Well, recognizing that there is much Good Living. That is, many alternative and practical notions of how to build decolonial communities. . . . Good living from their plural and intercultural condition will always be hybrids, networks, they will not be homogeneous or universalist, always historically situated, with multiple forms in embodied stories under the ethical premise of reciprocity (Guajardo Córdoba 2020, 14).

For the purpose of studying means of daily living to highlight the Good Living of colonized groups, decolonial methodologies are required.

Decolonial Ethnography

The information described in this book was gathered and analyzed using a decolonial ethnographic methodology that aims to highlight colonized groups' daily living, perceptions, and experiences in order to inform the conceptualization of everyday activities that have so far been mostly conceived from Eurocentric and privileged perspectives. My research aims to reclaim knowledge production by shedding a critical eye on prior research and theory through the stories of olive growers and my analysis of them, and by attempting to make the discipline of occupational science, the profession of occupational therapy, other social science disciplines concerned with human's daily lives and their well-being, and activism more relevant to marginalized global communities. This methodology is termed "decolonial" rather than "postcolonial" because the situation in Palestine has been one of ongoing settler-colonialism, as discussed above, and the land, people, and everyday life are yet to be liberated from the oppressions and injustices this entails. It nonetheless joins anti-colonial research in other settings, with other groups, and on other occupations, that aims to represent, and learn from, marginal groups and their daily living (Farias and Laliberte Rudman 2016; Frank 1996, 2012; Laliberte Rudman 2014; Whiteford and Hocking 2012; Núñez Valderrama, Hernández, and Alarcón 2022; Shetty and Nayar 2024). Ethnography as a methodology has a history of enabling and being enabled by European colonial and imperial ideologies and practices, and it is characterized by what Edward Said (2000) termed "a crisis of representation" (294), whereby privileged academics, professionals, and officials study colonized groups and, knowingly or unknowingly, contribute to their misrepresentation, othering, and oppression.

One way to counter this crisis is by decolonizing ethnography, which we might begin to achieve by focusing on and drawing from "the work of non-Western, colonized writers and intellectuals . . . [and] reach[ing] beyond the academy to valorise the knowledges of the colonized—ways of thinking that colonizers tried to supress or destroy" (Alonso Bejarano et al. 2019, 21). Alonso Bejarano et al. (ibid.) offered an alternative to mainstream ethnography through describing a study about undocumented migrants, and about the work of an activist group that provides services for this most marginalized of communities in the United States. The authors make a convincing argument for an ethnography that is not interested in "extracting" data from those considered "others" in society. Instead, ethnography is decolonized when members of the community themselves are interested in learning about their own group and its praxis, in the hope of achieving social and political justice. At the same time as these members are exploring their own practices, they are reaching out to migrants whom they might have never encountered otherwise. More so, the participant-researcher-activists are self-improving by acquiring new skills, such as interviewing, observing, documenting, and providing outreach services. Additionally, they are taking part in producing the means of making sense of their own community, and eventually transforming members' lives and offering new insights, knowledge, and practices to anthropology and the social sciences. One point of contention about ethnography, however, is the fact that it is inherently embedded in Western coloniality: whether it can be truly liberated as a result, or whether there is a hope in making it relevant to marginalized communities, is yet to be clarified (ibid.).

The concerns that led to this study were motivated by learning about the concrete manifestations of Israeli settler-colonialism and military occupation—described as "facts on the ground" (Pappe 2017, 185)—which include land confiscations, illegal colonies built on farmers' land, restrictions on movement, segregation, and violence by soldiers and settlers (UNHRC 2013). A United Nations Human Rights Council (UNHRC) fact-finding mission investigated the Israeli settlements' impact on the civil, political, economic, social, and cultural rights of the Palestinians in the oPt. It reported that 60 percent of West Bank land was under full Israeli control, and that since 1967 Israeli governments had led the planning, building, and development of colonies that are illegal under international law (ibid.). The report outlined how Israeli colonies built on occupied land—numbering about 250 settlements and housing approximately 520,000 settlers—impacted on the rights of Palestinians, and how this was negatively manifested in a variety of interrelated forms, such as restricting the right of native groups to self-determination; limiting equality and the right to nondiscrimination in the application of laws as applied to Palestinians and to Israeli colonialists; enabling settler violence and intimidation; allowing restrictions on religious freedom and related intolerance against native communities; dispossession and displacement of land and property of Palestinians; causing restrictions on freedom of movement, freedom of expression, and peaceful assembly, and restrictions on the right to water (ibid.).

The UNHCR report also studied the impact on the economic rights of the native population by addressing the agricultural sector, which has been the cornerstone of the Palestinian economy, although it has been in continuous decline since 1967. This, the report stressed, was due to land dispossessions, denial of access to land and water resources, as well as denial of access to local and international markets. The expansion of Israeli settlements and their related infrastructure caused further erosion of farming assets. The reduction in water resources, the high prices of transport, and the shrinking of markets—also impacted by the construction of the segregation wall (illegal under international law) and the segregation of communities—had led to a decrease in agricultural holdings, a move to less profitable and rain-dependent crops, and a decrease in productivity (ibid.). These factors were in addition to the recurrent attacks against farmers, animals, trees, and water installations, especially during the olive harvest season (ibid.). According to another United Nations (UN) agency—the United Nations Office for the Coordination of Humanitarian Affairs in the Occupied Palestinian Territories (UNOCHAoPt 2012), 48 percent of land in the oPt was planted with olive trees; olive oil production constituted 14 percent of agricultural income, supporting about eighty-eight thousand families. It documented seventy-three barrier gates that restricted access to groves, fifty-two of which were closed all year round except during harvest periods and then only opened for a limited number of hours. In 2011, for example, 42 percent of applications to access olive groves were rejected, and between January and October 2012, 7,500 trees were destroyed or damaged by settlers. That number was 9,500 in 2011, when only 162 complaints by nongovernmental organizations (NGOs) led to indictment, the majority of complaints being filed and closed by Israeli authorities (ibid.). During the olive harvest season of 2023, Yish Din, an Israeli Human Rights organization, documented 113 violent incidents against olive farmers and olive trees in the West Bank. For example, the report included at least 715 olive trees that were destroyed, twenty-four incidents in which settlers and soldiers assaulted farmers, fifteen incidents in which soldiers or settlers stole the crops, and half a dozen incidents during which settlers seized control of Palestinian farmland (Yish Din 2024).

As for land confiscations, an Israeli NGO used official Israeli statistics to investigate measures used to take over Palestinian land (Kerem Navot 2013). They outlined various ways in which land was expropriated, including declaring land to be a closed military zone, declaring land as state land, land expropriation from absentee owners, and forcible private takeover by settlers. The report found that the state supported settlers in taking over public and private land, and that during the previous decade tens of thousands of dunums (a dunum equals one thousand square meters) had been taken over by settlers, mostly from private landowners, in the central and southern hills of the West Bank (where my fieldwork was conducted). Other means of land confiscations employed by settlers were found to include setting up outposts in former closed military zones or former military-use land in the hope of developing them into colonies, building unofficial and unsanctioned roads leading to colonies that have developed into Jewish-only roads, and taking over panoramic areas to change them into tourist attractions (ibid.).

Decolonial thought conceives people as active survivors—rather than passive victims—who seek to maintain their own and their community's well-being

(Ramugondo 2015; Rasras 2005). Furthermore, occupational science has provided evidence that humans engage in daily occupations for purposes and meanings of doing, being, becoming, and belonging (Whalley Hammell 2004; Wilcock 2006). However, so far these ideas have predominantly been tested in Western or English-speaking contexts and on occupations of individuals diagnosed with physical or mental disabilities, and I wished to study these concepts (doing-being-becoming-belonging) in the context of olive-growing families in Palestine living under the aforementioned conditions.

Despite my suspicions about the "universal" applicability of these occupational science ideas—doing-being-becoming-belonging—which were conceived by Western English-speaking academics, I was interested in exploring them within the Palestinian context. I wished to do so because the Epistemologies of the South philosophy I have adopted does not seek to eliminate all knowledge created in the Global North. Instead, it is believed that Global North and South ways of doing and knowing should complement each other, seeking to create a "new universality" that enables coexistence between worldviews and means of interpreting the world (Said 2000, 430). This is hoped to lead to better understanding of the world, humans' daily realities and the injustices they experience (and how to resolve them), such as colonialism, capitalism, and patriarchy (Santos 2014). Moreover, my liminal positionality of living across Global North and South worldviews and ways of life allowed the process of intercultural translation, which enabled a bridging between these two worldviews.

But this comes with a warning: as two Native American scholars have claimed, decolonization is not a metaphor (Tuck and Yang 2012). Decolonial thought and methodology, according to Tuck and Yang (ibid.), should be combined with repatriation and redistribution of land and resources. Olive farmers, as will be seen in later chapters, have shown us that they do not only provide values and alternative knowledges but also actions by which they reclaim land and resources, and contribute to other actions toward the decolonization of Palestine as a whole.

Epistemology of Imperialism

The theoretical underpinnings of this book are rooted in the historical struggle of Palestinians against a European colonial ideology and practices often justified by scholarly work framed within Eurocentric disciplines (Masalha 2012; Said 2003). In an essay titled "The Politics of Knowledge," Edward Said (2000, 376) described the "epistemology of imperialism" that emerged in late eighteenth-century Europe. He referred to a philosophy of knowledge and knowledge production that has dominated many scholarly fields, and which coincided with an imperial perspective that separated races and cultures: between "developed" and "underdeveloped," or "civilised" and "primitive" ones. This separation has been dominant in Western-centric philosophies since the Greeks, Said (ibid.) added, but for the last five centuries (since the start of modern European imperialism) considerable credence has been given to these essentialist separations between cultures and races. What led to this was Western territorial expansion, which caused increased interactions with native populations globally, interactions that were mostly antagonistic in nature. Said claimed that this resulted in a "separation between people as members of homogenous races and exclusive nations that was and still is one of the characteristics" of this imperial epistemology. This "othering" is founded, according to Said, on the notion that "everyone is principally and irreducibly a member of some race or category, and that race or category cannot ever be assimilated to or accepted by others—except as itself" (ibid., 376).

There is a relationship between what Said (ibid.) called the "realm of interpretation" and the "realm of world politics"—each explicating the other, which has real consequences in the lives of people whose experiences are being interpreted. Said argued that knowledge founded on the confirmation of different identities is directly linked to ideologies and practices such as nationalism and colonialism. This dichotomous logic of Western-centric thought leads to policies of separation based on the nations individuals belong to and deems some groups as the "other" and not worthy of certain rights and privileges, as in the relationship between native colonized groups, who have been portrayed as savages and primitive, and the colonizers who are considered a superior and more advanced race. This relationship, between the dominant political structures and how people's experiences have been perceived and interpreted, has also manifested in Palestine whereby British, and after it Israeli, colonization was justified on a claim that native groups, being inferior, could not rule themselves and that it was for their benefit that they be ruled by a more advanced race (ibid., 379).

This epistemology not only separates people and creates hierarchies between European and non-European cultures, but also segregates human from other-than-human elements of nature, and perceives time, history, and territory as linear and binary features that can be quantified, reasoned, and rationalized to portray a version of history that conserves the elitist, Eurocentric, and "historicist"[8] truth (Anievas and Nişancioğlu 2015; Said 2000, 2003; Santos 2014; Scott 2012). Eurocentric philosophies, whether critical or not, are grounded in dualism and anthropocentric perspectives that consider nature as the other, distinct from, and existing outside of, human beings (Santos 2014). Humans are prioritized in this relationship, and thereby this conception considers nature a resource that can be available for people to control and exploit. Examples of the impacts of such modalities are in the policies that encourage "extractivist imperialism" (ibid., 26) across the globe, whereby powerful states or corporations cultivate foreign land, mine their precious metals, or fish in their territorial seas—these resources are extracted often from so called developing "Third World" countries and consumed by so-called developed First World nations.

Another example of a practice based on such an ideology is the standardization, or the institutionalization, of all aspects of life for people in the Global North and South. In his critique of the social sciences and their foundations in Western philosophies about the nature of knowledge and truth, Scott (2012) described the effects of this European colonial conception of reality on people's daily experiences. Scott (ibid., 54) described the project of "utopian image of uniformity" that resulted from the universalization and homogenization that the European nation states exported almost everywhere globally, which—in addition to structures associated with this "utopian image of uniformity," such as settler-colonialism and global market forces—led to a form of "institutional neurosis" (ibid., 79). This overstated belief in uniformity leads to enforcement of standardization, which is driven by what Santos (2014, 63) termed "high modern rationality"—an ideology based on presumed objectivity and rationality, and based on quantified scientific knowledge utilized as a tool to enforce policies on the everyday lives of communities, often authorized by the bourgeois elite controlling the lives of groups on the margins of society. Scott (2012, 34) saw the consequences of such a philosophy of knowledge as "order, rationality, abstractness, and synoptic legibility"—goals illustrated and achieved most clearly in the institutionalization of all aspects of daily lives for people all over the world, including the family, education, the factory, and the office. Colonialism, globalized market-capitalism, the nation-state, and their institutions were based on such instrumental rationality, which denied "vernacular"[9] forms of knowing and valuing that natives and non-European communities had relied on before the arrival of colonialism and the nation-state (ibid.).

Such ideology and practice, founded on neopositivist social science and supported by mainstream scholarly methodologies and methods, are contrasted by the morality and way of life of peasants and farmers living and working in smallholdings and family-oriented farms. As Scott (ibid.) demonstrated, they have been less affected than other occupational groups by the rule and control of the authorities because they rely on their land for substance, survival, and self-determination. Scott (1976, 1985, 2012) observed and analyzed everyday forms of cooperative political practices among such groups, and interpreted them within anarchist values, a philosophy founded on values of mutuality, creativity, and self-rule. He claimed that those values are shared among many communities around the world, who may not even have read or heard of anti-authoritarian thinkers advocating those principles. His observations come from the realities of farmers in the Andes and Southeast Asian peasants—those family-oriented smallholders who "are not merely producing crops; they are reproducing farmers and communities with plant-breeding skills, flexible strategies, ecological knowledge, and considerable self-confidence and autonomy" (Scott 2012, 40).

Vernacular (rooted in the everyday) knowledge and praxis, or "the practice of everyday life" as de Certeau (1988) termed it, are in constant struggle against European imperial ideologies and structures, such as settler-colonialism. Such structures are supported by and inform knowledge production in Western-centric social sciences, which leads to the creation of theories, knowledge, and oppressive policies that suppress the knowledge base and praxis of marginalized groups.

Peasants' nonhegemonic ideology, values, and actions are rooted in their need to negotiate their environments to maintain their collective well-being. Scott (2012) used Palestine as an example to illustrate how Zionism—as one case of a European colonialist project—enforced its ideologies and practices to eliminate native communities' claim to the land and vernacular lifestyle, for example, by removing all traces of their land-naming systems, which were rooted in everyday practices anchored in their natural environment. That erasure of native place names in Palestine was done following fieldwork conducted by Zionist scholars who gathered information from local Indigenous communities about their land-based knowledge and daily practices, in order to "Hebraise" places, or replace their names with names presented as empirically tested (Benvenisti 2000). Scott described how "the landscape has been comprehensively renamed in an effort to smother the older vernacular terms" (2012, 30). Other examples of how Western imperialism, capitalism, and nation states have contributed to the erasure of such vernacular knowledge and morality characteristic of rural communities are the near-universal enforcement of a patronymic naming system of families and individuals; numeric measurements versus vernacular measurements informed by natural phenomena; individualized freeholds replacing communal land tenure; and standardized national languages supplanting local dialects (ibid.)—all of which have also been applied by Israeli-Zionist colonialism in Palestine, and some aspects of which have been observed in this study as discussed in later chapters.

There were other practices, like forestry and farming that—informed by imperial epistemology—were homogenized and standardized for purposes of order, uniformity, and productivity, while denying the varied nature of humans and more-than-humans (Abram 1996), which are often values believed in by peasants or small-scale farmers (Scott 2012). For example, Benvenisti (2000) described how olive groves in Palestine have been uprooted in order to make way for more productive large-scale field crops. Similarly, Pappe (2006) reported on how European-style pine forests were planted by Israeli authorities on the sites of many ethnically cleansed Palestinian villages. Those practices were in contrast to vernacular epistemological and ontological understandings of human experiences and their relation to the land among native groups in Palestine, as well as in other groups in the Global South (Santos 2014; Scott 2012). As alluded to previously, peasants' daily means of doing, being, and knowing—described as peasants' "moral economy"—rely on principles of mutuality, spontaneity, creativity, and self-rule (Scott 1976, 2012). This morality has helped them confront Western farming methods and practices imposed on them due to the importation of market-led globalized forms of capitalism. They have been applied in what Scott (2012, xx) termed "infrapolitics," referring to those noninstitutionalized, often nonvisible but nonetheless influential resistive means to make sense of people's surroundings and enable their way of life to continue. This peasant moral economy is applied to ensure the continuation of the subsistence and survival of the peasant families and their communities (Scott 1976, 2012). Scott (2012, xx) thought of the peasantry as a class of their own, whose revolutions were ignored, and defined their infrapolitical practices as "forms of de facto self-help [that] flourish and are sustained by deeply held collective opinions." Peasants have not often had the opportunity to organize politically but that didn't stop them from "working microscopically, cooperatively, complicitly, and massively at political change from below" (ibid., xx–xxi).

John Berger (1979, 2007), another anti-capitalist thinker, similarly considered the smallholders and family-oriented farming communities as forming a class, whose way of life had been destroyed by dominant capitalist global structures. Berger, like Scott, believed that documenting and exploring such moral economies—knowledge, values, and practices—was critical at this phase of world history to inform more sustainable and ecological economies and ways of living. Scott's study of Southeast Asian peasants, and Berger's study of farmers and herders in the French Alps, pointed to a similar morality and similar ways of life based on the need for subsistence and survival. Scott (1985, xvii) conceptualized acts such as foot-dragging, sabotage, or unionizing against rich bosses—springing from this moral economy of the peasantry—as "everyday forms of resistance" to the market-led organization of farming (such as large-scale cropping) that help in realizing human dignity and freedom. Comparable forms of resistance were observed in this study. They are brought to light with the intention of contributing to epistemological and theoretical justice by highlighting such alternative means of knowing and being—all of which are key concerns of the epistemologies of the South described next.

Epistemologies of the South

In response to the epistemology of imperialism, Santos (2014, 15) described the "epistemologies of the South," which emerged as a movement of thought and praxis from marginal communities' resistance to injustices imposed on them by forces such as capitalism, colonialism, and patriarchy. These groups' lifeways and value systems offer alternative philosophies about the origins of knowledge created by the dominant Western-centric ways of knowing in the world. Epistemologies of the South act at all levels of experience: the ethical, political, cultural, epistemological, and ontological (ibid.). Epistemologies of the South originate from within colonized Indigenous groups, minorities, peasants, women, and other social movements who are resisting a form of what Santos termed "epistemicide," which he described as the destruction of means of interpreting human realities that did not suit "the dominant epistemological canon" (ibid., 238). The Epistemologies of the South perspective assumes that there are "plural systems of knowledge" founded on diverse ways of explaining the world, including the hegemonic positivist scientific method (ibid., 199). This diverse collection of means of knowing are based on the belief that no one method of evaluating human experience in the world is complete, and that there is a need to create new hybrids of ways to make sense of the world. Positivist, neopositivist, and critical paradigms—based on Western epistemologies—cannot fully explain the world, as "the understanding of the world by far exceeds the western understanding of the world" (ibid., 237).

Human freedom and justice are key goals in forming this constellation of hybrid perspectives, which aim for emancipation and social change and which "may follow grammars and scripts other than those developed by western-centric critical theory, and such diversity must be valorised [sic]" (ibid.). These perspectives are particularly needed at this moment of history, when societies are facing troubles on many fronts: human inequalities between and within nations, environmental degradation, human-made climate change, and oppressive effects of market-led capitalism and its value and practice of extractivism. Critical theories, such as the Frankfurt school and Marxism, produced some analyses of problems and their solutions, but were invested too much in European bourgeois modernity based on epistemologies such as the belief in linearity of progress, extractivism, and imperialism; above all, the key problem with these Western-centric critical theories was the fact that they did not acknowledge cognitive injustices caused by the denial of other ways of knowing and being, and of their role in interpreting human experiences and realities (ibid.).

What is needed, Santos (ibid.) claimed, is an alternative epistemology anchored in discourses and praxes that aim to confront oppression and offer a paradigmatic change at all levels of human experience: the ethical—ways of valuing and judging; the political—ways of deliberating and ruling and being ruled; the cultural—ways of providing meaning; the epistemological—ways of knowing; and finally alternatives should be proposed also in the ontological sphere, which conceptualizes reality or the ways of being of humans. He called for "cognitive justice," defined as the "radical demand for social justice, a demand that includes unthinking the dominant criteria by which we define social justice and fight against social injustice" and requiring delving into the roots of such criteria and their determinations at all of the levels mentioned above (ibid., 237). This paradigmatic shift, leading to cognitive justice, should be rooted in the experiences of unjust human suffering and the will to confront this suffering, according to Santos (ibid.). In order to allow this transition from the epistemologies of imperialism, or the North, to the epistemologies of the South, there is a need for an intellectual process involving two key processes: an intercultural translation and the construction of ecologies of knowledges (ibid.).

Intercultural translation is a process of interpretation of human realities that seeks and compares corresponding phenomena between different ways of being, leading to the forming of new means of intercommunications, in order to strengthen what Said (2003) called coexistence among new collective constituencies that fight for social justice and human dignity. Intercultural translations have to challenge dichotomies between forms of knowledge, such as scientific and nonscientific, and to confront the unequal status of some forms of interpreting the world over others (Santos 2014). There are, according to Santos (ibid.), different types of intercultural translations: those which concentrate on translating concepts or worldviews, and those that focus on alternative collective practices and on empowering communities engaging in them to be active agents contributing to the formation of hybrid forms of knowledge aiming at social change. Regarding the translational relationships, there are also two types: first, the translation to/from Western from/to non-Western concepts and practice; and second, the translations between different non-Western knowledges and praxes (ibid.).

When attempting to translate concepts from the Global South into discourses in the Global North, caution needs to be exercised. This is due to a history of more than five hundred years of European colonization of non-European lands, and a process of erasing value systems, cultures, ways of life and epistemologies (ibid.). In the Muslim-majority eastern Mediterranean, where Palestine is located, the "process of translation that colonial modernity ushered into Muslim-majority countries ... [was] always anchored in European colonial claims to universality" (Massad, 2016, 157). Consequently, this countercolonial possibility can be complicit with colonial logic (Spivak 1993). According to Walter Mignolo (2018),

Studying Olive Growing as Resistance

universality should be replaced with "pluriversality": "A world in which many worlds would coexist." Similarly, the concept of the "Sociology of Absence" suggested by Santos helps us focus on experiences that have not yet been totally colonized with Western-centric meanings. Another term Santos uses is "Sociology of emergence" pointing to the need to explore alternative experiences to expand knowledge and practice (Santos 2014).

The purpose of creating such ways of knowing is to expand ecologies of knowledges by stepping back from Eurocentric traditions to allow other analytical spaces that can explain reality (ibid.). This does not mean rejecting Western critical theories and advocating relativism, but rather broadening the possibilities of thinking about human emancipation. Santos (ibid.) claimed that the novel hybrid of means of interpreting the world "aims to create a new kind of relation, a pragmatic relation, between scientific knowledge and other kinds of knowledge" to allow maximum benefit from their respective contributions toward "another possible world" (ibid., 190). Said (2000), stressing the importance of continuing to work on the goal of widening the area of awareness in the study of everyday realities of people, warned against going to the other extreme by only highlighting the particularity of those diverse means of knowing rooted in the everyday of Global South groups. He stated: "Our point, in my opinion, cannot be simply and obdurately to affirm the knowledge and leave it at that, nor can it be to surround ourselves with the sanctimonious piety of historical or cultural victimhood as a way of making our intellectual presence felt" (ibid., 380). Such victimhood doesn't empower an improved sense of humanity, according to Said (ibid.). He saw the importance of testifying to a reality of oppression, but this was not sufficient unless it was invested in an intellectual process that universalized the situation to include all of the oppressed in the world. To deconstruct Eurocentrism in the intellectual sphere, Said believed that "ethnic particularity" did not provide the needed intellectual process. He said:

> It was never a matter of replacing one set of authorities and dogma with another, nor of substituting one center or another. It was always a matter of opening and participation in a central strand of intellectual and cultural effort and showing what had always been, though indiscernibly, a part of it, like the work of women, or blacks and servants—but which had been either denied or derogated (ibid., 381).

This process should aim to refine and extend the interpretations of realities that have been exclusively seen from a European observer point of view or consciousness. Said (ibid.) named this approach, which links different ontological stances, "worldliness," which he claimed is the reverse of separatism or exclusivism characteristic of the epistemology of imperialism. Worldliness counters that exclusivism by advocating for a "new universality" when addressing the issues of human rights, dignity, and freedom (ibid., 430). This new universality requires the will to frame those rights by employing similar language to that used by the hegemonic discourses in order to challenge their pecking order and tools, and to shed a light on uncovered facts and communicate what these dominant ideologies and practices had deemed irrelevant (ibid.). Said encouraged the critiquing of interpretations of human freedom, as they are analyzed in today's discourse, that relate to a specific national, ethnic, or religious identity whose freedoms are restricted within the territory of a sovereign national power that withholds those rights in the name of defending their national identity.

An example of this type of framing of human freedom can be found in Palestine-Israel. According to Said (ibid.) the international dimensions of the experiences of Palestinians and Israelis require this type of new universality and worldliness for the philosophical and political interpretation of human freedom. He claimed that there is a dominant consensus in world politics today that has been persistent since the Balfour Declaration was issued by the British government in 1917, which promised Palestine as a home for the Jewish communities of Europe. In particular, since World War Two, across the political spectrum of the liberal democracies of the West, there has been a framing of Palestinian rights that perceives Israel as a positive achievement for the oppressed Jewish populations of Europe without acknowledging the consequences and effects its creation had on the Indigenous population of Palestine (ibid.). This perspective of the liberal West, Said added, "was always very eager to deconstruct the Palestinian self in the process of *constructing* the Zionist-Israeli self" (emphasis in original) (ibid., 431). Writing as an "involved Palestinian," Said described Palestine as the "touchstone case for human rights"; he said: "I doubt that any of us has figured out how our particularly trying history interlocks with that of the Jews who dispossessed and now try to rule us. But we know these histories cannot be separated" (ibid., 435). Said concluded: "There is hardly an instance when the connection between freedom and interpretation is as urgent, as literally concrete, as it is for the Palestinian people, a large part of whose existence and fate has been interpreted away in the West in order to deny us the same freedoms and interpretation granted Israeli Jews" (ibid., 435).

Study's Questions

These deliberations led me to pose three research questions: First, I wished to explore how the structures, policies, and practices of Israeli settler-colonialism and its military occupation influence the daily activities of olive-growing communities in the oPt, such as traveling to and from grove and press; accessing land, harvesting, planting, and maintaining groves?

I hoped to learn about the specific activities that olive-growing individuals and families are engaged in: their daily routines, their seasonal and yearly routines, how and why they do them, and what they perceive to be the enablers and barriers to those activities. Those daily realities and facts on the ground created by a powerful outside force, as the above review of the literature has shown, would surely have specific impacts on the everyday realities and activities of olive farmers as they went about trying to maintain this important occupation of olive growing—vital in preserving their health, well-being, and community. I wished to learn about how these restrictions manifested in individuals' and families' routines, behaviors, relationships, and quality of life. I wished to explore the similarities and differences between individuals and families engaged in these meaningful activities. I also wanted to learn about the effects of the different circumstances of families in terms of where they lived and their family histories and backgrounds, and how these interlinked with the realities and restrictions they had to cope with on a daily basis.

The second research question I posed was: What are the means that communities adopt to enable the daily occupations of olive farming to continue?

I wished to explore what specific practical measures olive growers undertook to allow them to sustain the working of their land and production of olives and oil. I hoped to explore how each individual and family managed, or did not manage, to continue to travel to their groves, maintain their groves, and to plant and harvest their trees. I was concerned with the similarities and differences between individual olive growers and between families, and how and why they were similar or different in the ways they responded to those contextual factors.

A third question that this study aimed to answer was about the values that olive growers adopted and which they believed allowed them to cope with the daily realities they faced in order to continue farming olives. I became increasingly interested in studying the means of knowing and doing, and the motivations and values for the activity of olive growing, which are rooted in the specific ways of life and which were observed to be used as active responses—or resistance—to occupational injustices caused by settler-colonialism. This expansion in the issues I wished to study was inspired by ideas of occupational justice (Wilcock and Townsend, 2000), concerning differences in access to activities of daily living due to factors such as age, ability, or disability, gender, religion, nationality, sexuality, or any other contextual or identity dimensions. Moreover, this third question was influenced by decolonial scholars' interest in learning from communities that use nonhegemonic means of resisting social and cognitive injustice (Santos, 2014).

Santos recognized the value of knowledge and expertise conceived in the Global South by the communities themselves—rather than values and knowledge exported or enforced by privileged outsiders—to counter social injustice, including cognitive and occupational injustices—concepts that are further discussed in the following chapters.

An Introduction to the Following Chapters

Chapter 2 will discuss "*Sutra*," conceptualized as doing for well-being, which is a principle of action for olive growing that enables actual engagement in the doing of the activities of olive farming in order to survive economically and physically. *Sutra* also includes the subjective, emotional, social, and political meanings attached to this activity, which, combined, empower families to fulfill their roles and maintain their well-being, or *Al-'afya*, as uniquely understood by families in Palestine.

In chapter 3, Olive Growing for '*Awna*, or doing for belonging, will be explored. This chapter will introduce the concept of '*Awna* as the collaborative belonging principle of olive farming. The chapter interprets '*Awna* in light of the varied solidarities and coagencies I observed that enable this action, which in turn leads to the continuation of olive growing. This occurred despite the specific type of "occupational apartheid" families were observed to experience. Occupational apartheid (Kronenberg and Pollard 2005) stems from the systematic and direct imposition of limits on the daily lives of olive growers, which Israeli settler-colonialism and its military occupation aim to replace with a foreign settling community and way of life.

In chapter 4, *Sumud* as belonging for becoming will be explored. This chapter offers an analysis of the daily acts of *Sumud*—a means of resistive action specific to the Palestinian situation. *Sumud* will be conceptualized as the belonging for becoming principle of olive farming, which enables farming families to hold onto their land, trees, and daily doings, and stubbornly persist in finding creative responses to not only perpetuate their olive-growing activity, well-being, and communities but also to aspire to, and sometimes achieve, collective self-determination.

Chapter 5 will discuss the idea of a Palestinian Everyday Form of Resistance. This chapter discusses the interconnectedness of the three motivators and principles of action for the act of olive growing—*Sutra*, '*Awna*, and *Sumud*. The chapter will argue that, for Palestinian olive growers, *Sutra-'Awna-Sumud* do not exist separately in the real world; they interlink to form what I term "Everyday Forms of Resistance." Examples of resistive means will be offered from the olive-farming

Studying Olive Growing as Resistance 33

An Israeli settlement encroaching on Palestinian olive groves. Photo taken by Ahmad Al-Bazz.

communities in Palestine to the occupational science and occupational therapy communities, as well as to other disciplines and groups in the Global South who are studying and/or struggling against occupational, social, and cognitive injustices.

The conclusion ends the book with a discussion of possible implications for practice and theory, by offering some examples highlighting efforts to decolonize knowledge creation, dissemination, and practices in the fields of occupational therapy, occupational science, and sociology.

An Overview of Participant Families

Each of the following chapters is based on the experience of one of the four participant families who are introduced below. However, other members of the community, and activists, will be quoted throughout the book; therefore this overview intends to provide a summary of who the main families are, and where they are based. When I quote others not from the main families, I introduce them in the relevant sections of the book.

Chapter 2: Um Yasin, Abu ʿAttallah, and Yasin.
Um Yasin, wife and mother, is in her forties, and lives with her husband Abu ʿAttallah, in his sixties, and son Yasin who is ten. They live in Al-Raha.

Chapter 3: Um Weehab, Abu Weehab, and Weehab.

Um Weehab, wife and mother, in her sixties, and Abu Weehab, husband and
father in his seventies, and their son Weehab in his forties. They live in the village
of Al-Baydar.

Chapter 4: Um Nedal, ex-wife and mother in her sixties, Abu Nedal, ex-husband
and father in his sixties, and Nedal, their son who is in his forties. They live in the
village of Dar El Shoke.

Chapter 5: Nada, wife and mother in her thirties, Abu Kamal, in his fifities, Nada's husband and father of their children. The family lives in Beit El 'Ola.

All of the names of participants quoted in this book, and their places of residence,
have been altered for their safety. When I use the real name of a person, or a place,
I will note this in the text.

سترة

CHAPTER 2

Olive Growing for *Sutra*

> The remarkable continuity of peasant experience and the
> peasant view of the world acquired as it is threatened with
> extinction, an unprecedented and unexpected urgency.
>
> —John Berger 1979, xxvi

I begin this chapter by introducing the meanings and uses of the concept and practice of *Sutra* in Palestine, after which I provide the background for one of the participant families in this study, the family of Um Yasin and Abu ʿAttallah, how they
went about their daily activities of olive farming while living under the military
occupation and how they respond to it to maintain their lifeways and well-being.
In the remaining pages of this chapter, I describe an intercultural translation of the
theme of *Sutra* that illustrates that the concept of doing and being as aspects of
occupation (meaningful daily activities that contribute to people's health and well-
being) are captured in the daily lives of olive-growing families, but reflect collectivist, nonbinary, and liberatory ways of knowing and doing. That conceptualization
is shown as a contrast to the more individualistic and depoliticized ways in which
they have been conceptualized in Western literature. I further introduce more details, stories, and quotes from Um Yasin and Abu ʿAttallah's family, and others I
met, to test the utility of the concept of *Sutra*, which I translate as doing for well-
being, among Palestinian olive farmers, who were found to use it in a unique way
that challenges and extends the Eurocentric framing of constructs such as doing
and well-being and the relationship between them. The overall aim is to unpack
the term "*Sutra*" as a way of knowing and doing (a principle of action), which
communities here enact through olive farming and use as a means to motivate
them to do olive growing as an indispensable daily activity. I suggest that *Sutra* is a

needed Palestinian contribution to occupational justice theory, in that it expresses multidimensional purposes and meanings of everyday life, leads to a positive well-being for individuals and families, and expresses a nonbinary relationship between humans and their environment.

The term *Sutra* literally translates in Arabic as a cover, a shield, a wall or a fence built around a roof. Other meanings for this term relate to chastity, honesty, and righteousness (Dar Al-Mashriq 1986). In Islam (the religion most Palestinians identify with), *Allah* (God) is the ultimate *sater* (derived from the same root as *Sutra*), meaning the protector of all people. When used in conversation relating to a daily activity that leads to *Sutra*, it signifies securing the sustenance and survival of the person or the family. It expresses a means of action embedded in, and taken by, individuals and communities in order to motivate them to do useful deeds to secure their livelihood. Olive farmers I befriended expressed this principle in their conversations with me and through their actions, which I observed and took part in. They felt that olive growing done for *Sutra* leads to fulfilling multiple purposes and meanings, and that it provides positive health (in its holistic meanings) for individuals and families.

The Family of Um Yasin and Abu ʿAttallah

It was my first time driving alone to visit Um Yasin and Abu ʿAttallah. In my last two visits, Moneer—JAI (Joint Advocacy Initiative)[1] coordinator who introduced me to the family—accompanied me and directed me to the family's land. Driving southwest of Beit Lahem, I went through the town of Al-Khadir (real name) and onto the highway that bypasses Indigenous Palestinian communities to allow nearby settlers to arrive in Al-Quds for their work, leisure, and education without having to enter the Indigenous communities. I drove south toward Al-Khalil, but took the wrong turn, and I arrived at a colony entrance instead. I felt apprehensive, thinking it could be dangerous for a lone Palestinian man to enter an Israeli colony or ask residents for directions. I did a U-turn and headed back toward Beit Lahem, and turned right away from the highway onto roads mostly used by Palestinians and reached a gathering of taxis waiting on the edge of the road to fill up their cars with locals. I asked a taxi driver for directions and handed him my phone so Abu ʿAttallah could describe to him where I need to go. I reached the roundabout—the site last summer of the kidnapping of three young Israeli settlers, which the Israeli government claimed was the reason for the war on Gaza that year (2014). I noticed more army presence than usual, a watchtower with army snipers ready to shoot, and a large Israeli flag on the side of the opposite hill. I also noticed more CCTV cameras on the electricity poles on the sides of the

Olive Growing for *Sutra*   37

road, all of which were not there last time I visited the area. I arrived at the dirt road leading to Abu ʿAttallah's land. Abu ʿAttallah was waiting for me at the gate, and after greeting me and giving me three kisses on the cheeks, he got in the car to show me where I could park in front of his house. On the way there I saw Um Yasin picking leaves from the vine on the side of the path. While Abu ʿAttallah made me coffee, I met Yasin, who was eleven months old at the time and was already walking very well: "Like father like son, strong and likes nature," Um Yasin tells me.

The last time I visited them, Um Yasin was in her forties, Abu ʿAttallah was in his sixties, and their son Yasin was ten years old and already able to identify most trees growing on their land and to explain to me the benefits of terracing and the art of grafting fruit trees. The family live in Al-Raha—the name locals gave to the wadi (valley) where the land is located. Um Yasin was born in a nearby village called Soor, located about a twenty-minute drive south of Al-Raha. She moved to live on this land when she married Abu ʿAttallah. Abu ʿAttallah was born in Beit Lahem, which is the nearest large town. His siblings, and his first wife—from whom he is separated—and their five children lived in Beit Lahem. The main reason for Abu ʿAttallah's separation from his first family was that they were reluctant to move to the land and wanted him to sell it, which was out of the question for him. Abu ʿAttallah's mother and younger brother were killed by the IDF (the Israel Defense Forces, Israel's Army) in the early 2000s, after which Abu ʿAttallah was diagnosed with diabetes, which he attributed to his grief. Abu ʿAttallah said that he lost his "right hand" when his brother died. His brother had helped Abu ʿAttallah set up the land and worked by his side to reach the productivity levels they wanted. Um Yasin told me she visits her parents and siblings in her home village only when Abu ʿAttallah can drive her there, as she cannot drive and is fearful of settlers' or IDF's harassment, which, she often heard, happened to people using public transport.

Abu ʿAttallah told me about what enables them to carry on with the activity of growing olives, one of the main daily activities he engages in, and the reason I was introduced to this family:

> Of course, the family, or the persons around you, make it easier: your siblings, your children, your relatives, as manual labour today costs a lot of money; a worker today costs you, including getting here and going home, around 100 shekels and if you do your accounts, you will realise that you lose more money than you will earn by hiring workers. I have family [referring to his previous wife and children from his first marriage] but they refuse to come here to visit or help, so I turn to volunteers. Another thing that makes olive growing easier is when you

have financial means, but often the work you invest returns to the land; what you earn is maybe the things you eat.

In this part of the world the extended family acts as an enabler to the everyday activities relating to olive growing. As a result of sociopolitical and economic developments in Palestine caused by a combination of factors such as settler-colonialism, the military occupation, and the enforcement of neoliberal policies, family members are forced to look for work outside the family unit, and therefore fewer people are engaged in olive growing. Consequently, the families look for paid labor, or like the family of Abu ʿAttallah, they might need the support of local and international volunteers to allow them to continue with the activities of olive growing.

In the nineteenth century, Abu ʿAttallah's family had moved from the north of the West Bank to Beit Lahem, where Abu ʿAttallah was born. The family bought one hundred *dunums* (twenty-five acres) of land in Al-Raha in the early twentieth century. Abu ʿAttallah began to work the land in the 1970s to prepare it for cultivation. Before he moved to full-time farming, he owned a printing business in town. The printer closed down a decade ago due mainly to the PA (Palestinian Authority), which limited how much he could print and was increasingly monitoring and regulating the industry. In addition to this, more movement restrictions were imposed by the Israeli authorities, which made it difficult to transport his products. The one-bedroom house they lived in when I first visited was built in the 1970s. The other houses on the land belonged to Abu ʿAttallah's brother and cousins and were built during Jordanian administration that lasted in the West Bank until 1967; one house was built in the 1920s during the British Mandate, which ended in 1948. Abu ʿAttallah moved to live on the land all year round after he married Um Yasin a few years ago. Abu ʿAttallah and his family used two wells on the land, and a pipe from the Israeli authorities that delivered water pumped out from under Palestinian land and then sold back to Palestinian communities at inflated prices. The water from the wells was used to irrigate trees and vegetables. The water delivered in the pipe was for domestic use and for some of the vegetables.

Bordering Al-Raha on one side is what has been termed by locals the "roundabout of death." In the autumn of 2015, dozens of Palestinians were killed by IDF snipers stationed on the roundabout. When I visited the area in my second field visit, there was a surge of claims, by settlers and the IDF, of attacks by Palestinian youth, who are often accused of carrying knives with the intent to attack. In the early 1990s two colonies were built on the borders with Al-Raha. There was already a large colony at the other side of the road from the wadi, and since then the area has become a hub for ideologically motivated settlers, many of whom came

Olive Growing for *Sutra* 39

from western Europe and the United State. In the past, settlers have emptied rubbish and sewage onto the family's land. Um Yasin told me she worried a lot about settlers' attacks, as she heard about acts of violence elsewhere in the West Bank, as when a whole family, including a baby, were burned alive in their home by settlers.

The IDF's civil administration managed the local communities in Area C (the 60 percent of the West Bank that is under full control of Israel, where the family lived when I met them).[2] The officer who headed the local branch was based in a nearby colony. Since the mid-1990s the administration has offered the family vast amounts of money to tempt them to sell their land, or to swap it for another plot. Since the early 1990s, when the area containing this wadi was designated as part of Area C, all forms of construction were banned in the area; many activities the family depends upon, such as bringing in a water tank, required a permit from the authorities.

About the obstacles the family faces when trying to go about their daily activities, on which they rely for their living, Abu 'Attallah said:

> So far, we have never been stopped from farming, whether olive or apple trees or vegetables. Why? Because we are present on the land and created facts on the ground, we exist in this area as our right, and if the military authorities want it or not, we want to live on the land. But when we travel from here to Beit Lahem to sell the oil, sometimes there are checkpoints; sometimes they delay us, sometimes they don't, it depends on the situation on the checkpoint. One year we were offered to move, or swap lands, but we refused; this was in 2010, the military ruler came here and said, "You go to an area called *Kherbe*, there are asphalt roads, and there are proper houses built there"; I told him, "All these things are not needed for me," you see I didn't accept it. Other issues we have is whenever I turn the earth [dig] I need permission from the civil administration, but I don't cooperate, I dig the earth without telling them. Last year I was building a drystone wall, and they stopped the workers who were building it. They said that we needed to move 50 metres away from the colony's fence; I kept arguing with the colony's security man for half an hour. After an hour or an hour and a half, he came back to me and told me to go ahead [with building the wall]; he accepted because I was here first. I told him, "That's right, I am a citizen here and your God in his skies won't get me out of here." I said that to him, because I am a citizen, not a settler, I have ownership of the land. I showed him *koushan el taboo* (Turkish registration documents) and he couldn't say anything against it.

About living in this spot, Umm Yasin told me: "My life here is hard, like for example you can't go out, going and coming on the main road is risky because of settlers.

Because it's a settlements area here, it is not safe to stand on the road waiting for taxis or buses. If I stand on the road as a woman I might be harassed."

One of the key barriers to leading meaningful and purposeful lives for families here is the geographical distance between people's homes and their groves. Many of the plots of lands are situated a few to tens of kilometers from the village olive growers live in. Another factor is the village's distance from a main market town, and where all the essential amenities are. A further barrier is the military and set-tlers' violence against native Palestinians.

Um Yasin and her husband Abu 'Attallah harvest their olive trees between the middle and end of October. The season is a big event in the family's calendar, often described as "Palestine's wedding party," for it is a collective celebration across the country. It begins after the first rains of autumn arrive, when schools announce a two-day holiday so that children and teachers can help with the harvest. The family have a few groves of olives of different varieties, each planted on a different terrace. They have the *suri* (Syrian); the *baladi* (native); the *nebali* (a local culti-var); and, until recently, the K18, an Israeli cultivar that Abu 'Attallah replaced with apple trees because of its high demand for scarce water resources and its low productivity. Um Yasin and Abu 'Attallah press most of their yield to produce oil for their own consumption, and in a good year they make a small profit from sell-ing what oil they don't use themselves. The remainder of the olives are pickled to be eaten with their meals. Other families make soap from the low-quality oil, and use the waste products of pressing as fuel in the form of briquettes.

Abu 'Attallah and Um Yasin described a typical day and year working the land and farming olives:

> ABU 'ATTALLAH: My day begins at five in the morning, and I work on the land until eight, then I rest, and in the afternoon, I work for three hours and that's it; six hours is enough.
>
> The harvest begins any time after the 20th of October, when the fruit is judged to be at its optimum size. We spread sheets under the trees, and picking is best done by hand, we don't use a machine or a stick, or a comb. We use a ladder or we climb the tree if it can stand a human body weight. It's best for the harvested olives to be laid in the sun, not like the traditional saying "from the tree to the stone [press]," as today we don't press olives in stone presses. We use modern machines, and for modern machines the olives need to dry in the sun for a bit. In a typical year, it takes us ten days to harvest 365 trees with the help of volunteers. Before we started receiving help from volunteers, I used to hire workers. It used to cost me a lot of money, which I don't have. As for family help, of course it was me, my mother, my sisters and brothers. Then my mother

Olive Growing for *Sutra*

and brother were martyred, and after that, volunteers began to come to help. This year we don't have enough fruit on the trees to occupy the volunteers because of the snowstorm that came in December last year. The productive branches were broken.

UM YASIN: After picking comes pressing; most of what we harvest is pressed. We pickle olives only for our family's use, or for friends, and we don't ask for money. As for the oil, we sell it to local families from the same town. They come to the extended family house in Beit Lahem and pick it up from there.

ABU ʿATTALLAH: In the autumn there's also pruning. After that the trees are sprayed against pests; we spray them twice, once in the autumn after picking, and once when the trees produce buds in early spring.

UM YASIN: We fertilise the soil in November after picking the olives; we use compost from chickens or sheep; it is known that compost from chickens is better than any other compost.

ABU ʿATTALLAH: In February, if there's empty land, I will plant it with olives. Some saplings we buy with our personal funds, and some we get from the JAI, but after the snowstorm, we decided not to plant olives, but more grapes. In the spring we plough the groves. If we have young trees I water them in May, June, and July. To mature trees I don't give water, I leave them *ba ʾal* [fed by rain]. After three or four years, until the tree matures, I stop watering it. The tree begins to produce fruit by the fourth year; after its seventh year it starts giving you fruit every year.

When I met Um Yasin and Abu ʿAttallah, they relied on farming for their livelihood. Olive growing was just one part of the variety of fruits and vegetables they grew on the land. Prior to my visit in 2015, they received support from a local campaign organization to plant a grove of apples, in the form of saplings and volunteers to plant them. In total there were 365 olive trees on the land: each terrace had between sixty and one hundred trees. Um Yasin and Abu ʿAttallah owned sixty-five of them; the rest belonged to Abu ʿAttallah's siblings and their families. Abu ʿAttallah relied a lot on his tractor, which he maintained in a nearby village. When it broke down or when he needed a new one, which happened twice in the years between 2012 and 2015, he struggled to find funds for it. This worried him as any plot of land that is not being ploughed and planted is noticed by the authorities, who constantly monitor land use in the area. They can then easily expropriate it based on an old Ottoman rule that allows the authority to take from its owners what they deem to be unplanted land. Confiscation of land has been used by Israeli authorities as a tool to make life more difficult for farmers and force them to leave their land.

The family told me that the harvest is completed by volunteers, activists, and some members of the extended family. In some years the family picked more than in others due to natural changes in weather conditions. Abu ʿAttallah used long-handled shears to prune high branches during picking days. Olives harvested during the day were laid in the front court on a sheet in the sun until the harvest was complete and olives were cleaned from leaves and branches and loaded into the car to be transported to the press. When I joined Abu ʿAttallah on a trip to press the olives it took forty-five minutes to drive to the press in a village south of the wadi. The olives were unloaded from sacks in the back of the car into the weighing machines, then emptied into the first station of the room-sized machine. At the first station they were rinsed, then moved down the machine to be crushed. Next, the good oil was separated from the water and the waste product, known locally as *jefet*, which is often used for fuel. Finally, the olive oil came out of a tap at the other end of the room, and was filled into seven-liter containers.

Toward the end of spring and the beginning of summer other activities began in earnest, such as growing summer vegetables. At the end of the summer and after most of the produce was harvested, Um Yasin and Abu ʿAttallah prepared *mal-ban*, a local delicacy made of wheat flour, grape juice, pine seeds, and almonds that is eaten as a snack. In addition, they made jams and sauces, such as tomato sauces and *dibis* (grape molasses). Some of these products were stored for the family to eat in the winter months, and some were sold to locals.

Farming as a main occupation in the family is a purposeful daily activity as it produces food and contributes toward maintaining the health and well-being of the family. Working the land requires an ongoing orchestration of factors, such as the seasons, the climate, the soil, and the water. The fallah gains dignity and respect from the village for being self-sufficient, and moreover, specific to the situation in the oPt, the military occupation and the spread of the illegal colonies have caused this occupation to become a resistive one to challenge the control of the military authorities over all aspects of life here.

When I asked them how farming olives affected their health, Abu ʿAttallah said: "Health stays good because I work with energy and motivation, and because I am not forced to do it."

As for what motivated them to grow olives and work the land, they replied:

UM YASIN: To protect it so they (military occupation) can't dispossess us. As long as we protect the land, we protect ourselves, we will stay on our land; in the past and still today for some people the land was raped and taken by force. Today our land won't be taken by force.

ABU 'ATTALLAH: For me, there's this relationship with the land. If you ask me to do any other activity, for example if you tell me "take this football and play with it," I won't, but if you ask me to go for a walk in the mountain on the dirt road, I tell you, "yes it will be a pleasure." You tell me, "Take these keys and take the car for a drive," I don't have anything to do with driving, I won't go. I am in love with the land and trees, but generally with the work of the whole of the land, not only with the olive tree. In working the land there's a great pleasure for me.

When I asked about why their motivation and will to work the land were so strong, Abu 'Attallah told me: "My will is strong because I love the *a'rd* [land]; it springs from my love of the land."

We discussed their future as growers of olives and workers of the land, and they said to me:

ABU 'ATTALLAH: I want Yasin to become an agricultural engineer because I want him to stay put and not to abandon the land; this is a kind of resistance.

UM YASIN: It is our greatest jihad [effort to confront oppression]; if we are insisting on isolating ourselves to live on this land, isn't this the greatest jihad? All the things we needed to compromise on in order to stay here.

I was interested in other hopes they might have for the future, and Abu 'Attallah told me: "We want to live in our home in security and safety; there's nothing else I want."

In addition to the activity of olive growing being a source of purpose and health and well-being, it is also a source of meaning for the families I visited. Meanings that span the personal, familial, and the sociopolitical, and even the spiritual aspects of peoples' lives here. More importantly, being a resistive act is especially meaningful as a way to become an agent in your own life when all aspects of your life are restricted. Olive growing becomes a symbol for existence.

Sutra as Doing for Well-Being

Olive growers told me that the olive tree provides for many of the basic needs of their families. People here pickle the olives and eat them with most meals in the morning, noon, and evening. They press the olives for oil, which is used in most dishes, savory and sweet. In the past, before the widespread use of gas, olive oil was used to light lamps. Some drink a cup of olive oil in the morning to give them energy to carry out the day's tasks. The proverb says: "If you eat olive oil you will be strong enough to knock over a wall"—a saying that children are taught to encourage them to consume olive oil. Some use the oil to enrich and treat hair and skin. The olive tree leaves are brewed for medicinal uses for humans and animals. The wood is used to make tools and souvenirs. The pips and the waste products from pressing olives are used to make soap, and are made into organic fertilizers and fuel. The olive-growing families I met told me that in a good year they sell the oil and olives they do not use to families who do not own land or grow olives. It is important to state that families reported that olive growing does not make families rich, and that what they produce is often just enough to feed the family. Only one of the four main participant families in this study—Um Yasin and Abu 'Attallah's—relied on farming as their main means of income generation. Abu 'Attallah said: "What we earn is maybe enough for the things we eat. The earnings we take from the land often return to it." He was referring to the resources spent on maintaining the land and trees and on the picking, planting, and pressing of the olives.

In addition to the basic physical needs, *Sutra* through olive growing provides emotional wellness, dignity, and social protection. The tasks related to olive growing, such as picking, ploughing, and pruning, were described by participants as actions that induce calmness and a meditative state of mind. As Abu 'Attallah explained: "Working the land and looking after the olive tree is a pleasure for me. There's a feeling of calm, you understand? It often gives me a mental escape. When I focus on the task in hand, I stop thinking about anything, not about food, or about a drink, nothing." In addition to this immediate or acute state of emotional wellness, olive growing as *Sutra* gives the family longer-term emotional and social benefits. It is linked to feelings of security and self-confidence, as the family can provide for the needs of its members by growing olives. Abu Nedal told me: "When you have land and olive trees you are respected in the community. You have dignity." Just like a shield or a fence, which separates the house from other houses and protects it from evildoers, olive growing for *Sutra* leads to autonomy and self-reliance as the family will not need others to help them fulfill their basic household requirements. As a result, they feel self-respect and dignity. The family is esteemed by others as it can provide for itself and may even be able to do that for others, either by selling olive products or by allowing those without land to glean the fruit remaining on the trees after the harvest. More on the intercommunal aspect of olive growing will be discussed in the following chapters. However, *Sutra* is one of the essential means of believing and acting among the fallahi families I visited. They base their relationships to each other on this principle, among others rooted in their culture. *Sutra*'s meanings and functions relate to the term fallahin, which describes land-based, peasant, and farming ways of life. The noun *fallah/a* means a person who tills the land, or one who survives and betters her own, and her society's, circumstances in order to become self-reliant (Dar Al-Mashriq 1986).

Since the Israeli invasion and military occupation of the West Bank in 1967, and the increase in land grab and in colonies on Indigenous Palestinian land, *Sutra* in olive growing had acquired new meanings. Participant families felt that in working the land and growing the hardy and long-living olive trees, they protect their land from confiscation, and therefore farming olives conveyed a new resistive identity. Abu ʿAttallah told me: "The land you dig will pray for you, but the land you abandon will place a curse on you," relaying a spiritual dimension to growing olives in these terraced hills of Palestine. The olive tree is known to live for hundreds and even thousands of years, needing minimal care and irrigation, and as a result of land segregation and colonization, communities had begun to plant more olives to protect their land from confiscation (Qumsiyeh 2011; Rijke and van Teeffelen 2014). The olive tree and growing olives came to be symbols of persistence, of staying put on the land and of resistance to violations against land and trees. Moreover, olive-growing families had acquired a new role in society as land protectors and resisters against colonization and land segregation. The theme of resistance, or the daily acts of *Sumud,* will be expanded on in chapter 4. It is, however, highlighted here to illustrate that the motivator for action of *Sutra* in olive growing is linked to collective political and spiritual meanings and roles for the Palestinian olive-farming communities I met. It is a unique element of daily activities and offers fresh insights into how those activities are conceptualized within the social sciences, and occupational therapy and occupational science theory, and how they inform activism, and other areas of study concerned with human daily life, as discussed below.

Sutra as an Expression of Multiple Purposes and Meanings

The actions of *Sutra* relating to farming olives—as a daily occupation—correlate with the relationship between the aforementioned concepts: doing—a dimension of meaningful daily activity linked to survival and security; and being—a second factor of occupations associated with meaning and fulfillment of roles in the community (Wilcock 2006).

According to Wilcock (ibid.) daily occupations that represent the interaction between doing and being are considered to fulfill purposes such as providing food, shelter, and income, and meanings relating to the occupational roles people fulfill within their community. There is a mutual relationship between the acts and the feelings about them, which causes those who engage in the activity to feel well, and to express individual, social, and political meanings and functions (Wilcock

2006; Wilcock and Hocking 2015). This was indeed the case for olive growing done by the families I met, observed, and talked to in the West Bank. They grow olives to provide for the physical, emotional, social, and political needs of their families and communities. They participate in this activity as it makes them feel well and dignified. More specific and unique to their historical and political context, olive growing in Palestine under military occupation has additional political and spiritual meanings and roles for families here.

For an activity to be considered an "occupation," as articulated in the disciplines of occupational therapy and occupational science, it should have a purpose, such as caring for self, working, or recreation. It is also thought to have a subjective meaning for individuals, such as fulfilling a carer's role or being a learner, or a student (Whalley Hammell 2015). This sorting of the things people do into three categories: self-care, work, or leisure, is aligned with a normative role and based on able-bodied, Eurocentric ideas of prioritizing self-care (the phrase self-care here refers to activities of daily living performed for the purpose of looking after our bodies, e.g., washing and dressing, and toileting) and economically productive activities over other types of activities, such as those done for spiritual meanings and purposes (Whalley Hammell 2004). The "triad of privileged occupations [self-care, work, and leisure] has only partial resonance with the experience of people whose lives have been disrupted, for example, by impairment or illness, war, unemployment, bereavement or geographic dislocation" as Whalley Hammell stated (ibid., 297). I add to this list of disruptions: military occupation and land colonization, and structures and policies of segregation that disrupt the daily lives of families, as is the case of olive growers in Palestine. They are disrupted by policies and practices that lead to segregating land from its owners, land confiscations, and violence against trees and people. Unlike the understanding of occupation in mainstream Western thought, whereby it fulfills a single type of purpose and role, such as providing food or income, olive growing was observed to hold multiple purposes and meanings for each family. Observations and conversations during field work, as presented above, showed that olive growing can satisfy multiple purposes: providing food, fuel, medicine, hygiene, tools, and fertilizing. It was observed that during harvest and planting seasons, communities gather to work, eat, sing, and rest in the groves. During other times of the year, olive groves are used for picnics, hosting guests, and for exploration and play for children. Growing olives expresses a diversity of meanings and roles that span the emotional, social, political, and spiritual spheres of human experience.

It has been suggested that instead of this division into three types of occupation, it might be more beneficial to consider occupations as meeting "dimensions of meaning" that are "intrinsic" to the individual and meet internal or individual needs, such as self-maintenance, expression, and fulfillment (ibid.). Based on evidence from studies grounded in "client-centred" values and spanning diverse subjective experiences from around the world, Whalley Hammell (2009) identified four alternative categories that address these "intrinsic" meanings: restorative occupations, daily activities done for belonging and contributing to others, those that are done for engagement in doing, and those activities that relate to continuity of the past and hope for the future. Although the collective nature of human needs had been acknowledged here, this conceptualization remains individualistic and based on the experience of occupational therapy clients who have experienced a physical or mental disability. Moreover, the notion of meaning is individualistic as it often addresses a person's subjective experience as separate from other individuals' experiences or their environment (Dickie, Cutchin, and Humphry 2006). This limits the applicability of these dimensions, or categories of doing, in a collectivist society such as in the West Bank of Palestine. In particular, its relevance is limited when describing the daily lives of olive-growing communities who have not been diagnosed with a disability as those studied in Whalley Hammell's scholarship. In such communities, personal meanings are not necessarily separate from those of the family or the community, such as the spiritual significance and symbols that are expressed in the actions related to farming olives and are mainly conveyed in collective terms.

This holism between the internal and external, or individual and social meanings, was reported in the study of women engaging in craft production in Palestine (Frank 1996). In this research it was concluded that the preservation of crafts by women had personal and cultural survival functions for the community, who were fighting for their livelihood and against patriarchal and military oppression. As in other studies with Indigenous communities experiencing land colonization or similar contextual barriers to their daily activities, such as native communities in the northwest United States reported by Frank (2011), for olive farmers the boundaries between their internal subjective experience and their external realities seem less defined than what is often portrayed in mainstream Western literature about the division between the person and their environment. For olive growers I met, belonging and attachment to their place and context is integrally embedded into their identity and daily activities. This also resembles the findings of a study on turf-cutting in Ireland, a nation that has also experienced colonialism and changes to daily occupations as a result; turf-cutting was judged to be a meaningful daily activity driven by more than just practical concerns; researchers observed that cutting turf expressed tradition, and the preservation and transmission of cultural values and identities (McGareth and McGonagle 2016). Based on these findings and on my observations, it appears that what was beneficial for the family or

48   Chapter Two

the community of olive farmers was also beneficial for the individual. The needs of
the family, the local community, and the general Palestinian population were the
priority, and they were not expressed as different from the needs of the individual
member. The collective protection, dignity, and well-being were the priorities
when *Sutra*, as a medium for action, was expressed through olive farming. Moreover, participant families' understanding of well-being was specific to their circumstances, as analyzed in the next section.

Sutra for Well-Being and Occupational Balance

Olive-farming families I met told me about how they perceive olive growing for
Sutra as fulfilling diverse needs, purposes, and meanings, and leads to positive
health and well-being. I understood their conceptualization of their well-being to
express a balancing act between all spheres of their experiences, but that didn't
mean that for some this balancing act was easy to achieve. In this section I relate
the experience of farming olives for *Sutra* and well-being to the concept of occupational balance (as understood by occupational therapists and occupational
scientists), the specific conceptualization of Palestinian olive farmers' well-being,
and how their well-being was affected as a result of an occupational imbalance
caused by environmental conditions that occur outside of their control.

Most farmers I met have other paid occupations in addition to farming olives,
or if they worked in agriculture as their main paid occupation, they cultivated
other fruits and vegetables on their land. Prior to Um Weehab's retirement from
teaching, she used to work on the land during evenings and holidays. She would
fulfill the roles of mother, wife, and teacher, and now she was also a grandmother.
Um Weehab had recently added a new daily occupation that fitted in with her
other work and provided her with personal and collective meanings and positive
impacts on her and her community's wellness: she was acting as a community
leader in the newly founded seed library—described in chapter 4—where she was
teaching young people and teachers how to conserve native varieties of vegetable
and fruit seeds. About the relationship between olive growing and his well-
being, Abu Kamal explained how growing olives gave him a sense of "natural wellness" and that it matched, or balanced with, his other activities and capacities,
which in his case included working as a respected academic and his familial roles
as a father and a husband. Abu 'Attallah said he was satisfied with working six
hours a day on his land. The rest of the day he dedicated to caring for his son or
visiting family.

An activity is considered an occupation if it is found to lead to positive or negative well-being (Wilcock 2006). Well-being is defined as the "overall content-

ment" or "perceived state of harmony" between the biological, emotional, social, and political spheres of human experience (Whalley Hammell 2009, 108). Olive growing is an occupation that affects people's wellness or quality of life and, just like other land-based activities in other global contexts, it was found to have a restorative and healing nature. For example, Inuit communities in Canada who had experienced long-term consequences of settler-colonization found healing through traditional occupations, such as hunting (Thibeault 2002). The previously mentioned study of turf-cutting also reported the "restorative nature" of this traditional and collective activity (McGareth and McGonagle 2016). In contrast to traditional categorization of daily occupations and their links to each other and to health and well-being, olive growing as an occupation for *Sutra* is not separated from a person's other tasks and roles. Moreover, it is found to be well-coordinated and balanced with other actions and functions participants accomplish in the family or in society, and as a result of this it has positive impacts on their well-being.

The concept of balance between activities, for Whalley Hammell (2004, 303), refers to a "harmony" between the purposes or utility of the activity, and the meanings it expresses. For Whalley Hammell (ibid.), the right balance should be struck between "choice, purpose, meaning and self-worth" as they are experienced in everyday activities. This harmony through doing an activity is described as "occupational balance" and is usually achieved by not doing too much or too little of one type of activity, or when humans use just the right combination of sensory-motor, mental, or social capacities (Wilcock 2006). Occupational balance implies not being overoccupied or underoccupied, resulting in positive impact on wellness and health (Wilcock and Hocking 2015). Olive-farming individuals and communities I met demonstrated a specific understanding of this harmony that leads to well-being and expresses the being (well) dimension of occupations.

In Palestine this state of balance is named *Al-ʿafya*—a term that encompasses more than health or lack of disease. It has more of a social and a spiritual meaning than *Seha* (the word that signifies health in Arabic), which means a correct bodily state and is a term that is exchanged when people drink and eat together, or when they visit those who suffer an illness. *Seha* implies and expresses a wish for someone to attain a state of mental and physical wellness. *Al-ʿafya,* on the other hand, refers to healing from diseases, and more importantly it includes other meanings, such as doing righteous deeds that cause the person to be perceived as good. The verb of the root *ʿafya* (from which *Al-ʿafya* is derived) signifies giving, forgiving of sins, fixing corruption, doing good, and chastity (Dar Al-Mashriq 1986). It is often linked to feelings of well-being associated with getting involved in adequate, socially sanctioned, and satisfying work. When people visit each other or when they meet family members, friends, or strangers who are engaged in a task such as cleaning the house, making food, or fixing something, they greet them with the saying: "May Allah provide you with *Al-ʿafya*." *Al-ʿafya* relates to *Sutra* in that it implies doing something that is good for the individual and their community and harmonizes physical, mental, economic, social, and spiritual values and deeds. The term suggests equal worth for all those spheres. Achieving Al-ʾafya through an occupational balance is not the same as what is understood in the term "work-life balance," which is often cited in media or in governmental and corporate propaganda in the West as what people need to aspire to (Clouston 2014). A study found that occupational therapists experience occupational imbalance due to the demands of their job, based on a dichotomy between paid work and other occupations, the "social hegemony" of paid work and the culture of taking personal responsibility for performance measured by neoliberal standards—all of which are values embedded in the phrase "work-life balance" (ibid.). This term, therefore, gives priority to doing paid occupations for the purpose of producing monetary capital. Furthermore, it is based on the assumption that there are only two types of occupations: paid employment, and the rest of the rich array of human activities grouped under the second category, described as "life."

An alternative to this reductionist understanding is the conceptualization of harmony between personal and communal aspects of well-being achieved through traditional activity, as reported in Global South groups, including here in Palestine, and other Indigenous communities who have a unique understanding of health and wellness that encompass not only spirituality and cultural identity, but also harmony with the natural environment. For example, in an exploration of Māori health and occupations in Aotearoa (Māori name for New Zealand), Hopkirk and Wilson (2014) found that communities identified connections to, and being part of, the natural environment as essential to sustain and meet their wellness needs. This harmony between the personal and the natural environment was also observed among families of olive growers I met in Palestine. When people reported their feelings about growing olives for *Sutra*, they associated them with land, trees, soil, and other features of the natural surroundings.

Abu Kamal told me:

> In order for me and my family to achieve the natural balance for our personality, we work in the land and we plant and grow olives. The relationship with the olive tree was transferred to us in natural succession from the previous generation. I believe that the environment and geography are inherited by us. There is a natural relationship between the land and the human being, because the human body is made of the same elements the soil is made of.

Olive Growing for *Sutra*

More on this connectedness and belonging to land, nature, and other-than human communities will be discussed in the next chapter. It is briefly discussed here because of its contribution to achieving harmony between individuals and nature, and how it leads to being well through doing, or *Al-ʿafya*. Similar conceptualizations of well-being are increasingly being reported in studies with Indigenous communities, which experience colonization and environmental degradation in all corners of the world: from Ireland to the North and South Americas, to India, Japan, and Aotearoa (Aoyama 2012; Frank 2011; Hopkirk and Wilson 2014; McGareth and McGonagle 2016; Núñez Valderrama, Hernández, and Alarcón 2022; Shetty and Nayar 2024). The experience of olive-growing families in the West Bank of Palestine offers further evidence of the need of human societies to feel harmony with the natural environment through what they do.

Occupational imbalance results, as stated in the literature, from contextual factors such as economic and labor policy, or any other political, social, or cultural stressors (Wilcock 2006; Wilcock and Hocking 2015). For the Inuit in Canada, colonization, governmental policy, and climatic conditions caused changes in the occupational balance between those traditional activities they wanted to engage in, such as gathering and hunting for food, and those that were forced on them, such as permanent settlement and Western education. This caused many negative health consequences for the community, including obesity and addictions (Thibeault 2002). In Norgaard's (2019) study of the traditional occupations among the Karuk people in the Klamath Basin in modern-day California, she highlighted similar connections between colonizations, people, their natural environment, and their occupations: interconnections that help maintain people's health and food sovereignty. For the olive-farming families I met, the historical and political processes of land colonization and the spread of a globalized neoliberal economy have led members of families either to not find adequate and healthy activities to do, or to having to engage in demanding occupations at the same time without much choice. Nedal, for example, works in construction in Israel during the day, and on his family's land and in a barber shop in the evenings and weekends. He is not able to spend enough time with his family or friends, and for him occupational harmony, or *Al-ʿafya*, is hard to achieve. Nedal often expressed to me his shame that he works in Israel and his frustration he could not find other paid work. Nedal was also frustrated that he was not able to get involved in community work as he used to. His father, Abu Nedal, told me that as a result of the first Intifada (uprising), when schools closed for long periods of time due to curfews and violence, he convinced Nedal to go to work rather than continue his studies, as the family needed extra income.

Nedal said:

> I can't leave the land, I can't leave my job, but the thing that pains me inside is that I work in Israel. You plant a tree to pick the fruit, and if you look after it your children can eat from it. But when I work [in Israel], who eats my fruit? Our brothers the Israelis. The Israelis I work for don't appreciate my work. My boss always makes me feel inferior, that I am an Arab, and he is an Israeli, always and everywhere. When I work for them, nobody praises me for achieving this work. For example, now I plant and I want to feed the people of Beit Lahem [the near- est market town], and the people of Beit Lahem will say that person planted it and his produce is good. But when I work in building homes for Israelis, they don't tell me "You the Palestinian, your work is good," they will say to my Israeli boss that his work is good. Practically I am only a saw or a hammer. If I get sick and stay in my home, nobody cares. I will be replaced.

Nedal's frustration and shame result from the disconnection between what he wishes to do and what he feels he needs to do in reality. He does not, however, feel the same frustration and shame about olive growing, which he considers an occu- pation of necessity that he is proud he can still engage in. This was also found among land-based communities in Ireland. Traditional turf-cutting was observed to be an essential and ubiquitous part of life in the countryside, which was "seen as an occupation of necessity rather than an occupation of choice that people felt positive about" (McGareth and McGonagle 2016, 312). Despite the consequences of the imbalance between his various activities and capabilities, for Nedal olive growing meant he could provide *Sutra* and *Al- ʿafya* for himself, his family, and his community. He considered it an indispensable way of life that brought together all elements of his identity in equal measure: the familial, social, spiritual, histori- cal, cultural, and political. His father, Abu Nedal, who returned to his village after decades living in the nearby town where he was involved in several social and political activities, told me as quoted elsewhere: "I returned because this is my fate, my life, and there's danger in the village. I don't have a future in Beit Lahem. My future is here. I have my family and house here, in my land." He was referring to the ongoing land grab his village suffers from, caused by the nearby colonies, and to the almost daily violence the villagers face from settler-colonizers and the army. Nedal stated:

> Because I was born into a family of fallahin, I have to continue with the same lifestyle. The military occupation played a role in the story of work for us here. It was a leading cause for people leaving their land, and people got greedy for sala- ries. Even university students left their studies for work. I know a man whose

Olive Growing for *Sutra*   53

father died, and because he works inside the Green Line [in Israel], he has neglected the trees. Others hire workers to maintain the land for them.

When asked about possible alternatives to farming olives that her family could
choose, Nada told me:
    We are not placed in circumstances in which we have an option, and we cannot
be defeated. The other option we have is to be defeated. I don't know other choices
we can take. Maybe the alternative could be to leave the country, or to provide for
our children in another place.
    Olive-farming families I met, in engaging in their daily activities for *Sutra*, shed
a unique light on the conceptualization of occupation in mainstream scholarship.
In such works, doing an occupation is usually associated with individual choice,
and it is assumed that there is a personal agency—separated from the environment—at work (Dickie, Cutchin, and Humphry 2006). However, communities
in the West Bank reported that they had no choice but to continue with this traditional way of life. If there was a choice for them, then it was taken collectively
under adverse circumstances in order to provide for their livelihood, and to protect their families, communities, and their dignity. They had no choice but to be
well through doing olive growing in order to express the diverse meanings and
roles they acquired from previous generations, and which they were fighting to
preserve. This, for them, was a harmonious diversity of functions that spanned all
spheres of their existence: the personal, familial, economic, social, spiritual, and
political. In that sense they further our understanding of occupation, occupational
balance and imbalance by offering us their special way of doing through the concept of *Sutra*, and its positive consequences on individual and collective occupational harmony, termed here as *Al- 'afya*.

Sutra as an Expression of a Nonbinary Human-Environment Relationship

Alternative theorization of occupation and occupational balance have been attempted by critical thinkers adopting an occupational justice lens. They offer a critique of Eurocentric understandings of key concepts that has been helpful in going
beyond the dualistic notions of people and their environment that are dominant
in theory and practice. Some scholars have critiqued the term "occupation" as an
action of the person—an individual who is separate from her surroundings, be it
human or other than human. Dickie, Cutchin, and Humphry (2006, 85) suggested the term "occupational domain" to counter the reductionist and individualistic definition of "occupation" in the literature. They defined it as a process
located at the level of the situation rather than the person. They stressed that this

understanding of occupation is highly contextualized and inclusive of social groups, processes, and history. Their insights on how the process of being engaged in a meaningful activity brings balance or well-being links to what they called a "transactional" relationship between humans and their environment. For them, the links between humans, their context—place and time—and the activity is not a mere "interaction" but a mutual relationship "through which human beings, as organisms-in-environment-as-a-whole, function in their complex totality" (ibid., 83). This transaction implies that there is no hierarchy between those elements; that humans are part of their environment and that they influence it and are influenced by it through engaging in daily actions in a mutual relationship.

This rejection of the dominant dualism has been articulated by other critical thinkers in occupational science. Frank (2011) discussed this transactional relationship between occupation and place within Indigenous cultures in the southwest of the United States of America. Frank, like Dickie, Cutchin, and Humphry before her, referred to place as it was conceptualized by John Dewey, the pragmatist philosopher who defined place or site as a space where culture evolves through people's actions. The concept of place implies more than just the geographical location and encompasses social, cultural, and political meanings, according to this understanding (ibid.). This, Frank explained, is especially relevant to native societies who, as a result of European settler-colonialism, have suffered land alienation and its negative consequences on their health and well-being. The transactional relationship for those communities occurs between the place, site or society, and the individuals. In her review of studies on the consequences of settler-colonialism on Indigenous health and well-being in the southwest of the United States, Frank (2011, 3) proposed "viewing occupations as the sites within Deweyan situations where cultures undergo transformation through the actual doing of things." Indigenous tribes and individuals who were studied in the research reviewed by Frank (ibid.) were "thoroughly shaped by and through the possibilities of his or her language, family, [and] community" (6).

This strong mutual association between place, humans, and occupations was commented on by Kantartzis and Molineux (2012). They provided an alternative conceptualization of the relationship between humans and their context through their occupation to that dominant in the English language literature of occupational science. Their evidence came from Kantartzis's exploration of the meaning of occupation in a Greek town. Occupation was described as a process that is purposeful, but its purposes "may be enfolded, interwoven, emergent and complex" (ibid., 47). Similar to the analysis of my observations in Palestine, they stated that occupations in Greece "tend to arise as a vehicle for significant aspects of life such as sustaining oneself and one's community" (ibid.). Kantartzis and Molineux related this understanding of daily activity to the unique historical and political context of communities living in a specific location in a certain time in history. They based their argument on the concept of activity proposed by the sociologist Anthony Giddens who offered an understanding of activity as something that emerges as a continuation between spatial and temporal, and objective and subjective, levels of human action (ibid.).

Still, this utilization of Western-centric theory created by privileged white scholars mainly living in the anglophone world may be limited in its application to Global South settings outside the Western world. As a result of historical, global, and more specific local factors, Palestinian thought, however, adds to the conceptualization of daily activity by emphasizing the mutual interrelationship between humans, their doings, and the context they live in.

This mutual association between place and time, and the external and the internal elements of human experience through action, is illustrated in the experience of Palestinian olive-farming families in a particular form of relationship. The ongoing settler-colonialism and policies of separation led to Palestinian communities experiencing dispossession, violence, and other economic and social adversities that impacted on their daily realities (Said 2003). However, this did not stop them from utilizing their collective agency. Palestinians have been active survivors of oppressive policies and practices, who through doing this essential activity of farming olives, which leads to positive wellness, added a new layer to their roles. Farming olives came to express a resistive identity and motivation to take part in occupations that sustained their survival, which highlighted the social and political significance of such an act. Palestinian, Arab, and Israeli thinkers have theorized the daily lives of families and groups here as a social phenomenon that is highly contextual. They have stated that realities are created by communities themselves who are living in specific historical, social, and political circumstances. Scholars studying communities' daily life under military occupation concluded that people make their own destinies through their doing. They do this despite the human-made adversities forced on them. This unique experience of communities making their own realities despite oppressive contextual conditions that are imposed on them was termed the "Palestinian condition" (Rosenfeld 2004; Said 1999, 2000, 2003; Sayigh 1979; Zureik 1977, 2016).

Displaced Palestinian peasants were studied by Sayigh (1979), who analyzed the historical context of their everyday lives in a refugee camp in Lebanon. Her participants lived in land-based and self-sufficient communities before their displacement during the ethnic cleansing of 1948. She pointed to a historical and political consciousness that led to embedding strong links to land and rural ways of life among families and individuals who participated in her research. This inherited awareness, which led to intentionally adopting the doing for the well-being aspect of daily life, or *Sutra*, was evident in my conversation with olive-growing families. It was found to be an enabler to their continuation of doing olive farming to maintain their livelihood and their dignity through *Sutra*. Rosenfeld (2004), an Israeli scholar, analyzed case studies of refugee families in the oPt—most of whom were self-reliant fallahi communities before the *Nakba*—in regard to their daily occupations, such as wage labor, education, and political activism. Her study included quantitative and qualitative data that were contextually analyzed and interpreted on the basis of Marxist theory. She provided helpful historical evidence of stories of refugees uprooted from olive-growing villages. The study pointed to a past of dislocation and destruction, and an ongoing "underdevelopment" and oppression: conditions that may be expected to lead to social ills such as crime, educational failings, and despair (ibid.). The study aimed to make sense of the processes that led to a surprising situation: the development of social and political resources despite this history. Rosenfeld (ibid.) provided a historical analysis to illustrate the transformations in the fields of education, professional progress, and political organization in families she studied, which were achieved despite the hardships they lived with. Both researchers, Sayigh and Rosenfeld, theorized families' participation in daily activities as being strongly associated with an awareness rooted in history and in power dynamics in their society. This consciousness enabled them to go on being well through doing in order to create their own realities, rather than be passive victims of their circumstances. This intentional aspect of the daily occupation of olive farming, termed "occupational consciousness" (Ramugondo 2015), will be expanded on in chapters 4 and 5.

Further conceptualization of Palestinian daily lives, and their relationship with the historical and political contexts, was offered in a seminal paper titled "Toward a Sociology of the Palestinians." Zureik (1977) claimed that the specific phases of Palestinian history are particularly relevant to the study of society, whereby each stage typified a unique communal experience. The pre-1948 period was characterized by settler-colonialism, peasant land alienation, class transformation from self-reliant peasantry to controlled proletariat, and the imbalanced power relationships between colonialists and the colonized; while the post-1948 era, when Palestinians became a minority in their own land, resulted in experiences common to minority social identities (ibid.). Three key concepts were offered by Zureik (2016) to help highlight how Palestinians, wherever they are, go about their daily lives: liminality, colonialism, and resistance. Liminality was defined as "the ability to shuttle between contrasting worlds of experience, [and] lies at the heart of these studies that attempt to decode the ways that the colonised and the marginalised

Olive Growing for *Sutra*

cope and make sense of their everyday life" (ibid., 20). Resistance is another analytical term helpful in understanding everyday lives of Palestinians, and it will be discussed further in chapters 4 and 5. Both liminality and resistance are key to identifying a certain experience that unified a people through their collective historical and political circumstances, which were helpful in shedding light on the everyday lives of olive farmers and how they can be interpreted.

Palestinian doing for well-being, or *Sutra*, is seen as multiple, complex, secular (related to the everyday realities of people), and intersubjective, within historical and personal contexts (Said 1999). With his style of secular interpretation of human-made realities of everyday lives from an anti-colonial, or anti-othering lens, Said attempted to demystify everyday Palestinian life (Bayoumi and Rubin 2001, xxviii). He represented the multilayered daily lives of Palestinians to help think of their society as living in situations in which they are an integral part of creating their realities through their everyday actions. He wished to explore these realities to confront "all efforts to do away with us politically as a people," and to demonstrate how "we had continued to exist and resist as a people" (Said 1999, vii). For him, the key characteristics of the Palestinian experience were "exile, dispossession, habits of expression, internal and external landscapes, stubbornness, poignancy, and heroism" (ibid., xi). Said believed that recognizing these complexities help in understanding how identities are made: by combining the personal with the collective realities, which are influencing and influenced by the acts of the community. In this way, this understanding correlates with the "transactional" bond between people, their contexts and their occupations analyzed in critical occupational science theory. However, what is unique about Palestinian communities is that they are living under ongoing conditions of colonialism and liminality, and are engaged in daily forms of resistance as creative responses to these circumstances.

Despite the seemingly unendurable factors borne out of the specific place and time, and influencing the doing of daily actions in Palestine, communities here went on to create their own destinies. Olive growers demonstrated that they were occupational beings (a term that refers to the innate human need to take part in daily activities) who were actively seeking problem-solving and creative ways to orchestrate their environment through olive growing for *Sutra*. Said (ibid., 91) was specifically addressing the case of land-based peasantry, who were not passively oppressed people but "the reserve of a force building up out of a long, intense history, frustrated and angry about the present, desperately worried about the future." Said saw peasant communities as people who continue to go on working; their daily life is led upon a "resistant soil" that they created in response to the harsh climate they live in; they did so by consistently needing ceaseless effort to persevere in their way of life. What Palestinians do in their daily lives is termed "fragmented dignity" (ibid., 145, 146). Said (ibid.) wrote: "Here are people doing their utmost to address the everyday material world with purpose and grit."

The transactional association between the elements involved in the everyday lives of olive farmers can perhaps be described as a liminal bridging between the time (of day, season, year, or period in history) and space (place or society), and the subjective—internal thoughts, feelings, and values—and the objective—external circumstances—of human realities. This interplay between those elements can be key to understanding olive farmers' occupations. This mutuality was required due to settler-colonialism, which led to resistance, which in turn allowed daily meaningful actions to continue in creative and self-determined ways. This, in turn, brought dignity, health, and well-being to individuals and families. This dignity is perhaps fragmented and incomplete but, as will be seen later in this book, olive farmers do and live in a constant process of emerging, or becoming, aimed at collective self-determination. This dignity, which is achieved through doing and being, or *Sutra*, leads to an occupational harmony, or *Al- 'afya,* for olive growers in the West Bank.

Sutra, as a means and principle for action as described in the lives of Um Yasin and Abu 'Attallah's family and others, motivates olive-growing communities to continue to engage in this most essential and historic of daily activities. They persisted with this occupation despite the harsh conditions imposed by the military occupation, and the policies of segregation and settler-colonialism. *Sutra*, as a principle of action for farming olives, which is based on values of collective and multidimensional well-being, shows that the notion of doing for well-being as cited in Western literature has been utilized in Palestine for hundreds if not thousands of years. However, it was found to challenge mainstream Eurocentric conceptualizations of occupation, occupational balance, and well-being. This chapter showed how *Sutra* furthers these understandings from a unique Palestinian lens. It demonstrated how doing olive growing for *Sutra* signifies the expression of a diverse range of purposes, meanings, and roles for individuals and families in the West Bank. This included the biological, emotional, social, political, and spiritual aspects of human experience. I hoped to illustrate in this chapter an interpretation and a conceptualization founded on decolonial philosophy that challenged individualistic and binary thought dominant in Western disciplines. The daily lives of olive-growing families in Palestine provide an empirical example of how meaningful daily activities can lead to positive, harmonious experience that combines all the aspects of human daily life that sustain livelihood, meaning, and identity.

Olive Growing for *Sutra* 59

A gate blocking an entrance to a Palestinian community. Photo taken by Ahmad Al-Bazz.

In the next chapter the concept of ʿ*Awna*, another term described by farmers as a principle of action, will be analyzed through the lens of decolonial theory. *Sutra*, ʿ*Awna*, and *Sumud*—the topic of chapter 4—will try to advance understanding and use of occupation as a transformative concept for marginalized communities in Palestine and elsewhere in the world. This latter point will be the subject of chapter 5, in which those intentional, relational, and resistive elements of the collective occupation of olive growing will be synthesized as Everyday Forms of Resistance that have implications for occupational science, occupational therapy, and other disciplines and communities of praxis.

عونة

CHAPTER 3

Olive Growing for *'Awna*

> The image of a path is apt because it is by following a path,
> created and maintained by generations of walking feet, that
> some of the dangers of the surrounding forests or mountains
> or marshes may be avoided. The path is tradition handed
> down by instructions, example and commentary.
>
> —John Berger, 1979, xviii

This chapter focuses on the concept and practice of *'Awna* and how it manifests in the everyday activities of olive growing that are motivated by belonging to land, and other more-than-human elements of the environment, and local and international human communities. The chapter begins with the definition of *'Awna* and its meanings in Palestinian society, after which the family of Um and Abu Weehab is introduced. I present my observations of this family's daily lives and what they told me about the meanings of olive growing and how it is affected by the military occupation. The remainder of the chapter presents my intercultural translation of the concept of *'Awna* as manifested in the lives of Um Weehab and Abu Weehab and other olive-farming families. In the second section of this chapter, *'Awna* as the collaborative aspect of doing olive growing is defined, followed by relating it to the concept of belonging in Western literature. The theory regarding belonging is critiqued from occupational justice and decolonial lenses. Next, *'Awna* as a principle for action is shown to be based on values of belonging to more-than-human communities, and *'Awna,* as shaped by a multigenerational and intercommunal bond, is discussed. The final section of this chapter relates the term *'Awna* to the systemic attempt to deny access to, and opportunities for, the activity of olive growing, described as occupational apartheid.

Olive Growing for *'Awna*

'Awna is a noun derived from the root *'a 'wana'* in Arabic. One key meaning of this word relates to giving and receiving assistance, and to cooperation between communities. *'Awna* is also associated with an elder woman who is experienced and wise, and who acquired her knowledge through doing activities and using her skills (Dar Al-Mashriq 1986). When it is used in conversation in Palestine, the term *'Awna* (some pronounce it as *'Owna*, or *'Ouna*) means collaboration founded on solidarity with family, village, and community—including land, trees, and animals (Al-Batma 2012). *'Awna*'s ubiquitous nature in Palestinian culture is exemplified in its use in poetry and song, some of which I heard being sung in the groves during planting and picking olives. For example, *'dal 'awna'* [a call for *'Awna*] is a folkloric genre of song performed to a melody that people dance *dabke* to. *Dabke* is a group dance often performed at weddings and other important celebrations. Women and men hold hands in a semicircle while moving their legs and feet in different routines, and while circling around the center of the yard or dance hall at varying speeds.

The lyrics to one *dal 'awna* song go as follows:

Calling you all to gather and help, for olive is the best our country can offer
Calling you all to gather and help, for my country's olive is the tastiest
Calling you all to gather and help, for my country's olives and almonds
And sage and do not forget the za'tar [a local variety of wild thyme]
And dough balls when they rise and ready
Their flavour is the best with olive oil (ibid., 37, my translation).

The Family of Um Weehab and Abu Weehab

Um Weehab, Abu Weehab, and their family live in Al-Baydar. The drive there took us west of Beit Lahem through vineyards and groves, then through roads mainly used by Palestinians to the northwest area of Beit Lahem. We drove up and down steep and lush wadis lined with traditional drystone walls marking the terraces on which olive trees are growing. Before we reached the center of the village, the bus stopped and we all got off and walked a few minutes to Khirbet Al-Baydar—the area on the outskirts of the village where the trees we came to help pick are located—carrying with us buckets, ladders, and tarpaulin sheets. We arrived at the neatly weeded groves, with well-spaced olive trees said to have been planted in Roman times. The olive groves of Um Weehab and Abu Weehab and their family expanded over a few terraces and overlooked other terraces extending to the lower wadi, where I saw an Israeli railway line and pine woods planted on the hills opposite us. I was told that on clearer days it is possible to see the Mediterranean to the west, which locals can rarely reach due to travel restrictions.

When I first met them in 2014, Um Weehab and Abu Weehab were in their sixties. Um Weehab was a retired teacher who studied in a teachers' college in a city to the north of the village. She worked in schools outside and inside the village but also looked after her children and continued to work the land. Abu Weehab was a retired engineer who studied in a neighboring Arab country before he returned to Palestine. He was an elected councillor in their village of Al-Baydar prior to his retirement. He continued to grow olives and other crops all his life in addition to his paid jobs. They lived with their youngest daughter and son in an apartment above that of their oldest son, Weehab (in his thirties), and his family. Their homes stood in the same spot where Abu Weehab grew up with his family, and where Abu Weehab's ancestors lived before them. They had another son who lived and worked in North Africa, and a daughter who lived with her family in North America, where they migrated to seek a more secure life for their children. Um Weehab often talked of how much she missed them and how much she would like them to return to Palestine where they belong and where they are needed most.

Most of Um and Abu Weehab's extended family lived in the village. Residents of Al-Baydar were very proud of their community's reputation for being the vanguard of initiatives to protect their area's heritage, environment, and land. They were famous for valuing education, especially for girls and women. One of the first schools for girls in the area was established here in the early twentieth century by an influential local man who was passionate about his community and about education.

However, Abu Weehab told me in a concerned voice that not many young people in the village are currently interested in looking after the olive trees. He said: "You will notice, if you pass more than one grove, basically those people who are older are interested in continuing this activity. The youth have very little interest."

When I first visited Al-Baydar, it had a population of five thousand residents and Abu Weehab thought that there was approximately the same number of villagers, who were born here or whose parents were, who lived abroad. I was told some of the villagers who lived abroad worked toward improving their community, or sent money to build large and expensive houses, some of which I saw at the eastern entrance to the village. It was a village with pre-Roman Canaanite farming terraces and communal irrigation canals and pools that were still used when I visited. Al-Baydar is located a few kilometers to the southwest of the capital Al-Quds, and used to be called the "vegetable basket" of Palestine before the villagers were banned from entering it, following its occupation by the Israeli Army in 1967. Since then, villagers were also banned from using the train that passed through their land to transport their produce to markets, after the Israeli authorities

Olive Growing for *'Awna*   63

destroyed the station in the middle of the last century. During and for a few years after the *Nakba* of 1948, when the village was captured by Zionist militias, the villagers were expelled. They became involved in resisting the occupation, and eventually negotiated their way back to the village, in a process that resembled the experience of Dar El Shoke (see chapter 4). This was an unusual accomplishment among the majority of the five hundred or so villages that were forcefully depopulated during and after 1948.

Al-Baydar is located on the Green Line, and some of its land crosses this line. The community managed to negotiate an agreement with the Israeli and Jordanian authorities to permit them to access their land beyond the Green Line in the middle of the last century. There were no Israeli colonies immediately bordering village land, but there was a camera mast and an Israeli security vehicle permanently stationed on the opposite hill constantly watching the village. During one of my more recent visits to the village, in the spring of 2022, the villagers told me about a settler trying to set up a farm on village land. They were proud to declare to me that they managed to stop him.[1] The Israeli separation wall, when it is completed, was planned to cross and confiscate village land. However, villagers' efforts, such as collaborating with local and international NGOs and UN agencies, succeeded in postponing this from happening in the near future by successfully applying to place their village as a protected United Nations Educational, Scientific and Cultural Organization (UNESCO) World Heritage Site. Prior to that, villagers, including Um Weehab and Abu Weehab's family, had some of their land confiscated. Some of them, including Um and Abu Weehab, have taken the Israeli authorities to the Israeli high court with partial success. This legal process lasted decades and cost the families vast amounts of money.

One of the barriers to olive farming for Um and Abu Weehab's family I was told about is the lack of infrastructure in the village, including suitable roads that lead to the olive terraces. This situation pointed to a manifestation of occupational apartheid (discussed later in this chapter) as a systematic attempt to divorce farmers from their land, their trees, and their daily activities. When I asked about how they usually reach the groves, I was told:

ABU WEEHAB: The car can reach some parts of Al-Baydar, other parts the car can't reach. This track is not easy for the car as you saw. We parked the car at the bottom of the hill, then you have to bring up the equipment on foot, and as you saw, it is only Um Weehab and me today. The means of the Palestinian are limited. The Palestinian is an orphan. There's no party that looks after him. There may be a party that aims to sabotage him and his work. For example, this road may be opened, then the Israeli army will come and close it down.

Um and Abu Weehab have dedicated their time to food-growing activities since their retirement, but they felt that they were getting on in years and were not as strong as they used to be. Weehab was the only one of their children who supported them in land-based activities, though he was not always available due to other work commitments. He always tried to find a helping hand, either by contacting organizations who coordinate international volunteers, or by organizing some relatives or friends to help. When this failed, the family hired young men to help them in busy times, such as during the olive harvest. The family normally started their olive harvest from their groves near the center of the village from where they carried their tools by hand for a ten- to fifteen-minute journey on foot from their house.

When I enquired about why the family were interested in olive farming, I was told:

> ABU WEEHAB: Look, the first thing, the olive is a tree of resistance, which lives a long life, and for me she is a resistance to the [military] occupation. This is more important than anything else. I work in the land and pay for it from my retirement wage, so the land is not wasted, because when the land is not worked that's when the [military] occupation comes and confiscates it. Of course, we live here a case of struggle. A powerful occupation. A [military] occupation that looks for any reason to stop us growing olives. There are some people who ask, "Why are you planting this? If you plant grape or apple, which has a better economic value, it is better for you." I say to them, "I am all pain and hope that the future generations will come and continue the work." But what pains you is that the new generations are moving away from *Al-a 'rd* [the land]. So at least I plant the olive even if the next generation don't look after it, or look after it but not much, at least if they only do the ploughing, the land remains reclaimed. But if I plant it with apple, or almond, it will live 10 years or 15 years and then die, and the land returns to the uncultivated condition. And if there's nobody who reclaims it, it will be susceptible to confiscation. Our enemy, on the other side, that is the [military] occupation, by applying a deceiving, malicious policy, is using all tools in order to control the land and take it from us.

Regarding one of these tools the Israeli authorities use to confiscate land—and which to me pointed to another manifestation of occupational apartheid—I was told this story.

> ABU WEEHAB: I will tell you a story that happened to us here in Al-Baydar. In the year 1983, the military ruler comes and tells us that there is some land, of 700

dunums, that is now confiscated. And pretends to be fair and very democratic. What he does, he said, "You have 20, 25 days to object to this decision via the court." We hired a lawyer and we went to submit an objection. The lawyer submitted an objection on villagers' behalf, as the land belonged to some of us in the village. Because when the [military] occupation comes, it doesn't discriminate between families. It [the military occupation] wants the land. We formed a committee that worked on locating the documents that prove our ownership, in order to be able to defend ourselves in the Israeli military court. Here we notice that we have a problem in Palestine. Israel considers that proving ownership of the land comes in the form of the Turkish *Taboo* registration, but here very few of us have the documents to prove this. When the Turks ruled, they registered all of the land, but I didn't have any paper to show registration. We surveyed the land, marked on the maps our plots, in order for the lawyer to retrieve its registration.

The military occupation submitted maps detailing the plots which are cultivated in one colour, and the parts which are not cultivated in another colour. I tell you, in the 1940s, they photographed the land, and then the percentage of cultivated land was 70 percent, and the English law [from the period of the British Mandate in Palestine], and before it the Turkish [Ottoman] law, doesn't permit it [the military occupation] to confiscate land with such a percentage of use. After 10 years, in the 1950s, they took a second picture of the same piece of land, showing that the percentage of land use had dropped to 60 percent. After eight years the use dropped to 50 percent. After that it was 40 percent. In the late 1970s, the percentage of land use had dropped to 30 percent. There's an English law, and before it a Turkish law, which allows them to confiscate unused land within that percentage of use. See how it [the military occupation] uses all the tools in order to confiscate our land? As if they were waiting day after day until the percentage of land use allowed them to claim the land as their right.

The court proceedings took a very long time, eight to nine years: from 1983, until maybe 1991, or even 1992. What happened in the end is that the court ordered this land to be expropriated to the state. I tell you they are a state who claims to represent democracy and justice! We had, as they claimed, an opportunity to appeal to the high court of justice, as if this "democratic" state is very just! So, we appealed to the high court, and the high court of course requires another lawyer, and it requires additional financial resources, and people's financial means are limited here. Despite all of that, we appealed. And after a couple of hearings, it was decided to return the case to the military court. Then the Intifada began, and things happened which stopped us from pursuing this case. Then we were surprised to find out that there was a ruling in favour of the confiscation.

When I asked how they responded to this, Abu Weehab told me:

Now I am talking about my personal experience. I know that according to their own law [Israeli law], if there was a 10-year period during which they [the Israeli authorities] haven't utilised the land, then the previous owner has the right to utilise it. After 10 years I went to the plot of land that is my own, and dug it and I planted it with olives and other fruits and until now it's used. When I reclaim land, I make sure I build dry stone walls because they [military occupation] rely on taking pictures from the air, and when the plot of land is walled, it shows that it is cultivated. If there were no walls, they will want to say that it's not cultivated. I will tell you, simply, the land in which this tree is planted is saying "I am utilised, I am planted." In this way I pull a small rug from under the attention of the military occupation because here my land is planted. You are the occupier, you can bombard airports, you can bombard and occupy anywhere you want, I can't compete with you, but you can't claim you are law abiding and come to take my land.

When asked about other meanings they attached to olive growing, Abu Weehab said:

From a social aspect, look, there are many things. Firstly, there's the *'Awna* or the collaboration between family members and the villagers. There's also the *tasyeef*, which allows people who don't have land and trees to take what is left on the trees after the owners have harvested them. There's also something called *el'giri* [following the example of your neighbours]. When I see my experiment had succeeded and I managed to reclaim land, and no one attacked it, the others will try and do the same. Finally, there's the awareness that we try and implant [consciousness] in our offspring to educate them about the importance of the land and olive growing.

Finally, I asked them what they thought about recent projects that were achieved by some of the young people in the village. For example, the villagers led a successful UNESCO application for a World Heritage Site, the rebuilding of the old houses to turn them into guesthouses and other projects, such as establishing an ecological museum whose team had built walking paths in the nearby hills to maintain their use and thereby limit the possibility of the land being confiscated, or the setup of a souvenir factory that employs local women. They replied:

UM WEEHAB: These are simple tools of resistance. People don't have permits to travel and work, so they make sure an old, abandoned building is utilised and provide an income to the village council. And from that they are able to build or make other projects.

ABU WEEHAB: The plan since 2005 has been to talk about the [separation] wall. From the military court to the high court, Al-Baydar residents went to the high court, which took the decision to halt the construction of the wall on village land for now, due to the UNESCO decision; and that was a political decision. This is a ruling that occurred in 2014. The issue lasted from 2005 until 2014. But we will continue to be watchful and concerned as this enemy [the military occupation] is unreliable.

This consciousness that passes from past and current generations to the next generations relates to communal daily living and the preservation of traditional life ways that maintain the community's health and prosperity. This awareness often leads to resistance to structures that limit their traditions by a diversity of means, which will be detailed in this and the following chapters.

Abu Kamal told me about his family's bond with the land and with olive cultivation, which summarizes the theme of ʿAwna—the focus of this chapter—well:

What connects us to the land as a family is our fallahi roots. Before their displacement, our parents owned vast lands, and large parts of them were in the hilly areas, and in common with other hilly areas of Palestine, it was planted with olives. After the *Nakba*, an Israeli settlement was built on the land. We loved the olives since we were small, even after our parents were forced to leave our ancestral village. When we were children living in the refugee camp in town, we had no land and we lived in tents. During the olive harvest season, because of the poverty we lived in, we went gleaning to gather unharvested fruit from the trees. Part of the olive picking period we call here in Palestine, *tasyeef*, a word which means that families who own land and trees leave some of the fruit on the trees and allow those without land to pick them. It is an ancient tradition that continues to this day. My siblings and I used to walk to the wadi nearest to the camp to pick olives.

One year we gathered enough fruit to produce two full containers of oil [equivalent to 14 liters], and this is something I will never forget. It was a big achievement as we had a large family and needed from six to eight containers of oil a year. We consumed a lot of it. We used to even drink the oil. Our relationship with the olive began in this way. Our dream was that when we grew up and saved money, we wanted to buy land, and this actually happened several years ago. My siblings and I were educated, and acquired qualifications in respectable professions that earned us some money. We bought some terraces in that same wadi we used to glean olives from. We began to look after this land, and we planted other things in it as well. We use the fruit and other produce collectively as an extended family, and we donate the rest for the needy in the camp. It is an adventure to buy land in this part of the world, especially here in Area C. This area is controlled by the Israeli military occupation and all of the farming land here is under threat of expropriation.

Abu Kamal and his family demonstrate this practice of *'Awna* as part of their daily resistance to enable their survival and maintain their health, but also for this family and others I met, *'Awna* is about creating new means to ensure their future and their flourishing.

'Awna as Doing for Belonging

Adding more on the collaborative aspect of the occupation of olive farming, Abu Kamal told me:

> You know, we Palestinians are a hospitable nation. We like inviting friends and neighbours to our homes. When we didn't own any land in the wadi, we invited people to our apartment, and in here you can see the space is limited. Palestinian families are large families and when they gather, they need a large space. Now we started inviting our friends to our land, so this is a form of influence on social relations.

For Nada, Abu Kamal's wife, Abu Kamal and their family, the olive grove and the doing of the activities of olive growing became harnessers of social relationships and the community's collective wellness.

Abu Weehab told me about the social aspects of olive growing for him, his wife Um Weehab, and their family:

> There are many social aspects to this activity. For example, when I finish picking my grove, I will help my brother, then I will work with my cousin who hasn't yet finished harvesting all his trees. Not for money or for any other benefits, but for something we call *'Awna* [cooperation]. It creates a good social atmosphere between people. If someone needs to rebuild a drystone wall, his relatives and friends will help him. This collaboration is very essential.

The concept of *'Awna* implies a collaboration, which is based on a way of life that necessitates a relationship of solidarity and mutual aid (Spade 2020) within and between families, the village, society, the nation, and between different global groups. It requires a strong historic bond between generations and between human communities and nature, land, trees, and animals. Doing indispensable daily activities, such as those relating to farming olives, requires this means of action to be embedded in society. Families need it to enable their survival, their dignity, their identity, and the strong alliances that rural communities have developed throughout their history. Moreover, ʿAwna as a way of life has survived and is still prevalent despite, or perhaps because of, the ongoing military occupation and settler-colonialism rural communities have experienced since the nineteenth century. This motivator to doing olive growing, termed ʿAwna, will be analyzed here in relation to the notion of belonging in occupational therapy and occupational science literature, which has two main aspects: first, the connectedness people feel to their community, and second, the contribution they make, through their participation in society, to others' well-being (Whalley Hammell 2004, 2014). Belonging expresses the importance of reciprocity and of relating to a network of social support, which form the basis of the skill or ability to engage in actions, and of the promotion of others' well-being through this action (Whalley Hammell 2004). Belonging as a contribution to well-being through doing has been discussed in the literature studying collectivist societies' values, such as Ubuntu, which in southern Africa means: "I belong, I participate, I share" (Whalley Hammell 2014, 41). More on this notion and practice of Ubuntu will be discussed later on in this chapter and in chapter 5. Furthermore, Whalley Hammell and Iwama (2012) defined the notion of belonging as connectedness to land and nature. It was understood to be more important for those Global South traditions than the doing and the being aspects of occupation that are prioritized by modern Western thought and practices in occupational therapy (Iwama 2006).

Abu Kamal's story of how his family have returned to growing olives despite their expulsion from their ancestors' village and despite living in a refugee camp for most of their lives, points to the transformative aspect of ʿAwna. For Abu Kamal's family, their belonging to their land and community and their cooperation have led to their lives being improved socially and economically.

This dimension of doing for belonging was mostly avoided up until recently in occupational therapy and occupational science writing, due to the dominant individualistic theorizing of occupation and the Western-centric binary logic in understanding the relationship between humans and their environment (Hitch, Pépin, and Stagnitti 2014a, 2014b). When it was addressed, the term was studied in research among individuals who sought occupational therapy services for their needs related to their physical and mental disabilities (ibid.). Wilcock proposed her theory of the occupational nature of humans in the 1990s, in which she suggested doing, being, and becoming as occupational determinants of health (Wilcock 1998, 2006). Belonging as a motivator for doing was initially suggested to further this theory by Whalley Hammell in 2004. Since then, Wilcock has acknowledged the benefits of belonging briefly in a paper published in 2007, after which she and Hocking (2015) cowrote a chapter about it in the third edition of the book, *An Occupational Perspective of Health*. In it they termed belonging as an aspect of occupation and well-being, which they described as "belonging through doing." They portrayed it as a universal need that spans age, gender, income, and other criteria of difference. They stated:

> Doing and being enable the maintenance and development of satisfying and stimulating relationships with family members and associates and within the community in which people live. Whether our doing engenders a sense of belonging is a matter of health and well-being of the whole planet, because human life is embedded within the global environment (Wilcock and Hocking 2015, 232).

Doing and being are still, for Wilcock and Hocking (ibid.), the main aspects of occupation that contribute to belonging and well-being. Without the doing and being aspect, according to this definition, relationships are assumed not to be formed. Although Wilcock and Hocking acknowledged the holistic associations between humans and nature and with the global community, this conceptualization is still limited. One issue is the claim for the universalistic and essentialist nature of belonging. The idea that one notion fits all communities in the globe in the same way is problematic. Another concern with this analysis is its key focus on how belonging contributes to the health and well-being of individuals, rather than pointing to the transformative social, political, and spiritual functions of it. This is a function of occupation that occupational science has been increasingly producing evidence to support, using critical research studying marginalized groups. This work is advancing understandings of belonging beyond the biomedical and dualistic lens in occupational science. Such studies include those that were conducted with Global South communities: people seeking refuge, colonized native communities, and minorities all over the world (Frank 2012; Kronenberg, Simó Algado, and Pollard 2005; Kronenberg, Pollard, and Sakellariou 2011; Núñez Valderrama, Hernández, and Alarcón 2022; Sakellariou and Pollard 2017; Shetty and Nayar 2024; Whalley Hammell 2015).

I hope that the findings of this research with olive-farming families in the West Bank of Palestine will contribute to evidence supporting the importance of the social and political roles of belonging. The form of doing for belonging that was observed in this study such as in the story of Abu Kamal and his family has been utilized because of their love and attachment to their heritage, land, and olive trees that motivate them to improve their circumstances, which led to them buying land and farming olives and other produce, despite the historic and ongoing settler-colonialism that aimed to divorce them from this tradition. But just as *Sutra* challenges Western-centric understanding of occupation as the relationship

Olive Growing for *'Awna*

between the doing and being dimensions addressed in the previous chapter, *'Awna* extends the notion of belonging from a Palestinian perspective. *'Awna* among olive-farming communities was found to represent an intentional and relational aspect of daily activities based on three main types of associations: the one between humans and the natural environment; the historic bond between humans across generations, including ancestors; and the third between different human communities.

'Awna as a Bond between People and the More-Than-Human

'Awna is founded on a relationship of interdependence between people and their land, trees, and animals. This relationship was illustrated through metaphors used by participants in their conversations with me, such as describing caring for trees as if they were their own children, or relating to the olive tree as a bride being prepared for her wedding. Bilal, another olive farmer I met, told me about maintaining his trees using the metaphor of his beloved woman to refer to the tree:

> I see the tree as being my woman whom I want to look after and make look beautiful. I want to prune it, to water it, and make it healthy and pretty. In the same way a woman or a man goes to the hairdresser who makes them look nice. For any person whose nails are long, and their hair is long, you want to trim them. And for the tree that's the same thing. How does a tree differ from a human?

Also, on this relationship with the tree, Abu Weehab told me: "I tell you honestly, when I climb the tree, my mood relaxes completely, as if I am looking after my son, and this emotional bond between the tree and me is very powerful." Analogies and metaphors such as these are evidence that families here do not separate the human race from other beings with which it shares the earth. It is a connectedness that spans species, a level of belonging beyond the human family, and has pagan spiritual origins.

This strong alliance has premonotheistic roots: it existed prior to the establishment of Judaism, Christianity, and Islam when a belief in one God, rather than a group of gods, became the norm. To enable them to make sense of natural forces influencing their lives, communities strongly related to, and identified with, their natural surroundings. They worshiped gods who provided rain and fertile soil for their crops, and others who protected them from adversities (Masalha 2013; Nashef 2002). One of those gods whom the Canaanites, Philistines, and other native societies of premonotheistic Palestine believed in was *Ba'al*. He belonged to a pantheon of gods and was worshiped for his power to bring storms and rain, thereby controlling food production (Ra'ad 2010; Thompson 2000). Today *Ba'al* is a term used in everyday speech and refers to any grain, vegetable, nut, and fruit produce that is naturally irrigated from seasonal rains.

Indigenous populations across the globe express this interconnectedness to nature and land through doing wanted and needed activities. McNeill (2016) described how the spiritual relationship of Māori communities to the natural environment is expressed and maintained through their everyday lives. McNeill's paper described a process of land alienation as a result of a history of colonialism, which resulted in losing some of the spiritual aspects of that strong link between humans and nature. These resulted in negative impacts on occupations such as education and employment and led to negative health consequences. However, McNeill showed how a revival of this spiritual bond between land and people provided a basis for negotiating a deal with the New Zealand government that allowed Māori communities to access their ancestral land. Whereas more-than-human communities are viewed in traditional occupational therapy theory as resources to be exploited (Iwama 2006), olive growers and Māori communities consider them an integral part of the community and their destinies as mutually connected.

This mutual link is essential for the maintenance of everyday activities of olive growing in the hills of southern Palestine. In these hilly areas with narrow and steep country lanes, narrow paths between buildings in villages and towns, and restrictions on building infrastructure, donkeys have become essential in helping with ploughing and transporting tools, produce, and people to and from the groves. As a result of these circumstances, people form interdependent bonds with animals, as did Nedal's grandfather. He died shortly after his donkey died because, it was said, of his grief at losing his lifelong companion. The donkey and the fallah share not a master-slave relationship, but one that relied on mutual connectedness that allowed the two to maintain their lives and belonging to community and nature. Another example is the strong links farmers develop with their land, such as the story of an elder in Dar El Shoke who decided to live in a shack on his land outside the village in order to be connected daily to soil and nature until he dies.

Palestinian traditional ways of living in the countryside are founded on a strong link to the natural environment: a relationship of love and ongoing interactions, according to Al-Batma (2012). Writing about the unique qualities of rural Palestinians, Al-Batma (herself from a local fallahi community in the oPt) addressed their bond with the natural environment as a relationship leading to the development of theoretical and practical expertise. This knowledge and skills provided information about periods for preparing the land and other key times in the farming calendar, such as those for picking olives. Farmers know when to expect a productive season or a good yield, and when the weather is going to settle after the

Olive Growing for *'Awna*

winter, by watching the stars or the movement of birds (ibid.). For example, fallahi families know when the harvest season is approaching by looking at the sky. They look for a star named *eshail*, which appears at the start of autumn. This star has always been associated with the beginning of the olive-picking season as it predicts the coming of the first rains, after which the summer dust is washed off the trees and olives are harvested (ibid.). Communities here associate their daily and seasonal farming routines with spiritual, religious, and cultural events strongly linked to natural processes. These rituals and celebrations are all linked to the months in the year and to the movement of stars and birds (more on these celebrations will be discussed below). This way of life, and the values it is founded on, such as this important alliance with the more-than-human communities that helped in explaining daily realities, developed and was transplanted into each generation (ibid.). This inherited association is an essential element of the notion of *'Awna* as a means of action and motivation for farming olives, which also has a historical and a multigenerational dimension that will be discussed next.

'Awna as an Intergenerational and Intercommunal Collaboration

In addition to a relationship to the more-than-humans, *'Awna* has an intergenerational aspect for olive growers. This was demonstrated in the experience of Abu 'Attallah, who was inspired by an elder in his family to love the land, work it, and become self-reliant. Nedal described the intergenerational element of olive growing when he told me: "We were brought up to see our grandparents grow olives. When the first rain came people knew it was olive harvest season—a beautiful season with memories of everyone helping and sharing food."
Nedal continued:

> I have land which I inherited from my grandfather, and that wasn't planted with olive, but I planted it with olive trees. We reclaimed some other land with the help of organisations who helped us plant olives there. Another one of our plots where the spring water dried up, I planted with olives because they don't need irrigation. People ask why I didn't plant anything else that makes more profit, for example grapes? For me, there's this connection, something in the unconscious happened between me and this tree, it is a historical relationship.

The connectedness to former generations has also been noted as part of the belonging aspect of occupations that other formerly colonized societies express in land-based activities. McGrath and McGonagle (2016, 317) found that turf-cutting in Ireland, like olive growing in Palestine, had a "generational consciousness" element in transmitting cultural values. Whalley Hammell (2014, 43) summarized some research evidence for this "desire to honour and remember loved ones" (43), which provides a motive for people in many cultures to participate in specific daily activities. Examples of activities through which people do this included lighting candles, giving flowers, and maintaining skillful activities handed down from previous generations. In Malta, for example, people play certain musical instruments to express solidarity with ancestors (ibid.). In the West Bank, however, the challenge for families is to continue to pass this intergenerational and historical awareness of attachment to community, land, and trees to their offspring. Many of the farmers I met told me about how they are worried that "the old will die and the young will forget," which is thought to be what David Ben-Gurion—a leading Zionist who became Israel's first prime minster—wished the policies and practices of the state of Israel to achieve (Winstanley 2013). Fallahi groups believe that there is an attempt to erase their heritage and way of life by the military occupation and the ongoing colonization of their land—a situation that I understood as an example of occupational apartheid (see below).

Together with the other consequences of human-made problems olive growers complain about, such as human-made climatic changes and globalized capitalism, Israeli policies have caused an incremental degradation of ways of knowing and doing that are essential for their survival. The structural contexts causing ʿAwna as an ancestral and historic bond to degrade are also paradoxically triggering a revival of this type of relationship between the different types of human communities. Olive farmers told me how they are frustrated by relying on the "big powers that be" to protect their values, daily occupations, and livelihood. Even the Palestinian Authority (PA), some of the participants in this study believed, was formed with the intention that it be used as a tool of further oppression. They are, therefore, looking to revive an old way of connectedness to ancestors, heritage, and traditions they believe is a key to maintaining their way of life. Examples of such initiatives, such as Bilal's family farm and the seed library, will be expanded on below. More on how people are coping with this, and on the theme of hope, community aspiration, determination, and belonging for becoming will be discussed in the next chapter. Before that, I turn to the final type of ʿAwna, or doing for belonging, found among olive farmers: the connectedness between the individuals and other human communities.

Olive growing for ʿAwna requires solidarity and interdependence between communities, including local and international groups. This needed bond is aided by a "coagency," which provides support that contributes to the wellness of the groups of people involved (Zureik 2016). This intercommunal aspect of ʿAwna in olive growing was found to occur at three different levels: the familial, including

Olive Growing for *'Awna*

the extended family or *hamoula* at the village level; the local or national domain; and the global sphere.

Interfamilial (*Hamoula*) Connectedness

Um Weehab and Abu Weehab coordinate their harvest with Abu Weehab's cousin, whose family co-owns some of the olive groves with them. I joined them and some local and international activists one weekend in the middle of October to pick their olives. The atmosphere was celebratory, and there was chatting, singing, and drinking of tea and coffee among the branches of the ancient *rumi* (Roman) trees, some of which are strong enough to be climbed for pruning. We learned how to use tools for pruning, and received a tutorial from Um Weehab, Abu Weehab, and their cousin on trimming the trees. It was during this afternoon that we talked about the term *'Awna* and about its history in their village and the local area. It was a collective moment in which we were discussing a belief and practicing it in real time—a phenomenon that Abu Weehab and most other participants in this study felt was under threat due to the attempt to "do away with us" as a culture and people. This solidarity between the core and extended family members was an agent or a facilitator to this type of *'Awna*, the one that was performed that afternoon through the doing of olive picking. Families told me that due to their social and political ills and the ongoing military occupation, they felt that this traditional way of living was at risk, and this threat was a key topic of discussion in my conversations with them.

One aspect of this intercommunal attachment is the importance of the core family. Family identity, and its role in the daily lives of rural communities in Palestine, was studied by Tawfik Canaan, a Palestinian scholar who researched local peasant communities, and subsequently in Finnish anthropologist Hilma Granqvist's ethnographies—both published their work in the early twentieth century (Nashef 2002). They described everyday and seasonal activities, and rituals in villages in the Beit Lahem region, portraying them as routines that express the importance of the core family and of the home in Palestinian culture. Most important celebrations studied in those villages were found to be related to the family and home, for example, the birth of a baby, especially if it was a boy who would carry the name of the family. Other key events in Palestinian villages were marriage and the building of a house, which traditionally housed both the humans and the animals (Nashef 2002; Sayigh 1979).

The *'Awna* between communities here is based on a hierarchy of solidarity, or "layers of kinship" as Sayigh termed it. Sayigh (ibid., 21) wrote about the differing priorities of belonging in traditional Palestinian society. She showed that the solidarity of the family is at the top of this scale. A core family, or a household, in Palestine often includes three generations of patrilineal blood relatives: a father and a mother, their offspring, and their sons' families. It also usually consists of the grandparents from the father's side. The second-most important type of belonging is the relationship to the extended family or *hamoula*. A *hamoula* can be described as the clan to which the family belongs, and in some cases the whole village is made up of one or two *hamoulas*. After that, the village identity, and solidarity with fellow neighbors in the village, follow in the scale of alliances. The village was termed by Sayigh the "family of families." She illustrated how the peasant family and the solidarity between members of the clan constituted an effective form of defense against oppression forced on them by imperialism, distant landowners, and the higher socioeconomic classes. Factors contributing to the *hamoula's* strength in pre-1948 times were found to be the lack of a strong state, raids by Bedouins, tax collectors, and merchants' power. This, Sayigh stated, "formed the structural setting within which the peasants' culture" of "moral familism" developed (ibid., 21). According to this moral code, the family unit, and the belonging to the *hamoula* and the village, are the bases of Palestinian groups, whereby "all relationships between people of the same village were translated into kinship terms" (ibid.).

This deeply rooted morality of family is expressed through terms referring to the home or the *hamoula* in Arabic (ibid.). The words used for house—*beit* or *dar*—are often used to refer to the extended family a person belongs to. For example, my surname is Simaan, and our *hamoula* is referred to as *"dar el Simaan"*—meaning the house of Simaan. Moreover, names of villages and towns often have the prefix of *dar*, or *beit*: such as Beit Lahem (Bethlehem), which refers to the house of the Canaanite god of the southern hills *Lahm* (Ra'ad 2010). This key role the family plays in forming the values and the daily activities in rural Palestine is founded on the reality that the "family collective" is both the unit of production and the unit of consumption. According to Sayigh, "Its [family] economy was based primarily on its rights to family and communal village land, its labour power, and the social ties that could be converted into material aid when needed" (1979, 22). Therefore, "the size and structure of the peasant family collective fitted Palestine's system of agricultural production and land tenure, both of which called for a year-round, medium-sized labour force" (ibid., 22).

Women had more activities to do in the house than men, such as domestic and childcare tasks; drying and storing food for winter; looking after the orchards around the village; and caring for hens and ducks; but they also worked with men in the fields and collected water and firewood (Rosenfeld 2004; Sayigh 1979; Seger 1981). The working "peasant mothers" are symbolically associated with the

Olive Growing for *'Awna*

home and land in daily language in this part of the world. "Women were its [the home's] basis not only through their childbearing function, but also through their economic contribution. And more than men, it was the women's job to maintain the network of social relations on which village and family solidarity depended" (Sayigh 1979, 23).

This strong role that women played contradicts the inferior status they hold in the patriarchal order of the family. The story of Um Weehab in this study, and how she worked outside of the house in schools and how she had to manage her family land duties, testifies to the accuracy of this analysis.

Vivien Sansour (her real name), a local woman who was in her thirties when I first met her, and who works with farmers, gave a description of a day in the life of a peasant mother—based on the story of a farmer from Jenin in the north of the West Bank:

> Mother fallaha wakes up at five in the morning to clean the house, then she goes outside to bake the bread in the oven, after which she does the laundry in the yard in front of the house. The mother of the house then goes down to the kitchen garden and to the field to gather some wild and grown produce. This is called *sarha* [the term used to describe walking in the field to gather food]. If she needs za'tar she goes to collect it from the land, and she stays there for a few hours. By then her husband had gotten up. She feeds him breakfast and makes his coffee, and now he needs to go to work, but she needs to prepare lunch, of course. Father goes down to the land by now. The point is that she has already done 100 things and her husband is still asleep, she is so industrious, it's insane. Mother makes the lunch before her children come back from school, and then she helps with their homework. Next, she goes to the field for the afternoon, then she needs to prepare dinner for everyone. And she's already done the washing up and everything else. She is ploughing—literally and metaphorically—all day long, you understand me? She does several things: she is the one that picks the fruit, she makes preserves and stores food.

It is beyond the scope of this book to discuss the position of women in rural communities, and their experience of inequality—an experience sadly still shared across the world to a varying extent due to the patriarchal order dominant in globalized capitalist, colonialist, and religious institutions (Federici 2014). The specific roles and experiences of Palestinian rural women are illustrative of the intersectionality of all forms of identities and injustices that the local communities suffer from (Davies, 2016; Grillo, 1995). Vivien often told me about how, as a woman in the West Bank, she simultaneously faces several forms of control over her and what she does. She told me the sources of this oppression come from the global agribusiness that floods the markets with commercial seeds, chemicals, and produce from Israel and denies her and her society the delights of native varieties; the Israeli military occupation and the colonies that restrict land-based occupations and other daily activities; and institutionalized religion and patriarchy—both of which consider men superior to women, and therefore limit Vivien's potential and capacities. However, after studying and living abroad for some years, she decided to return to work with local farming communities to revive old ways of knowing and doing. Vivien hopes there can be a collective fight against those types of oppression she identified. Vivien began to achieve some of this through the doing of meaningful daily activities related to preserving heritage seeds and working the land in traditional and sustainable ways. Vivien called this "agri-resistance," or daily-acts-of-*Sumud* (Simaan and Sansour 2016), which will be described in the next chapter.

Another fundamental element of the family, associated with growing olives for '*Awna*, is the descendants or the offspring. The value of children is considered key to the future of the peasant family, as they guarantee the care of land and parents in old age (Rosenfeld 2004; Sayigh 1979). Sayigh explained the habit of early marriages and rearing large families as phenomena that result from economic and environmental factors: labor force, infant mortality, and conscription [as the case was under the Ottomans]. All these conditions led to the central role of descendants in rural society, and "there is also the Palestinians' profound love of all fertility, natural or human" (Sayigh 1979, 23). The importance of reproduction has always been present here, based on pagan fertility traditions that existed in historical Palestine before the advent of the monotheistic religions (Thompson 2000).

Familism in Palestine, nonetheless, consists of some aspects that became irrelevant because the connection to the clan, the land, and its role in the families' sustenance have changed since settler-colonialism arrived here. For example, the so-called code of revenge, which refers to when a member of a family is killed and whereby the family of the victim has a duty to kill a member of the perpetrator's family as an act of revenge. Another problematic custom relating to this family consciousness is the notion of honor, according to which women who are suspected of having extramarital sex are killed by male relatives because they are thought to have harmed the honor of the family. By forming such "illegitimate" affairs, women would not be able to find an adequate husband, as this value and practice dictates. Such customs are not the norm any longer, but they still occur in Palestine, and civil rights organizations are increasingly seeking to combat the phenomenon (e.g., Musawa, Al-Qaws, and Aswat[2]). Other more benign aspects of family solidarity, and mutual aid, relate to traditions such as helping the

Olive Growing for *Awna*

members of the extended family in time of illness, or lack of work. There are a few concepts and habits that are still practiced relating to this familism, such as the terms of *qareeb* (kin) and *g'areeb* (stranger). The popular proverb states: "My brother and I protect each other against our cousin, and my cousin and I protect ourselves from the *g'areeb*." Another value relating to this way of life is the concept of duty, or *wajib*, referring to responsibilities that individuals have to perform for the family, for example, offering gifts on days of celebration. Another one of those values, which can also be negative when taken to its extreme or abused, is the concept of manhood or *roujouleya*, relating to a man's duty to protect his family, *hamoula*, and village (Sayigh 1979). Family, clan, and village associations were the basis upon which the value and practice of *Awna* has been maintained throughout the histories of groups here. However, as a result of the displacement and disposition of the *Nakba*, people have sought additional alliances to strengthen their own communities and to feel belonging and to contribute to the wider world. Their national and international bonds that support, and are supported by, olive growing will be discussed below.

Local and National Belonging

Prior to 1948, fallahi families identified themselves and their loyalties mainly with their ancestral village, and this persisted even after many of them were displaced to refugee camps, where they transferred this solidarity to the next generations. Camps, or neighborhoods within them, for example, are often named after the villages from which the refugees came. According to Sayigh (ibid.), the solidarity of the village met two key needs: The first was the defense of the communities by the ongoing work of the land; the second was the administrative functions imposed on them during the Ottoman era. Ottoman authorities recruited *mukhtar*s, or chiefs, from the village to enact the differing forms of oppression practiced upon villagers, such as collecting high rates of taxes on their land and produce; villagers, due to their *hamoula* loyalties to the chiefs, accepted this as their fate (ibid.). This continued into the British Mandate period to some degree, though they were also ruled by British generals and officials who were based locally in these communities. During the British rule the role of money-lending and banks increased, and as a result villagers relied on outsiders for loans to pay their taxes or buy seeds, for example (ibid.). In that way the British Mandate, and after it the Israeli regime, led to the increase in dependence on capitalist systems, such as cash and loan masters, rather than on the gift economy and the *hamoula*, which rural families had relied on for their survival previously. In other words, settler-colonialism, which led to the adoption of globalized capitalism, had started to usurp the earlier reliance upon the support of the family and the *hamoula* in the previously self-reliant fallahi communities.

In studying former peasant families in the refugee camp of Dheisha, Rosenfeld (2004) showed that as a result of the Israeli occupation and the expulsion and dispossession of whole villages and towns, the role of the family evolved and people developed links to their local and national community. Rosenfeld found that individuals and the collective community in a refugee camp she studied had created significant social and political resources based on values of interdependence and collaboration. For example, she observed impressive educational achievements, professional skills, and organized political activism as a result of newly formed relationships with the local camp and regional communities, such as in forming work committees and joining national political parties. Sayigh (1979) argued that clan solidarity had shifted to a more national consciousness when people here faced an existential threat to the whole nation by the establishment of the state of Israel. For the purpose of resistance, people were driven to adopt alliances that expressed and allowed the practice of national solidarity, which is increasingly becoming essential among communities in Palestine in order to stand up to the Israeli occupation and worsening land colonization and segregation of land and communities.

My observations of olive growers' local affiliations, which '*Awna* is based on, showed that this local belonging—to people with whom they share a geographical area—is core for them. For example, the aforementioned story I was told by Abu Weehab about his village of Al-Baydar that had recently been awarded global protection through a UN organization. The villagers had worked together with local and national organizations to apply for this status. After a long process, and much opposition from the governments of Israel and the United States against the application, they succeeded in having their village listed to defend their ancient terraces and collective water irrigation system. They aimed to protect them from colonization and the segregation wall, the route of which was planned to pass through village lands. Without the collaboration with other local groups based in local towns and villages, and the exchange in expertise and skills this provided, the villagers would not have been able to secure the protected status. There was also outside support received from international individuals and organizations, the topic of the next section. Another example of this local solidarity is the agricultural committee that was founded in the village of Dar El Shoke. The aim, when it was established in the 1980s, was to provide support for farmers to maintain their land-based livelihood in the face of the increase in Israeli colonies. This committee proved to be effective in providing experts and volunteers to help farmers care for their trees and crops in an environmentally sustainable way. It continues its work

Olive Growing for *'Awna*   81

today and has spread nationally, and currently works with farmers all over the West Bank.

This national alliance is further exemplified in Damir's family farm, mentioned elsewhere, which provides educational and voluntary programs for local children and women. The family also advises other local farmers on legal processes as they have been involved in court cases for several decades to try to defend their lands against the military occupation's threats of confiscation. The family have managed so far with some success to hold off the land grab, and their experience has been used to advise local farmers in similar situations. The custom of gleaning, mentioned above, is another illustration of the strong connectedness fallahi communities feel and practice toward other local people. As Abu Weehab reflected:

> After I finish these trees, I assume that people come here to look for the fruit that I left on the trees. Why not? This is the nature of life. A bug can find the olive that dropped on the ground and eat it. A bird can come and eat it. In our religion we say: "What you gather for your survival and livelihood is enough, and what is left doesn't belong to you." This is the nature of life. Why would I prohibit someone from their right to survival?

Not all families I met allow their olives to be gleaned by others, as one olive farmer I talked to told me. Hanna is a single man in his thirties who looks after his family's groves with his mother, because the other members of his core family have migrated to Latin America. He told me he does not permit people to glean olives from their trees. Nonetheless, when I was helping them pick their olives, he asked me and some other volunteers to go and help his cousins who were harvesting their trees in a nearby grove. For Hanna, his mother, and extended family who come from a Christian minority, *'Awna* through olive growing is perhaps practiced within the extended family and the smaller community of those who belong to the same faith for protective reasons. Because they belong to a Christian minority that has experienced emigration and reduction in land and financial resources, Hanna and his family felt less able to afford participation in this tradition of allowing gleaning by strangers. However, all other families I spoke to, such as Um Weehab and Abu Weehab, Nada and Abu Kamal, and even Bilal and his Christian family, demonstrated instances of intercommunal *'Awna*.

This shared destiny that moves beyond the family and the village collectives, and includes wider national connectedness, is interpreted by Zureik (2016) according to his postcolonial conceptualization of human agency. In his research, he referred to the technological advancement of human networks through social media, and their use by Palestinian youth to advocate for solidarity with the Palestinian struggle for freedom and justice. He called the enabler of this emergent means of intercommunal communication and collaboration a "coagency," which refers to the "empowerment and resistance by marginal groups through a combination of technology-people networks" (ibid., 42). Coagency is a useful analytical term that helps to explain the medium that fuels participation in wanted and socially sanctioned activities done by groups of people who are challenging injustices, such as settler-colonialism. This participation—enabled by a collective agency—is "indivisible from both occupation and belonging" and is driven by a shared agency located among individuals, families, and their community (Whalley Hammell 2014, 43). For Whalley Hammell (ibid.), it is a form of a doing for belonging, fueled by a coagency that mediates between the humans and the task in-hand, to enable engagement in activities essential for their and their society's continuation. This coagency within human communities occurs due to the reality of a group sharing a culture, heritage, history, and structural forces that the members live in.

This shared sphere of experience creates codependence expressed through doing important actions that require collectivism, such as in olive growing. In this sense, farming olives as a daily activity might be described as a collective occupation relying on solidarity, coagency, and interdependence (Kantartzis 2017; Ramugondo and Kronenberg 2015). The concept of collective occupations was informed by the idea of Ubuntu as an African ethic, which refers "to human interconnectedness, or how people's humanity is constantly shaped in interaction with each other, assigning responsibility to both the individual and the community for the other's existence" (Ramugondo and Kronenberg 2015, 496). Based on such a value, the construct of collective occupations links individual and collective, as well as oppressive and liberating elements of occupation as individuals can influence each other's wellness. It also combines intentional and relational aspects of our daily doing: human beings need to relate to each other, and in order for them to interact they engage in activities together (ibid.). The intention of these activities is to maintain human relationships and the individual and collective well-being that these occupations are hoped to lead to. It is a concept that combines terms that illustrate the communal elements of occupations.

Ubuntu in South Africa and 'Awna, practiced through olive growing in Palestine, were shown to express purposeful daily activity done by the family or the community for each other's wellness and benefit. In that way the main intention for engaging in such an activity is a relational one: people grow olives to stay connected to their family, village, land, nation, and globe.

The aforementioned study of daily occupation in a Greek town found that collective occupations were essential in maintaining the social relationships and collective well-being on three different levels (Kantartzis 2017). This included the family, at what was named the micro level; the intermediate or local level,

Olive Growing for *'Awna*

described as meso; and a macro category of social fabric at the global and institutional level. The researcher described the meso level, found to be dominant in the Greek town. Collective occupations in Greece are mediated by a coagency at a level beyond the family, in common with Palestine, where this interdependence is founded on the value of *'Awna*. The coagency acts as a vehicle for "doing for belonging," or *'Awna*, in order to enable an "occupation that provided support, information and identity across the community" (ibid., 21). Due to factors explained below, the coagency in Palestine needed to move beyond the local, or the meso level, to include also the macro level. The solidarity, as a value that *'Awna* is informed by, has been expanding to involve international individuals and organizations, as observed in this research and discussed next.

Belonging to a Global Community

Since the early 2000s (around the time of the second Intifada) there has been an increase in solidarity activism and grassroots support for ordinary Palestinian communities, including olive farmers, by voluntary organizations and individuals who visit the oPt to see for themselves the impact of the military occupation on people and their way of life (Qumsiyeh 2011). Reflecting on the support of international activists who visited his family's farm to help with working the land, Damir said to me:

> We felt we're not alone. Solidarity by people from abroad is very important. For example, when we hosted 40 people, those come from 40 families, who come from 40 towns. Solidarity with the Palestinian people is widening, as these people go back home and tell a story [about Palestine] in a positive way. Not the stereotypical picture they see in the news about Palestinians. I tell them about what happened to us, they experience Palestinian hospitality, and these things give an alternative picture of our situation to the outside world. They come and see, and go and tell.

He was referring to witnessing injustice by ordinary people from around the world that many Palestinians believe useful in resisting the dominant narrative that portrays them as "uncivilised" people or "terrorists" in mainstream media and academia (Said 2000). This collaboration between global communities helps in standing up to and resisting the colonization of their land, by raising global awareness regarding everyday injustices, and by forming bonds of solidarity. This interdependence, between the local and the global, has evolved throughout Palestine's history. Families', villages', and communities' mutual support were the cornerstone of life in rural areas of Palestine before 1948 due to its geography, climate, and the small size of the communities (Sayigh 1979). These types of connections and belonging continue, as shown above, but as a result of the ongoing colonization, military occupation, and the lack of state welfare or support from the PA, solidarity has evolved to include, more recently, grassroots organization and international connections sought by local groups. The Joint Advocacy Initiative (JAI) works with international church groups to galvanize support for olive farmers from around the world. *Ta'ayush* (coexistence)[3] is an Israeli-Jewish organization, whose members I met while planting olive saplings with a farming family. They were present on the land to support the family by monitoring and documenting IDF and settlers' behavior toward them, to help the family to communicate with the IDF in Hebrew, and to physically assist with the task of planting olive trees. The landowners *Ta'ayush* members were helping that day had been struggling to access their land due to restrictions and violence (against both trees and people) inflicted on them by the IDF and nearby settler-colonizers.

Not all people I spoke to agreed that this aspect of international collaboration in the activity of olive growing will always yield positive results for the farmer. Hilal was an activist working with farmers and a former project coordinator at the JAI who worked with families such as Abu Weehab's and Abu 'Attallah's. He and other locals I met, who worked with other NGOs in the area, told me how they felt that these organizations risked making farmers dependent on their support rather than facilitating their autonomy and self-reliance.

Hilal said to me:

> NGOs make farmers wait for aid in order to reclaim their land, rather than be on their land and do it themselves like Abu Weehab does in Al-Baydar. The fallah has to have monetary resources to spend in order to be supported by some of these organisations. Some of the farmers take loans and fall behind in debt just to pay their part in aid projects. Alternatively, they can be provided with the money and sign a contract committing themselves to working their land. We need to help people defy restrictions rather than add more burden on them. All NGOs work within the system of the Israeli occupation, and they should do everything to defy it. The commitment should be to farmers' needs not to the donors' needs. Funding from abroad is OK as long as it is used as an enabler. Human and natural resources are more important than financial resources, and a good example I have seen is The Land Institute[4] that concentrates on human resources by prioritising humans rather than funds, exactly like Palestinian fallahi way of life in the past. The JAI used to do this, but fell into the trap of what we term as the "financial missionary model" which most NGOs work according to; the classic fallahi model, on the other hand, is the wanted model. For example, Abu 'Attallah can

now survive without aid because we worked hard to facilitate his self-reliance. He needed some support in the beginning, and he now has hundreds of olive trees, but started only with 50. One of the causes for my departure from the JAI was the shift in prioritising what's best available naturally to what is economically available. In that way elite organisations including NGOs and the PA serve the top elite, the Israeli occupation, by increasing the financial burden on farmers and making them reliant on aid. After growing for a while, NGOs get stuck and then their aim shifts to maintaining the status quo and the salaries of the employees. Good NGOs are those who cease to exist as they fulfill their aim. The best NGO is the one that began yesterday and will close in 2–3 years.

Hilal's experience shows how well-meaning Western-funded organizations that are motivated by human rights and social and occupational justice as understood in the West may be harmful to Global South communities. Hilal articulated well an issue I was aware of from the start of my field work. I saw that the international support, which includes funds for projects such as the "olive tree campaign" at the JAI, is helpful in providing subsidized saplings and human power to harvest and plant trees—both of which are needed due to the poor financial situation of most farmers I met, and due to the need of helpful hands as other members of the family might have needed to look for wage-labor or other work elsewhere in order to survive as a family. On the other hand, I also saw that farmers lived under military occupation and a system of segregation, and their land is constantly under threat of being expropriated, and perhaps as Hilal suggested, what is needed is an organization that works with farmers at all levels of their struggle. Global support through organizations might provide appropriate financial support; some human power to help work the land; and, most importantly, organizations should also be working to end the military occupation and its policies that are causing the situation of occupational apartheid. In some respects, the JAI and other NGOs have a stated aim to do just that, and what Hilal was referring to was the risk of that becoming a tokenistic aim without proper actions toward it. However, all farmers I spoke to saw the importance of forging these international alliances and solidarities. This importance lay in seeing that people empathized with their cause and were prepared to support them financially, and most importantly by being present on their land during critical times when the risk was highest for violence against people, land, and trees, such as in planting and harvesting seasons.

On the one hand, this global solidarity expressed by having allies from Israel and the world present on the land is helpful in reducing farmers' vulnerability and exposure to such violence, as I was told by participants. On the other hand, participation in olive-growing activities was observed to benefit the international activists who joined olive-growing families in their fields. This experience, as many of them told me, was an "eye-opener," which taught them about a situation of global and local injustice and helped in correcting the dominant narrative they had been given about it by mainstream media. Moreover, it enabled them to feel valued by contributing in their small way to bringing about social and political change. Several of the international activists I met told me that their experience working with farmers made them consider other marginalized communities or situations of injustice in their own countries. Many of them, through their experience of *'Awna*, were able to fulfill the famous idiom, "think globally and act locally," a phrase I heard used by some of those volunteers.

Solidarity with global communities reflects what Said (2003, xxi) termed a "collective constituency"; through these alliances of people who share social and political interests, communities fight oppression of all kinds by employing collaborative means, such as sharing and exchanging ideas and practices connected to how to preserve land rights and traditional daily activities essential for communities' survival and well-being. The aim of this constituency is the opposite of the "othering," and of the notion and practices of settler-colonialism and nationalism, which Said criticized as an import of Western colonial powers. He saw these as ideologies based on essentialist and xenophobic ideas about race and ethnicity. Said told us that not all is doomed, however, and that global communities share common concerns such as those for the environment, poverty, equality between genders and for minority groups, and health and human rights. He continued: "No one can possibly know the extraordinary complex unity of our globalized world, despite the reality that, as I said at the outset, the world does have a real interdependence of parts that leave no genuine opportunity for isolation" (ibid., xxi). He suggested that instead of the human-made clash between cultures, societies need to focus on the ways cultures, or ways of doing and being and belonging, resemble each other, share with each other, and coexist "in far more interesting ways than any abridged or inauthentic mode of understanding can allow" (ibid., xxii). This brings about what Said, and Zureik after him, called worldliness, an attitude that human groups adopt and which expresses "an appreciation not of some tiny, defensively constituted corner of the world, but the large, many-windowed house of human culture as a whole" (ibid., 382).

This sharing and exchanging between world communities has been described as expressing a respect for "global wisdom"—a phrase that refers to ways of knowing and doing of specific communities of the Global South—and has been discussed as a useful source for theory and practice (Whalley Hammell 2014). Learning about means of action such as *'Awna*, or doing for belonging to a diversity of world communities, can be transformative for all. Specific to this study, this expe-

Olive Growing for *Awna*

rience can help activists and scholars interested in daily human doing to move beyond the Eurocentrism that has produced notions and practices not always applicable to all groups of people. Witnessing and being witnessed through *Awna*, or doing for belonging, can help in decolonizing ourselves from theoretical imperialism through learning how communities are resisting settler-colonialism on the ground. The ways in which Palestinian olive farmers resist occupational apartheid through their daily lives is the topic of discussion in the next section and the next chapter.

Olive Growing for *Awna* as Means to Confront Occupational Apartheid

An incident I recorded in my field notes provides a good illustration of a situation of structural injustice influencing olive growing I observed, and how it was challenged by the principle of *Awna*.

I joined the JAI to help with the harvesting of Abu Samir's olives from his grove in Dar El Shoke, a grove that borders the latest construction site in the nearby colony. The grove was dusty because the rains were late in arriving that autumn, and because of dust drifting from the nearby building site in the colony. The grove was littered with rubbish, including unwanted furniture dumped there from the colony. We finished harvesting the small grove before noon, and I offered to help carry the sacks on my back using the only dirt path leading from the trees to where the car was parked. The path was steep and narrow and could only be used by humans or donkeys, as the rest of the field—and the wider paths leading to and from it—had been fenced off by the military. On my final trip to Abu Samir's car at the top of the path on the edge of the main road to the village, I noticed some settlers—whom I could identify by their distinctive religious attire—standing at the bottom of the hill. I was later told they were bathing in one of the few remaining village springs that hadn't dried up or been occupied by the settlers. A few seconds later we saw four army jeeps and some half a dozen heavily armed soldiers on foot, who approached us and asked who we were, who our leaders were, and where we were from. Their manner was aggressive, and it made me and the other volunteers feel intimidated. We were advised by the group coordinator to board the bus and let Abu Samir talk to them, because if we were to get involved, he might "be punished" for it after we had left the village. From the window of the bus, we watched the soldiers approach Abu Samir with documents in their hands. He later told us they were instructions written in Hebrew, which he couldn't read, and a map, which were used as their evidence that his land had been declared a closed military zone. He said we were lucky to have completed the harvest before they arrived; they might have come at any moment to announce a ban on access to the field and to evict us from the land. This would have stopped his family from benefiting from the harvest this year, as had been the case in the past, Abu Samir told us. He felt lucky because they let him keep his yield this time. Abu Samir thought this might be because of our presence there, as internationals witnessing the situation.

Participant families were observed to enact the principle of '*Awna* to empower them to cope with the structural and systematic attempts to segregate them from their land and trees, their heritage and communities. They demonstrated how, despite the specific occupational injustice imposed on their belonging, they adapted and found ways to harness this collaborative principle through olive growing, and in order to maintain and even develop this activity further. In this section I will discuss the specific form of injustice, termed here as occupational apartheid, and how it was manifested in the daily lives of participant families.

Olive growing as doing for belonging, or '*Awna*, is systematically restricted by policies of control and segregation that lead to occupational apartheid. This study shows empirical examples of constraints on participation, such as imposing closed military zones in olive groves by the Israeli military occupation, that discriminate against the native Palestinian community. Occupational apartheid was defined as the following:

> The segregation of groups of people through the restriction or denial of access to dignified and meaningful participation in occupations of daily life on the basis of race, color, disability, national origin, age, gender, sexual preference, religion, political belief, status in society, or other characteristics. Occasioned by political forces, its systematic and pervasive social, cultural, and economic consequences jeopardize health and wellbeing as experienced by individuals, communities, and societies (Kronenberg and Pollard 2005, 68).[5]

This construct was introduced in 1999 by Frank Kronenberg, based on his work in Latin America with street children who were denied access to meaningful occupations such as education (Kronenberg and Pollard 2005). This type of injustice imposed on people's daily activities is associated with geographical, territorial, and social segregation and enforced on groups for a significant length of time (Pollard, Kronenberg, and Sakellariou 2008a). It is linked to political forces that include "discourses and circumstances" that prioritize the needs of some groups over the needs of other communities (Durocher 2017, 11). The term "apartheid" was borrowed from the racial segregation system of the apartheid regime in South Africa imposed from 1948 until 1991, and was intended to enable a liberating stance by providing the language to describe and express a situation of injustice related to restricting communities' daily living (Pollard, Kronenberg, and Sakellariou 2008a). This liberation could be achieved by confronting this injustice and highlighting "contributive" justice—a structure that enables equitable social and collective benefits for all in society (ibid.). Pollard, Sakellariou, and Kronenberg (ibid.) outlined some examples of the phenomenon, including South Africa and Israel, whereby regulations and laws, as well as assumptions and attitudes, discriminated against and excluded some groups from doing what they wanted or needed to do, to the benefit of other groups. Despite the negative effects it has on the oppressed group, this form of injustice is maintained to preserve the status of powerful groups (ibid.).

Occupational apartheid applies to Palestinian olive-growing families whose everyday lives provide evidence of such a phenomenon that can be helpful in substantiating this concept and furthering it from a unique perspective. Due to their belonging to the Indigenous fallahin, olive growers have been systematically restricted from participating in the most essential of activities for them. They are limited from gaining access to such an occupation through a variety of tools. Examples of these include policies and practices that allow the confiscation of what the IDF deems as "unworked land," or declaring land owned by native families as a closed military zone, or uprooting trees to make way for the construction of the separation wall or for roads restricted for use by Israelis only (Manor 2017). Moreover, settler-colonizers—a growing minority in the oPt that includes many recent migrants from western Europe and North America—can travel and work anywhere they wish within the oPt and inside the Green Line. Palestinian olive growers, nonetheless, were observed not to be passive victims of these injustices. As shown in the previous chapter and in this one, they have acquired and adapted means to allow them to maintain this historic occupation. They were empowered to do so through their principles of *Sutra*—doing for well-being—and *'Awna*—doing for belonging. As the next chapter will show, they also can teach us how to resist occupational apartheid through their creativity, persistence, and hope for self-determination and justice.

In conclusion, *'Awna* is defined as a motivator for action that is shaped by values of connectedness to others and that Palestinian communities enact to enable everyday activities, which are done together and influence everybody's well-being. Doing for belonging was described from decolonial and occupational justice perspectives, and it was suggested that it is based on different types of associations. Alliances that humans form with nature, ancestors, family, village, locality, and the globe were linked to stories from the field and compared to previous studies in the literature. The terms solidarity and coagency were used to interpret this collaborative aspect of olive growing, and were related to occupational science discourse in order to further understanding of the concept of doing for belonging from a

Ancient olive terraces in the West Bank of Palestine. Photo taken by the author.

unique lens. *'Awna* was shown to be a dynamic and adaptable phenomenon that has evolved to embrace new relationships in response to changes in society and changes in how oppression is manifested. This openness that allows the principle of *'Awna* to be applied in new, shifting, and overlapping ways, with different kinds of allies and in different forms of community, has helped to give Palestinian resistance a kind of nimbleness and agility that has prevented it from being extinguished. Moreover, it was shown in this chapter that the case of olive growers in the West Bank can offer an example of a specific type of occupational apartheid. In the next chapter, I will discuss how this phenomenon is being confronted through a way of knowing and a means of action described here as daily acts of resistance, termed *Sumud* in Arabic.

صمود

CHAPTER 4

Olive Growing for *Sumud*

The work of *Sumud*, from childbearing and building to
testifying and fighting, continues.

—Edward W. Said 1999, 113

This chapter discusses the practice of *Sumud* among olive-growing communities
in Palestine. I begin by defining *Sumud* and its meanings in daily life in Palestine. I
then introduce the family of Um Nedal and Abu Nedal and their experience in
living and working on the land as an example to a resistive way of life that is motivated by the practice of *Sumud*. The rest of this chapter presents the process of my
interpretation that involved comparing and contrasting *Sumud* with corresponding ideas from the literature. I offer more observations from the field that I understood to represent manifestations of this resistive means of olive farming, which
pointed to the belonging for becoming dimension of meaningful daily activity. In
the second section of this chapter, *Sumud*, as used in Palestine, will be defined as
resistance to injustice. Thereafter, I relate it to other notions of resistance, followed
by a discussion of the changes in its use and meanings throughout modern Palestinian history. In the following section, I show how it is used in the daily lives of
olive-growing families I met. Then I address the different values that inform this
principle that drives the daily acts of resistance olive-growing families were shown
to enact: the idea that it stems from a necessity rather than a purely individual
choice; the need for selfless compromises to be made; the sociopolitical consciousness it requires; and that it aims to lead to communal self-determination. Following that I discuss the daily-acts-of-*Sumud* as further evidence of the political and
resistive aspects of meaningful daily action emerging from recent literature. In the
following section *Sumud* will be compared to the relationship between belonging

and becoming in Western literature. The final section of this chapter will discuss two examples of daily activities other than olive growing that I came across during field visits and that I saw as representing daily acts based on means of *Sumud*.

Similar to *Sutra* and *'Awna*, and as is the case with most words in Arabic, the term *Sumud* stems from a root of a verb. The root *samada* has several meanings: one, it relates to a person who can be relied on; two, it refers to something that remained as it is, or survived; three, it has a meaning associated with a fight, or a physical confrontation; four, it signifies a cover for a bottle or for a person's head; five, it refers to a high rock, or seating on a high place; six, it is associated with the process of gradually saving money, or things that are savable; seven, it means a person who never gets hungry or thirsty in a war (Dar Al-Mashriq 1986). This plurality of literal meanings of the term mirrors the diversity of its uses and the complexities of its meanings in the daily lives of communities in Palestine. *Sumud*, like the concept of *Sutra* and *'Awna*, is a term that is omnipresent in Palestinian daily lives. It has developed to mean different things at succeeding stages of historical events, and as a result of everyday realities interacting with sociopolitical conditions. It is a word whose uses have stemmed from the living conditions and the everyday realities and activities of communities here.

The Family of Um Nedal and Abu Nedal

The drive to Dar El Shoke, where Um Nedal, Abu Nedal, and Nedal and their family live, took me west of Beit Lahem through the town of Al-Khader (real name), past a fence several meters high, a part of the separation wall, followed by a tunnel for the use of locals, and onto an Israeli-built bypass road connecting the nearby settlements to Al-Quds. I passed the gated entrance to the large colony described as a "huge city" by Heyam, Abu Nedal's wife (at the time of my visit) and passed a new construction site that will expand the colony.

When I first met Um Nedal and Abu Nedal, they were in their sixties and were divorced. Abu Nedal had since married and divorced twice more. Nedal, Um and Abu Nedal's only son, was in his late thirties and was married to Nahed, with whom he had three daughters and a son. They all lived in the small village of Dar El Shoke. Um Nedal lived in a small house across the garden from the ground floor apartment Abu Nedal lived in, which was beneath the house Nedal built for his family. Nedal had four sisters who lived elsewhere. In the vicinity there was a one-room building facing the road, which Nedal used as his barber shop and where he worked in the evenings. Nedal was the main breadwinner for the family, which included his mother and father. Nahed used to work as a social worker but took a break to raise her children. As described earlier, Nedal had a permit to

Olive Growing for *Sumud* 93

work within the Green Line (the armistice line separating the West Bank from Israel), where he worked during weekdays. He cut villagers' hair in the evenings and at the weekend (in a recent visit to the family, I learned that Nedal had turned the barber shop into a stationery shop). Nedal worked either on the land or in the house doing maintenance and building work during the little free time left for him. Nahed came from a nearby town and moved to live in the village when she married Nedal several years ago. When I visited, most of the villagers still farmed the land that was left under their ownership and had not been expropriated, but I was told that they all needed other sources of income, which they often found in construction or other menial wage-labor. Um Nedal spent her days either in the garden and the vegetable plot, or with her grandchildren or with other women relatives and covillagers. She was also a member of the local women's cooperative, where they made foodstuffs such as wild hawthorn jelly and wove baskets out of leftover olive shoots.

Abu Nedal returned to live full-time in the village just before I visited them for the second time, before which he lived in the nearest large town. Before that he moved around because of his political activism and his career as a journalist, and spent some time in hiding from the Israeli authorities. He also spent time in jail and several years under house arrest. This was not unusual in the oPt, I was told, where four in ten of the men have been in Israeli prisons.[1] For a few years before returning to Dar El Shoke, he worked in a community center in one of the large refugee camps in town, and on land and some terraces belonging to Nada and Abu Kamal's family, which owned land in a nearby wadi. Regarding his return to living in the village and his occupational history, Abu Nedal said:

> I came back last year to permanently live in the village, but even when I lived in town I didn't completely stop coming and working the land here. I moved to Beit Lahem because of work, because of my income. I used to work as a journalist at a national newspaper. And besides journalism, I was an activist in a political party. And I worked in Gaza, in secret political work, it's not a secret anymore, I worked there for a long period. When I used to come back here, I lived secretly in a monastery in town. A sympathetic priest gave me shelter until they [the military occupation authorities] arrested me, when they raided the monastery. The charge was that I was an inciter.

When I enquired who was looking after the land in his absence, he told me:

> My ex-wife Um Nedal and my son Nedal. After we divorced and Um Nedal returned to her home village, I asked her to come back, I told her "This is your land, work in it, live in it, and build on it; live in dignity and respect." So, she did and of

course Nedal helped her, that's why Nedal, unlike most villagers his age and younger, is a good fallah.

The family told me the history of Dar El Shoke, which is a small and an old village of 1,200 residents, who belonged to a few extended families from two *hamoulas* (clans). Their ancestors were thought to have lived in this valley for thousands of years. The village is located near the east side of the Green Line. It was occupied by Zionist militias in 1948 and declared a closed military zone. Most residents fled the village and lived in caves or nearby villages and refugee camps. An international agreement in the 1940s between Israel and Jordan (which governed the West Bank until 1967) allowed the villagers to work their land but not live on it.[2]

Several villagers were killed and injured during that period while working on their land. Later the village was attacked by Israeli forces, and most buildings were destroyed. The locals, including Abu Nedal's family, were expelled to the largest refugee camp in the area, where they stayed until the early 1970s, when they decided to attempt to return to their village. They formed committees responsible for agriculture, education, construction, and water to help resettle the village. I was told they managed to successfully negotiate their return with the Israeli authorities. Village families shared a system of irrigation from natural springs, whose water was collected into pools from which tunnels transport water to the vegetable plots on the wadi's flat plains. This collective water use allowed each extended family a slot of a few hours during the day to collect water in their pool.

Two illegal Israeli colonies were built on villagers' land on the two hills that surround Dar El Shoke. One of these colonies consisted of tens of thousands of settlers, I was told. Settlers in this colony, as in other colonies in the area, are armed, and they are protected by watchtowers, fences, walls, private security guards, and the IDF. Villagers were worried about the colonies, and they feared that more land will be confiscated in order to expand them. They were proven right when, in 2014, hundreds of acres were confiscated, and immediately afterward they began to see cranes in use to extend roads and build more houses in the colony. The larger of those colonies reached very close to the buildings in the village. Some of its houses were only a few meters from the village schoolyard, and pupils were often hassled by settlers on their way to and from school. Villagers often complained of settlers hiking through the village with firearms, which made them feel intimidated. In a visit to the village in the spring of 2022, I saw how a new Israeli-only road being dug to connect the colony to other nearby colonies to the east was swallowing up more stolen Palestinian land.

Abu Nedal reflected on how he saw the military occupation changing the activity of olive growing:

The [military] occupation firstly is practically trying to confiscate as much land as possible; the focus now is on all land that is planted with olive. It [the military occupation] started targeting all land that doesn't suit anything but olive growing. Secondly, I think, I don't have a proof for this, this needs evidence honestly, but from experience, most of the pesticides and herbicides that are sold to farmers to combat diseases, most of it comes to us out-of-date or ineffective, and that increases the problems. They come from Israel, the same happens with the saplings, they cheat us with saplings, they sell them to us diseased. But now the settlers are the biggest danger for the olive trees; they uprooted many of our relatives' trees. The most recent confiscation of land suitable for olive growing happened four months ago. The authorities expropriated 4,000 dunums [each dunum equals 1,000 square metres] in this area, most of which was from our village.

[He took a pen and started drawing on a paper]: Look, roughly, our village is shaped like the number 8. This is all confiscated land [indicating the surrounding outer areas]. What's left is the populated area of the village, the cultivated fields and the orchards. They reached the edge of the fields. All of this is confiscated. From all directions, from the north, from the south, and from the west and the east, all of it is surrounded by the colony. The edges of the colony reached the village houses here, the last house here is on the border exactly. Even the road from the right and left, the road you came through, is confiscated. Nothing connects us to Beit Lahem [the main town in the area] but that road on the top; the other one is for the settlement, it's confiscated.

Abu Nedal, who spent most of his days in the field, told me: "I go to the field every day from the morning, and I won't return home until the imam calls for the evening prayer. At the moment [February], I am rebuilding the drystone walls around our olive grove."

Abu Nedal returned to the village to work on his land and to spend his remaining years in his place of birth. However, in his absence it was Um Nedal and Nedal who had been the main caretakers of the olive growing and other land-based activities. Abu Nedal considered Nedal a good fallah, unlike many of the villagers from Nedal's generation. Many of them sought work elsewhere, mainly in menial jobs or in construction in the nearby colonies—or, if they were lucky, they were given a permit to work beyond the Green Line. When Abu Nedal returned to the village, he took over the majority of the growing activities. He spent most of his days on his vegetable plot near a water-collecting pool where he made himself a makeshift shelter and a newly built toilet—the first in the village on or near farming land, he told me.

When asked why they grew olives, Abu Nedal replied:

> Historically the olive tree and other native species, like fig, provide the family some food sustenance. Adding these sources to what the family might grow in the field or gather from the wild, such as za'tar, will provide some food security. Plus, the main reason for planting olives in our village in particular is the culture of resisting settlements. Any vegetable you plant, when the season ends and you harvest it, the land goes back to being not cultivated. Grapes and many other types of fruit trees such as almonds, you plant them and after 5, 10, 15 years they die. There has been a targeting of all land in this area of Palestine since the 1970s, and people were encouraged to plant it with olives. Most of the olives in our village were sourced by the agricultural committee. Practically the process of planting more olives started in the early 1980s.

When I enquired about why people were returning to olive growing, he said:

> Olive plays an important role in the life of farmers. When you come and uproot trees or forbid people from planting olive you increase the burden on the families. People today live in hard working conditions. The employment market is almost closed in Israel, the value of the currency is low, what's left is the reliance on farming for those who have trees, and when you deprive him [the fallah] of his olive, how would he survive? Tell me how can he live? Today there are people who can't work, and only plant olive so they can live from it, so they can produce 100 containers of oil or even maybe 50 or so, so they can sell them, you see? I am currently looking for any dot in the land that is not planted to plant it with olive. Not only me, the whole village. I returned to live here because this is my fate, my life, and there's danger for the village. I don't have a future in the town, my future is here; I have my home here in my land.

On his thoughts and feelings about their future, Abu Nedal reflected:

> I am very worried for the village. Nobody knows what the destiny of the village will be. There is talk that our village has already been annexed to the greater area of Al-Quds [the capital that was occupied and annexed by Israel], the land not the people. This means that what the future of the people will be, nobody knows. Are they going to keep us in Israel, or transfer us to the PA areas? Nobody knows, no one can answer the question: what is the destiny of the people of Dar El Shoke? An unknown destiny, and a very dangerous and hard one.

Olive Growing for *Sumud* 97

When I asked how he responded to this, he told me:

> I rehabilitate the land, what for? To renew it and rejuvenate it, so I can plant it and so I and those who come after me can survive. I also keep talking to the media, I spread the word on Facebook, on Twitter, on WhatsApp, everything about the village and its people.

Abu Nedal's answers pointed to an example of how olive growing's doing for belonging (*'Awna*) aspect includes a strong attachment to history and heritage. They also further illustrated how occupational apartheid is manifested in his village, and how the resistive principle of belonging for becoming (*Sumud*) motivates, and is enacted through, the doing of olive growing.

Sumud as Individual and Collective Resistance to Daily Injustices

"As for the Israeli state, we exist and live on this land in spite of its will for us not to be here. We are the reality here whether they want it or not. We want to live on this land. For them, they would uproot us from our land today before tomorrow." This was what Abu 'Attallah told me regarding what he saw as the aims of the military occupation. On what he does to counter this, he told me a story about when he was offered an opportunity to join the armed resistance. He contemplated it and weighed it against the other options he had, such as farming his land. Abu 'Attallah told me he sat for three days with the rifle that the organization had given him, mulling over the dilemma. "At the end of the three days I called the guy from the *tanzim* [organization] and told him to come to pick up this piece of metal [referring to the weapon he was given]. I don't want to be deprived of my land." He was concerned that his involvement in armed resistance would provide a reason for the authorities to destroy the family home or confiscate its land as a collective punishment, as in the case of other families in the oPt (Kremnitze and Saba-Habesch 2015). For his wife, his extended family, and himself, he decided to stick to farming as a way of responding to and confronting the ongoing consequences of settler-colonialism.

Farming olives as a way to resist the military occupation has a hopeful aspect that Vivien pointed out to me. She told me that for her, olive growing means that "when you plant a tree you are saying 'I have a future.'" In this way olive growing is motivated by an optimistic view of a future collective self-determination. As for the belonging aspect of *Sumud*, Bilal reflected on why he should fight for the land: "For the Palestinian people all of this goes back to that basic and principal thing: it originates in our relationship to our mother, *Al-a 'rd* [the land]. She is our land, our mother, and that's why we need to keep looking after her, protect her, be steadfast and *samidin* [the plural present tense of the root of *Sumud*] in it. We can do this by taking care of her and by being creative." Bilal was referring to that strong bond discussed in the last chapter between fallahi communities and the land. He was also speaking of the conviction that he cannot leave the motherland—which produces everything he and his family need—and instead allow it to be dominated by settler-colonizers from the west or Israel. Bilal, in this statement, expressed the need for the attitude of *Sumud* and its resistive and creative qualities that are essential for the survival, resistance, and flourishing of olive-growing communities. It is a means and a value that farming communities have inherited, and have now revitalized despite, and because of, the military occupation.

Sumud as a principle for action in Palestine has been discussed by scholars and writers from a variety of academic disciplines. Rijke and van Teeffelen (2014)—international development and education scholars—carried out interviews and focus groups with Palestinians from diverse backgrounds, aiming to analyze the complexity of meanings and uses of the concept. As with how it is interpreted in its daily use, *Sumud*'s plurality of meanings, they concluded, made it "almost impossible to develop a strong common definition—even though the concept has a "feel" that is directly recognizable to Palestinians." It "is not an easy concept to grapple with intellectually, it resonates within deep layers of Palestinian struggle for freedom, justice, community, and care" (ibid., 96). When used in conversation, *Sumud* refers to values and actions through which people persevere, persist, and hold on to their land and trees to enable the continuation of their communities, and to express all aspects of their identities: the physical, emotional, social, cultural, and political. *Sumud* is sometimes translated into English as "steadfastness." Shehadeh (1982, 6) introduced *Sumud* to English readers in his book based on his personal journal about life in the oPt. He described acts of *Sumud* as the "third way" for "defeating the defeat": an alternative to hating and to leaving the land. Shehadeh described examples from his personal life and from the lives of others in his community. They included stories of everyday creativity, personal acts, and small rebellions, such as when he maintained his fake smile and politeness despite the great anger he felt when passing through a checkpoint one day. He related stories of the *Sumud* of families when their homes were raided in the middle of the night without justification, or of friends who lost innocent loved ones who were shot by soldiers. As a lawyer who founded an organization—Al-Haq—to defend land rights,[3] Shehadeh had many stories about the *samidin* (adjective of *Sumud*) of the fallahi communities who were resisting the confiscation of their lands, which resembled many of the stories I heard during field visits.

Olive Growing for *Sumud*

As for Shehadeh's own personal *Sumud,* he expressed it through the writing of his memoir. He explained the inner process leading to this attitude:

> Anger gradually, through the years of occupation, [has] given way to despair. Anger fuels memory, keeps it alive. Without this fuel, you give up even the right to assert the truth. You let others write history for you, and this is the ultimate capitulation. We *samidin* cannot fight the Israelis' brute physical force but we must keep the anger burning. . . . It is up to us to remember and record. . . . But if my *sumud* as a lawyer is to mean anything, I must at least be able to tell my people's stories (ibid., 68).

For him, *Sumud* acts both as a motivator for and as means of actions:

> [It] had been practised by every man, woman, and child here struggling on his or her own to learn to cope with, and resist, the pressures of living as a member of a conquered people. *Sumud* is watching your home turned into a prison. You, *Samid* [steadfast in the third person], choose to stay in that prison, because it is your home, and because you fear if you leave, your jailer will not allow you to return (ibid., viii).

The notion of *Sumud,* according to Shehadeh, is born of an internal struggle people face in deciding how to respond to their daily conditions. They have to choose between either "acquiescing in the jailer's plan in numb despair" or becoming madly hateful of "your jailer and yourself, the prisoner" (ibid.). It is from this foundational inner dilemma that *Sumud* "is developing from an all-encompassing form of life into a form of resistance that unites the Palestinians living under Israeli occupation" (ibid.).

Said (1999, 100) described *Sumud* in the daily lives of workers and peasants in Palestine as "a form of 'elementary resistance' that turns presence into small-scale obduracy." In their everyday lives, Said observed Palestinians continuing to participate in their meaningful occupations "often without much hope or horizon, with the result that alienation from work is now gradually being assimilated and transformed into a prevailing attitude" (ibid.). This phenomenon was identifiable in the emotions of despair Nedal and his family were confronting through the daily acts of olive growing. Nedal told me: "In the end [my father] returned to farming. He is interested in agriculture, because we have a problem. We have a problem in the general situation here. There are no prospects, there's no future, there's even no aspiration to think forward, and this is also a problem." Nevertheless, Nedal and his family persisted and persevered in farming olives despite this desperation.

Sumud, in this way, is a mental action taken by the oppressed to stop the abuser from having influence over their minds (Shehadeh 1982). In the field of talking therapies, Allan Wade (1997, 23) described a similar mental strategy. He termed these actions as "small acts of living," or "everyday resistance." Wade believed that survivors of oppression such as domestic abuse or racism respond in their own special ways against these injustices. He explained that they are spontaneous and personal resisting acts, as opposed to instructed or prescribed interventions others advise them to take. Another quality of these acts is that they are calibrated shrewdly, in an effort to avoid causing further harm to the situation the person is in. Determination—the insistence upon continuing with such attitudes and acts to transform their lives—was another quality Wade (ibid.) ascribed to these survivors. However, according to Wade, the actions were taken despite not being expected to succeed immediately in stopping the oppression. Wade reflected on an Ethiopian proverb that James C. Scott wrote about in his book, *Domination and the Arts of Resistance*: "When the grand lord passes the wise peasant bows deeply and silently farts" (ibid., 29). Small acts of resistance, for Wade, are spontaneous acts that have an immediate effect on the mind of survivors of oppression. One of the instances Wade wrote about as an example of these acts is when abusers are not able to control the minds of their victims as they are assaulting them physically (ibid.). In such cases the oppressed still have agency in their autonomous mental activities, and in that way, they may fart metaphorically in order to feel that the injustice is overturned in that moment.

Palestinian olive-farming families, by doing olive growing as an act of *Sumud*, stop the Israeli military occupation from fully dominating their lives, if not physically through the dismantling of fences, for example, but mentally through their determination to continue ploughing their fields despite the fence being built to divorce them from their land. Their land and geography may be dominated and occupied, but not their minds and their agency to go about their daily life in inventive and creative ways, in order to resist that control in their own ways. Their actions are spontaneous and are judged by them to be helpful, or to not cause more harm to the situation they are in. For example, when the path is blocked to their groves and they cannot use a car to get there, they will instead find creative solutions such as the use of a donkey, or by staying in caves on the land. Some of their actions, such as Abu Weehab's land reclamations—discussed in the previous chapter—are not expected to yield immediate results but are hoped to help in the long term toward self-determination. To sum up *Sumud* as daily resistance in Palestine, Said noted that it is practiced by people as they go about their routines, day after day. He concluded:

> [Palestinians'] cares and anxiety set in nevertheless. The amount of unguarded reflection is also the moment of deepest vulnerability. Will the children be picked

Olive Growing for *Sumud*

up for taunting the settlers? Will "they" take another piece of land? Limitless worries, for which there is no truly effective antidote except going about your work tomorrow, again, beginning again (Said 1999, 100).

Sumud in Comparison to Other Notions of Resistance

Notions of resistance and the diversity of their meanings and utility have developed throughout modern world history. For instance, anti-colonialism resistance historically referred to peoples fighting the ideology and practices of imperialism in order to replace it with self-rule through nationalism. In the later years of the twentieth century, the idea of resistance began to relate to peasants' and workers' rebellions, and to fighting injustices including dominant forms of knowledge. Colonialism did not end with the successful fight for a nation-state that many peoples achieved, as in India or Algeria. Those independent postcolonial nation-states remain under the hegemony of globalized ideas and practices created by Western-educated middle classes, which led to praxes of resistance that include the fight of oppressed groups, such as women, peasants, workers, and minorities (Santos 2014). Those groups who are marginalized by patriarchy, capitalism, and racism aim to free themselves from systems and institutions, as well as from forms of knowledge and ideologies, which cause their oppression (ibid.). People's resistance comes in multiple forms; they organize collectively and adopt selfless principles (Qumsiyeh 2011). Some aim to lead to a revolution, but all forms aim to negate the foundation of domination.

James C. Scott (1985) studied other types of resistance that show new spaces where human agency and action can be expressed in culturally specific contexts and are led by values rooted in everyday experiences. This kind of resistance that Scott discussed is an idea and practice exercised in the everyday life of ordinary people. Scott (ibid.) described everyday forms of resistance in the face of adverse socioeconomic conditions in his seminal book, *Weapons of the Weak*. In the case of the Malay paddy farmers discussed in this book, resistance came about as a consequence of the dramatic changes to land tenure and methods of farming brought by the Green Revolution in the 1970s. The study focused on class struggle rather than settler-colonialism—as in Palestine—but both in Palestine and in Malaysia, people responded to a spectrum of forms of oppression by finding space in which external forces of control over their life and everyday ways of doing do not triumph, and where they can confront and challenge their oppressors, such as their bosses and the rich landowners. For Scott (ibid.), these daily forms of resistance are common in class relations, and "they are not an outright collective defiance" and do not lead to a rebellion (ibid., 27). Examples of daily resistance among the

Malay rice farmers included activities that were informal, covert, and more focused on immediate gains. Such acts included false compliance, slander, and sabotage against their bosses. Daily acts of resistance consisted also of some more
collective and organized forms such as boycotts or organizing and unionism
among the peasants in Malay. As in the Malay case, the acts of Palestinian olive
growers are rarely reported or analyzed, and it is important to do so as "something
of a testament to human persistence and inventions" (ibid., 33).

The daily activities of resistance carried out by olive farmers do not refer in this
book to organized and planned rebellions that aim to dismantle the military occupation as their immediate outcome. However, some of these actions require
organization and planning, such as when families decide to go to court against
land expropriation. It might be that their ultimate aim is for collective self-
determination and self-rule, and that they hope that their resistance will act as another small step toward that goal. However, daily acts of *Sumud*, as analyzed in
this book, are done with the indispensable attitude of the idiom: "To resist is to
exist"—a motto that is often seen drawn as graffiti on the segregation wall in the
West Bank.

The Historical Developments of *Sumud* in Palestine

Like the other notions of resistance that evolved to signify a variety of activities
across the globe, *Sumud* as a means of action has developed throughout the modern history of Palestine to mean a diversity of things. Rijke and van Teeffelen
(2014) studied how the concept moved from nationalist symbolism and strategic
debate to a way of life. *Sumud* as a national Palestinian notion has been part of the
collective consciousness here since the British Mandate, during which there were
two large rebellions led by peasants in the 1920s and 1930s. By the 1960s, it became more commonly used among Palestinians and was particularly linked to refugee camps in Jordan and Lebanon, where, despite their exile, people held onto
their right to return to their land and villages. During the 1970s, it became associated with the Palestinians who were living as an oppressed minority within the
Green Line and was expressed in cultural and artistic forms. For example, the poetry of Tawfiq Zayyad from Nazareth, who portrayed the olive tree as a symbol of
Sumud, "with its deep roots in the land, bearing fruits only after years of growth"
(ibid., 87). The olive tree, in this way, was used as a metaphor for the *Sumud* of the
deeply rooted native communities living within what came to be known as Israel.

During the civil war in Lebanon, in the 1970s and 1980s, the *Sumud* was
mainly associated with armed groups defending Palestinian refugee camps there.
In the late 1970s, it began to refer to those living under military occupation in the

West Bank and Gaza. It was then used as a strategy for action "moving beyond the symbolism of the struggle and the land" (ibid.). Grassroots movements began to form committees for farming, for women's rights, and for health, like the story of the agricultural committee formed in Dar El Shoke I described earlier. This provided *Sumud* with "a more bottom-up and activist meaning" aiming at increasing self-sufficiency and decreasing reliance on Israel (ibid., 88). This strategy reached its peak during the first Intifada in the 1980s, and since then it has acquired a broader strategic role related to tactics including active noncompliance.

Rijke and van Teeffelen (ibid.) provided "prototypical" instances of these deeds of noncompliance that infiltrated popular awareness, such as stories of farmers who would replant their olive trees after their uprooting by settlers or the IDF. *Sumud* also evolved to refer to images of Bedouin families who rebuilt their communities after their homes, clinics, and schools were repeatedly destroyed by the Israeli authorities. In the 1980s, the notion of *Sumud* developed to be used as a "conceptual window to communicate Palestinians' humanity to non-Palestinians" (ibid., 89). Books and publications began to be written in English to describe the daily lives in the oPt, such as Shehadeh's work mentioned earlier. A common theme of these books is "the small issues of daily life, a wry humorous sense of the absurdity of life under occupation, and the attempt to cling to basic human values under extremely testing circumstances" (ibid.). The Oslo Accords, the so-called peace process commencing in the 1990s, and the subsequent unhelpful practices of the PA leadership had almost managed to cause the notions of *Sumud*, as resistance and a way of life, to lose its role as daily principle adopted in the everyday lives of communities (ibid.). During this period, the idea of *Sumud* risked becoming part of an institutional jargon used by political leaders as a justification for neoliberal social and political policy. This was illustrated in the abovementioned paper in the neoliberal program of Salam Fayyad, a former PA prime minster, who started to form state institutions based on capitalist and consumerist models to portray a government ready to be granted statehood by the international community. These institutions were claimed to be for the good of the people and their *Sumud*, while actually benefiting a small elite of ministers and large corporations (ibid.). In the last ten years, however, *Sumud* has been revived in grassroots discourse and has come to represent a popular resistance struggle against the wall, the expanding illegal colonies, land confiscation, and house demolitions. Such renewed ideas of *Sumud*, as a value and means of action for confronting oppression, are illustrated in the movement for Boycott, Divestment, and Sanctions against Israeli institutions involved in the military occupation, known as BDS.[4] Civil society organizations and trade unions in the oPt, inspired by the anti-apartheid struggle in South Africa, argued that people should take matters into their own hands and show politicians that they could influence the processes and structures of the military occupation (Davies 2016).

In this way *Sumud's* meaning has shifted to refer to the struggle for civil and political rights for all in historic Palestine, rather than a fight for a nationalistic state. These and other nonarmed struggles were described by Qumsiyeh in his book, *Popular Resistance in Palestine: A History of Hope and Empowerment*, published in 2011. "To resist is to exist," for Qumsiyeh, means taking direct actions that intend to accomplish pressure on opponents, decrease their grip on power, and make communities stronger. It requires a positive "can do" attitude and will eventually lead to self-sufficiency and a better quality of life. Qumsiyeh (ibid.) argued that daily forms of *Sumud* are hoped to eventually lead to self-determination and the right of return for refugees. The notion of daily acts of resistance in this sense also includes Israeli and international solidarity, and one of the examples Qumsiyeh used was of international volunteers picking olives during the second Intifada in the early 2000s.

Daily *Sumud* in the Lives of Olive Growers

I observed one powerful instance of an action based on *Sumud* when I was helping a family to plant olive saplings in the winter of 2015/16. Amir, a family member who is a teacher during the day and a farmer in the evenings and holidays, related to me an event he described as "a nightmare come true":

> In the night between the 16th and 17th of February I dreamt that something bad had happened to our olive trees. I went to the land on the morning of the 17th of February, and found all of the newly planted olives had been uprooted. The 500 olive trees were donated by the JAI to us and were planted by 40 volunteers on Friday 13th of February, 2015. My family own a few hundred *dunums* in this wadi, but we come from a village near Al-Khalil. I love this wadi and the trees in it as it is my second home. I lived on this land with my parents in a cave for some of my childhood, especially during harvest time. I felt shocked and devastated when I saw the terraces empty of trees in the morning. My family began facing problems from the Israeli authorities and settlers in the 1990s, but we eventually managed to prove we owned our land with documents from the Ottoman, British, and Jordanian eras, which we luckily had kept safe. This is unusual as most Palestinian farmers in the area rarely manage to find papers to prove their ownership of their land. Our land is surrounded by two colonies. Settlers from these colonies have beaten up members of my family, and one day my brother had to be hospitalized as a result. The last attack on us took place last autumn. One year we planted apri-

cots, apples, almonds, and other fruit trees, most of which died as we were unable to access the land to look after them as a result of settlers' violence. This year we decided to plant the land with olives, and we have been working on the soil for some months to prepare it. We ploughed the land, removed the thorns and weeds, and prepared the soil before planting day. On the morning of the planting day, we had to park our cars hundreds of metres away as usual, and walked up and down the steep rocky terrain before we arrived. We walked that way because we were worried about settlers or soldiers attacking us if we used the road leading to the two colonies, which also leads to our land. At least a dozen heavily armed IDF soldiers were surrounding us in the nearby hills on the morning of planting day. Shakir, the IDF commander, approached and warned me: "Next time don't bring with you all these types [referring to international volunteers], they are trouble. You should only come with your family." He also told me that he shouldn't be surprised if our trees were damaged.

On their way back to the bus after we finished planting, some of the volunteers were nearly run over by dangerously fast driving settlers, who shouted at them, "Go back to where you came from" in an American accent. One volunteer noticed their American accent and replied: "You should go back to Brooklyn." This morning when we arrived here, what we found looked like a massacre. What's left of the 500 trees were broken branches, severely damaged saplings thrown out of their holes, white plastic covering laid on the ground, and most of the wooden sticks still standing by the empty holes, looking like a mass grave. Most of the saplings have been taken from the land, and I think it must have taken them a few hours to remove. I think the IDF soldiers manning the checkpoint and the watchtower bordering our land must have seen them and turned a blind eye or helped them even. I plan to go to the civil administration in a nearby colony to make a complaint, but I don't expect much from them because if your oppressor was also your judge how do you expect justice to be achieved? We will not give up, and we plan to work with the JAI to plant this field again, as we did twice before. We will not despair, no matter how strong they are. It is our right.

Indeed, the following year, when I visited and called Amir to ask about how the saplings were, he reported that the trees they had planted the following season were still there. As expected, they had not heard from the civil administration about finding the perpetrators, and the family did not expect any compensation. They simply hoped that the trees they had replanted would grow well and that they would produce good fruit in a few years' time to feed the family and protect the land.

Other examples of daily activities of resistance seen during my field work include finding an alternative way to access land that is fenced, gated, or where constructing roads is banned, such as by the use of donkeys or by finding holes in the fence; looking for alternative materials to build needed structures that the IDF bans, such as using stone already present on the land to construct a storage space, rehabilitating old wells for storing rainwater, and using caves in the hills for shelter and storage. Other families appealed to the courts and UN organizations to gain their land rights, with some successes. Others accessed confiscated land clandestinely to reclaim it by planting olive groves.

Not all stories I heard in the field represent examples of daily acts of *Sumud* among olive growers and the farming community in general. This is true in particular among the younger generation, many of whom found no other option but to abandon growing olives for other more profitable opportunities in order to sustain their families. Nedal told me about a man from the village whose father died and, because he works as a wage laborer in Israel, their land and trees had been neglected. Abu 'Attallah's children from his first marriage had also decided not to work the land and wanted their father to sell it and stay in town. Abu Weehab told me a story about a man from a nearby village who used to cultivate very good yields of grapes, and when the neighboring settlers saw what he was capable of he was offered a job within the colony with a good salary, so he neglected his grapes, and his yields became less and less productive with the years. Abu Weehab thought of this story as a parable for the ideology and practice of Israeli settler-colonialism that has an interest in native communities leaving their land. Abu and Um Weehab themselves were worried that among their own children only their eldest, Weehab, was interested in olive growing.

I asked Abu Weehab about what was unique about him, Um Weehab, and their son Weehab who were able to continue farming olives. He told me that they felt rooted in the land, and that they were fortunate to have some financial means to be able to spend on maintaining the land without expecting profitable yields every year. He also told me that he developed political consciousness as a young man in the 1960s and 1970s, when Palestinian resistance against the military occupation became more organized. This was similar to what Nedal told me when I asked why, unlike most men his age in the village, he was interested in olive growing. He told me that as the only son of his father, who had left him and his mother to live in town, he was embedded in an environment of fallahin and that he helped his grandfather look after the sheep and grow fruit and vegetables. Nedal also was part of a youth political organization that campaigned for workers' and farmers' rights before the establishment of the PA in the 1990s. According to Nedal, his involvement in the youth organization increased his political consciousness and

Olive Growing for *Sumud*

attachment to the land and to olive growing. He believed that the establishment of the PA has led to politicians and political parties seeking financial means as the main motivator for getting involved in social and political activism. Nedal thinks that political organizations have not been helping in developing that sort of awareness among the young that is important for people to maintain their belonging to the land and their will to resist in their daily life in order to maintain the activity of olive farming. Nedal and his wife, like Nada and Abu Kamal, however, continued to try to nurture this awareness in their own young children by taking them to the land and by getting them more involved in the activities of growing olives and other fruit and vegetables.

The Characteristics of Everyday-Acts-of-*Sumud*

For those who maintained the activities of olive growing and were challenging the military occupation through the everyday-acts-of-*Sumud*, these means had certain qualities, demanded specific skills, and were shaped by a variety of values. These specific characteristics of olive growers' daily acts of *Sumud* are discussed below, followed by links made to relevant studies on the concept of resistive occupations from an occupational justice perspective.

First, *Sumud* is a position and an action that families adopt as a necessity in the face of occupational apartheid. *Sumud* allows them to survive, maintain their identity and belonging, and work toward a future vision of a more just society. Participants talked about a revival in olive growing since the 1970s, calculated to counter the increasing land grab and the expansion of colonies on land owned by Indigenous families. Nedal's story of working three jobs reflected the need for *Sumud* in his daily life, whereby he persisted and held on to their land and the other jobs in order to provide for his family. Damir and his family had to be creative and problem-solve in what they could do with their land and how they could use their time as a family doing this—this is another example of how vital this attitude and means of action is. If olive growers are not to lose their land, they do not have a choice but to be on and work their land. Due to Israel's use of the centuries-old Ottoman rule that allows the expropriation of land that it deems unworked by its owners, many families believe that being on the land and working it is essential to reduce the chances of it being confiscated. Therefore, in adopting the value of *Sumud*, families had no choice but to find means to access and work the land, as when Abu Nedal and his family, with the help of the agricultural committee in their village, rehabilitated a terrace and a well at the top of the hill and planted it with grapes. If Nedal had an opportunity to choose, he might have worked full-time on their land, or he might have opted to work for his own community in the village, as he often told me. What allowed him and his family to hold on to their land, and to survive and continue to belong (to their land, family, and community) and to grow, were the daily acts of *Sumud* that he could not afford not to adopt.

The second characteristic of *Sumud* is the selfless efforts that it requires from communities and individuals. *Sumud* as a necessity required sacrifices of the families I met. Um Yasin and Abu ʿAttallah left their families and moved to their land to protect it. In justifying these sacrifices, Um Yasin said: "As long as we protect the land, we will preserve ourselves. We will stay put on our land." She added: "Staying put on the land is our only jihad." The term "jihad" in Arabic originates from the root meaning to make an effort to fight oppression (Dar Al-Mashriq 1986). Many of the olive growers stated that this was their way of fighting the occupation, rather than by means of protesting or carrying arms. Damir's family had to find vast amounts of money for legal representation for court cases to challenge the Israeli authorities' attempts to confiscate their land. Abu Nedal left town and other jobs he had there to return to his village to work and protect the land and his own community, which was at risk of "being swallowed by the colony," as he explained. This effort was selfless, and in some respects was not guaranteed to yield immediate results, but families I met were determined to practice it as their right and duty because they were the owners and workers of these lands, and their ancestors had been doing this activity for thousands of years. They felt they could not afford to not practice this duty, as they would lose their livelihood and ways of life. Qumsiyeh had equated this selfless attitude to the story of Jesus, as told in the New Testament, and considered Jesus to be one of the first documented examples of popular resisters to domination (by Roman rule) in these lands (Qumsiyeh 2011).

These needed and creative selfless acts are oriented toward the third characteristic of *Sumud*, which is communities' self-determination, as Damir reflected:

> The future will be difficult. I believe that despite these circumstances we should be able to change our own reality. What we can do is a small stone in the large mosaic of liberating the land and ourselves. You add another stone, and we add another one, then we can hopefully complete the whole picture. We need to have a vision for the future, and be realistic at the same time.

His family's land was under threat of confiscation, hundreds of their trees were uprooted, and their solar panels and wells were destroyed by the IDF. Their vision included developing an organic farm, educational projects for local communities, and a volunteering program for international activists—a vision they had been working on for the last decade. Their daily acts of *Sumud* were based on a hope that functions as fuel for the family's daily lives. This can-do attitude was adopted by olive growers seeking a better future in which they could practice a degree of self-rule over their daily lives and activities, and it was a fundamental factor in contributing to the motivation for taking part in daily means of *Sumud*. This process of becoming that leads to dreaming about, and planning for, a greater collective self-ruling and self-actualizing future will be further explained later in this chapter.

Self-determination requires sociopolitical awareness, which is the fourth characteristic of *Sumud* I observed that olive growers have developed through education and the renewal of traditional practices. Abu Weehab said: "The future needs social awareness and feelings of belonging to the land. Because if there is no awareness, everyone will migrate. Those who have it, even if they go away, will come back. We have no life apart from the one in this country, and we need to preserve it." Um Weehab, his wife, a retired teacher who had always worked on the land, said: "The role of the teacher comes into play here. Teachers with this awareness will engage pupils who don't read this in books. They will teach the things that the other side is hiding, and this will open their eyes." She was referring to attempts by the Israeli authorities to monitor school curricula against anything that is perceived as a threat to their dominance, which includes learning about Palestinian history and heritage (Masalha 2012). She was worried that Israeli policies, aiming to preserve the status quo of segregation and colonization, would cause younger generations to forget their heritage and lose their connectedness to their native land and traditional practices.

This type of awareness was described as an "occupational consciousness," which refers to a recognition of power relationships of dominance between the colonizers and the colonized, and the awareness that this can be maintained but also confronted through people's daily activities (Ramugondo 2015). Ramugondo (2012) discussed this construct as she studied families in South Africa who, as a result of the history of colonization and apartheid there, needed to negotiate long-term issues of power and find ways to confront this in their everyday lives in order to improve their and their community's well-being. The term "consciousness" was borrowed from Marxist, postcolonial, and liberation thought, and aims to illuminate a situation of ongoing disparities in relationships between groups of people in society; the appending to it of "occupational" signified that these relations "lay out through human occupation" (Ramugondo 2015, 422). Ramugondo's study on intergenerational play within families in post-apartheid South Africa demonstrated some lasting effects of Western forms of colonialism in the daily habits of Black families; these effects were expressed in routines adopted by the youth in shantytowns and found to be caused by feelings of inferiority about their identity in relation to "white" identity (Ramugondo 2012). This manifested as Black youth favored imported consumerist occupations, such as watching television all day. This frustrated the families studied, especially the older generation, as it prevented them from continuing traditional forms of play based on mutuality and cooperation—based on their values system of Ubuntu. This led Ramugondo to explore the concept of occupational consciousness as "a critical notion that frames everyday doing as a potentially liberating response to oppressive social structures" (Ramugondo 2015, 489).

The notion of occupational consciousness can aid in increasing people's awareness of sociopolitical and historical influences over their daily occupations, by supporting them to articulate their own situations and thereby enable self-directed activities that lead to their individual and collective well-being (Ramugondo 2012). Black communities in post-apartheid South Africa still experience the colonial legacy in financial and living conditions disparities, and in feelings of inferiority among some individuals. Through her postcolonial lens, Ramugondo was able to illustrate how both the oppressed and the oppressors can reinforce unjust systems; she saw this as "implicit consent" in the family she studied when she observed how they were prevented from self-determining a narrative about their own occupation (Ramugondo 2015, 492). However, the territorial segregation and separation in work and education imposed during the apartheid era is no longer the law in South Africa. In Palestine, olive-growing families are still living under a segregating structure enforced by the official policy and practice of settler-colonialism and military occupation; they are constantly aware of it, which provides the motive to act. Their challenge against this situation of injustice is expressed through values and means of action they have carried over from previous generations, with some contemporary additions, such as the incorporation of global solidarity, discussed below.

Palestinian families I spoke to, unlike the South African family in Ramugondo's study, were alert to such a situation and continuously articulated this awareness to me. However, it can be argued that some Palestinians might have adopted the othering and self-demoting stance that sees them as inferior. This has led many to leave olive growing and seek some other daily occupations, such as consumerism or professions that led them to leaving the village. This implicit adoption of attitudes of the colonizers can also be seen in the partnership of the PA with Israeli forces or when the PA adopts practices and institutions based on Western capitalist ideologies that proved harmful to Indigenous Palestinian communities, such as those agribusiness policies cited by Sansour and Tartir (2014) (see below).

Communities I visited recognized the hegemony of Israeli policy and ideology over their daily lives. They resisted it by ensuring that acts of *Sumud*, based on

Olive Growing for *Sumud*

their people's historic experiences and ways of living, were practiced despite land colonization and segregation designed to erase these ways of life. To this end, they engaged the young and found ways to preserve their belonging and resisting activities to enable their survival and emergence as a unique people who belonged to their specific context but also to the wider global community, by communicating and sharing their own special way of daily resistance, as discussed next.

Additionally, the process of intercultural translation performed in this book is intended to also contribute to this type of awareness-raising of this specific type of a Global South occupational consciousness within other marginalized communities (marginalized by capitalism, racism, colonialism, patriarchy, and other systems of oppression), activist communities, the discipline of occupational science, the field of occupational therapy, sociology, and other social sciences concerned with meaningful daily actions.

Daily-Acts-of-*Sumud* as Further Evidence of the Political and Resistive Aspects of Occupations

The stories of the *Sumud* of olive farmers belong to the larger world insofar as they resemble situations in other parts of the globe. The realities of other communities, their occupations, and their contexts were presented in the series of books, *Occupational Therapies without Borders* (Kronenberg, Simó Algado, and Pollard 2005; Kronenberg, Pollard, and Sakellariou 2011; Sakellariou and Pollard 2017). These volumes were an inspiration for this study and motivated me to think about my own community through an occupational justice lens. They included a collection of theoretical and empirical explorations of global groups facing adverse sociopolitical conditions, and how these impacted their daily doing. Their meaningful occupations were restricted, but despite that or because of it, they have been using these activities as socially and politically transformative tools for their own liberation. The books told stories from all corners of the globe, including Latin America, South Africa, and Palestine. Communities studied included ethnic, religious, and sexual minorities, people seeking refuge, people with mental health issues, and people with physical disabilities. Occupation emerged as a concept that encompasses resistive elements that counter the status quo of domination, oppression, and different forms of injustice. This resisting agency was expressed through individual and collective activities, and with political consciousness and determination to achieve justice of some kind. These occupations variously had immediate or long-term outcomes, but all aimed at changing structures or transforming the community. The social and political transformation aspect of daily activities was evidenced, for instance, by a study of domestic workers conducted by Galvaan

(2010), a South African scholar. The women in this study maintained their other occupational roles as mothers and members of their communities, and organized in unions. They managed to participate in all these activities and roles, despite and in response to the harsh working conditions imposed by employers' rigid rules and the long-standing issues of racial and financial segregation (ibid.).

The topic of occupation as a tool for social and political change was discussed in Gelya Frank's work (1996). She studied craft production among Indigenous Palestinian women and among Israeli women from communities who had migrated from non-Western countries. Women in Palestine have a long history of realizing forms of self-determination through doing their daily activities collectively. Documented examples of such acts include when in the 1920s women led direct actions against British rule, such as demonstrations, petitions, and letter writing to influential politicians (Frank 1996; Qumsiyeh 2011). These collective acts of resistance were done by women aiming to free themselves and society from oppression, and were and still are pivotal in the general struggle for occupational and social justice in Palestine (Qumsiyeh 2011). Frank (1996) showed how in the late 1970s women established work committees that were restricted and limited by political, social, and economic structures, including Israeli policies and patriarchal domination. Such oppressive measures were exemplified in Frank's (ibid.) study in the case of the closing down of an embroidery workshop by the IDF during the first Intifada. Craft production by women in Palestine, it can be argued, is an instance of a daily act of *Sumud*, as it is a collective and historic occupation done with coagency and solidarity between local women. It aims to counter the status quo of domination. Its outcome is to maintain and improve livelihood. Craft production is similar to the collective occupations done by other colonized people, such as when Indian producers attempted to be self-sufficient in making their own clothes on spinning wheels rather than relying on imported British supplies, enabling a boycott of British produce to counter the British occupation (ibid.). This aim of becoming more self-sufficient adds another level of resemblance between the cases of craft-making and olive growing—both of which are daily acts of *Sumud* with wider global connections and relevance to other communities who are experiencing historical and political injustices and seeking ways to resist such injustices.

Frank (ibid.) conceptualized craft making as a resistive occupation, and her study was the first I could find in the field of occupational science to append the term "resistive" to occupation. She wrote that "individuals continue to use crafts to adapt to oppressive situations and groups to mobilize resistance to political and economic domination" (ibid., 56). She claimed that in these instances, the "lexicon of culture" was contested, and she wished to explore what occurs when "naming

Olive Growing for *Sumud* 113

daily activities and interpreting their meaning becomes a political act" (ibid.). She defined culture as the "patterns of meaningful everyday activity" and argued that it was a phenomenon that requires analyzing from political and economic perspectives (ibid.). In that sense resistive occupations, such as craft making and olive growing, express a culture that is at risk of being disrupted or lost. It is a political phenomenon because it is a communal act and is done for collective self-actualization, therefore enabling people to fulfill their potential through their daily occupations. This was demonstrated when Damir told me how he and his family decided to adopt the approach of "non-violent resistance" by finding creative ways to enable them to continue working the land, and in that way they "chose the path of hope," as Damir told me, to become more self-sufficient. They also work with nearby villagers to do the same, to achieve their collective potential.

In sociology and environmental studies, these means of resisting in the everyday lives of communities have recently been highlighted by Norgaard (2019), who studied the native communities of the Klamath Basin in modern-day California. Specific to Palestinian communities and from the field of psychoanalysis, Sheehi and Sheehi (2024) examined the practicing of resistance among Palestinians and psychotherapists living under Israel's military occupation. In occupational therapy and occupational science, and apart from Frank's work mentioned above, some have discussed phenomena they called "wicked problems" from an occupational justice perspective and came close to terming occupations to counter them as resistive activities (McGrath and McGonagle 2016; Wicks and Jamieson 2014). Wicked problems were defined as socioenvironmental issues that impact people's wellness, such as climate change (Wicks and Jamieson 2014). Settler-colonialism in Palestine can be classed as a "wicked problem" given its definition as a major issue without clear solutions (ibid.). More specifically, in regard to land-based occupations, Cabell (2012) studied agro-ecological farming in Canada as a way to counter the status quo and contribute to alternative ways of being. This study came close to describing ecological farming as a form of resistance, highlighting the belonging and spiritual elements of the transformative occupation of growing local and seasonal food using environmentally friendly methods (Cabell 2012). Núñez Valderrama, Hernández, and Alarcón (2022) examined the impacts of coloniality on rural and fishing communities in Chile, and these communities' resistance through collective occupations, such as fishing. Shetty and Nayar (2024) wrote about stories of resistance in people's everyday doing. Located in India, Dadra and Nagar Haveli is a union territory primarily inhabited by tribal communities for whom farming and forestry are defining cultural occupations. The paper aimed to contribute to the growing literature addressing the intersections between occupations and humans within the Global South.

Frank and Muriithi (2015) studied singing and sit-ins in the U.S. civil rights movement and during the fight against apartheid in South Africa. The authors stressed the need for empirical evidence to further the conceptualization and theorization of occupations as socially and politically transformative. In this theoretically considered paper, the authors proposed "a theory of occupational reconstructions"; borrowing John Dewey's meaning of "reconstruction", occupational reconstructions were defined as "what people do together to restore or remake ordinary life in response to a shared injustice or other problematic situation" (ibid., 11). They adopted Dewey's philosophy of Pragmatism to address how collectives, in this case civil rights and anti-apartheid activists, face a problematic situation that leads to a process of inquiring, experimenting, and acting. They offered seven criteria for, or principles of, occupational reconstruction: it should be a shared activity; it is about problem-solving to improve a situation; it is an embodied act that people are motivated to do and they personally take part in it; it has a story structure, adopting a concept of narrative with an imagined future that is anticipated, uncertain, and unfolds with time and space (Mattingly 1998); it involves creativity; it is carried out by choice; and finally occupational reconstruction should be an optimistic trial aiming to achieve positive change (Frank and Muriithi 2015).

All of these criteria can be found in the occupation of olive growing in Palestine. Farming olives is a communal activity, though not with one purpose but with multiple aims and meanings, as shown in chapter 2. Olive growing is carried out to solve the problem of feeding and financially supporting the family in the context of socioeconomic, historical, and political hardship. It is an embodied action that is holistically engaged in by individuals in their bodies and minds. It has a story structure—timeline, places, and different characters, as conversations with olive farmers showed. In terms of the start, middle, and end structure of story that occupational reconstructions have, olive farming, unlike direct actions done for solely political reasons, does not have a period of time when people decided to begin it. However, as shown above, there was a particular period in recent history, the late 1970s, when olive growing began to be associated with decolonial struggle. This points to a moment in time when farmers took a conscious decision to reengage in such an occupation as a way to confront the military occupation. The creative element of olive growing is illustrated in the skill of problem-solving and adopting innovative actions such as in the story of Damir's family. Cultivating olives was not found in this study as an occupation that was forced on individuals and families in the oPt; rather, just like the activities described by Frank and Muriithi (ibid.), they felt the need to engage in them by their own choice. Finally, olive growing is done with a hopeful attitude despite the negative prospects. People

Olive Growing for *Sumud*

do it to self-actualize, and they are willing to trial different things in order to achieve positive change as a result.

There is, though, one conflict between occupational reconstructions as analyzed by Frank and Muriithi (ibid.) and olive growing as conceptualized in this study. Cultivating olives is not an act that is solely done for political ends, as is the case with sit-ins in the United States, or boycotts against South Africa. Olive farming in Palestine, as observed in this research, is a political act, and some of the motivations for doing it are collective, but it was not planned as an act of civil disobedience. It might include some direct actions such as reclaiming land, or protests against the uprooting of trees, or using holes in the fence to pass through to one's land. These direct acts of protest are not the ultimate goal of olive growing as an act of *Sumud*; instead, they are done for purposes of holding onto their land, trees, and community (belonging) and to enable them to become more self-ruling (becoming).

Sumud as Doing for Belonging and Becoming

This emerging theoretical discussion about the concept of resistive occupations in the literature leads me to an exploration of how the daily acts of *Sumud* described in this book relate to other theoretical insights in occupational justice discourse, and how the unique act of resistance through olive growing can expand these understandings. The daily occupations of *Sumud* were interpreted in this study in relation to the interlinking of becoming and belonging, as presented in "the theory of the human need for occupation" (Wilcock 2006). In this theory, the relationship between these two dimensions of occupation represents the future-oriented determinant interacting with the need to connect and contribute to communities' wellness (Hitch, Pépin, and Stagnitti 2014a, 2014b).

The foundation of the concept of becoming is challenged and extended by the experience of Palestinian olive farmers as interpreted in this book. Becoming in Maslow's work on the hierarchy of needs and his theory of human motivation, which Wilcock based her theory on, refers to concepts such as change, development, and transformation—all drivers and outcomes of what people do in their daily lives (Maslow 1970; Wilcock and Hocking 2015). Maslow's theory assumes a move from meeting lower order needs to satisfying those higher ones, all of which are biological needs humans are born with. The lowest of them are the physical and emotional needs of the human body, and at the top is the highest fulfillment of the human potential, termed "self-actualisation" (Maslow 1970). Becoming is constant, as humans never reach an optimal endpoint of their progress, according to this view (Wilcock and Hocking 2015). To challenge such ethnocentric and anthropocentric notions, Santos (2014) called for epistemologies that are based on ways of knowing and doing rooted in the daily lives of marginalized communities in the Global South, such as Ubuntu in South Africa. Western-centric intellectuals, including those on the liberal left (e.g., Dewey and Maslow), according to Santos, have provided the wrong answers to the world's troubles (ibid.). Some of those answers, such as "development" or "education," "democracy" or "human rights," are seen as solutions that fit all societies with no attention to specificity of place and time. Further, such ideas are founded on epistemologies—ways of seeing and knowing the world—that, if imported to groups such as olive farmers, may not help their situation and may even lead to more oppression.

One example of how Western-centric notions of development and progress were imposed on Palestinian farming communities was reported by Sansour and Tartir (2014). In the name of economic development, the PA created industrial zones in the West Bank, which allowed it to confiscate land from farmers. These zones have been found to be profitable for agribusiness, mainly Israeli companies, rather than for the farmers themselves (ibid.):

> Like many farmers around the world, Palestinian farmers are the victims of a top down neoliberal development approach that attempts to dispossess them of their land and seeds in service of banks, multinational corporations, and agribusiness giants. An instrument of this approach has been the Palestinian Authority's creation of industrial zones that will entrench Palestinians' dependency on Israel and sustain the current detrimental economic framework (ibid., 1).

Palestinian rural families, like other Global South communities, are facing a situation of injustice as a result of an idea of progress or development forced upon them. They are also creatively living and resisting under these hardships by using means deeply rooted in living in harmony and mutual transactions with other beings. An alternative term, rooted in the Palestinian experience, was offered by Said (1999), who discussed the concept of "emergence," or *intilaqah* (a beginning with eagerness and force). "In place of some Archimedean magic principle outside history or society," Said suggested emergence as a way to interpret the daily existence of Palestinian communities (ibid., 125). Palestinian olive-farming communities, as observed in this research, are living under a continuing process of land colonization, land and community segregation, and other ideologies and policies that have been forced on them in the last century. Because of and despite this negative trajectory, Palestinian individuals and communities have been responding through their patterns of daily living, or culture (Frank 1996). They go on doing what they need to do, aiming to collectively self-determine and emerge as more self-ruling and self-actualizing. Said (1999) associated this ongoing emergence with workers and peasants, who were a "force of recovery" through their daily doings (ibid., 116). Their daily acts of *Sumud* represented a combination of the emergence element—doing for becoming—with the doing for belonging dimension discussed below.

The belonging aspect of this interaction of doing for becoming and doing for belonging refers to the duty of all individuals in society to build and harness social relations (Rijke and van Teeffelen 2014). These bonds are embodied in family and in local and international relationships, which have a function in keeping the Palestinian way of life alive. Belonging is achieved by mutual alliances creating a situation in which people share each other's burdens and form a community based on solidarity and caring (ibid.). Evidence of this aspect of daily lives in Global South groups was shown in a study by Kramer Roy (2011). She used participatory action research to learn about occupational justice issues within families of British-Pakistani background who were raising children with disabilities. This study highlighted a community's experience of occupational injustice, how their "belongingness" suffered due to negative views about disability within the community, and how the positive changes in their beliefs and ways of doing enabled the acceptance of their children and better caring for them (ibid., 390).

The belonging aspect of *Sumud* does not only represent those who live in the oPt, but also Palestinians who live abroad who have connections to the nation, Palestinian culture and history, and Israeli and international solidarity activists (Rijke and van Teeffelen 2014). *Sumud* relies on this belonging aspect to act in conjunction with the future-oriented element of doing for becoming. "The resistance expressed through *Sumud* represents a way of believing in a better and more human future, and a rejection of the unjust relationship between occupier and occupied," as Rijke and van Teeffelen concluded (ibid., 93). Olive growers demonstrated this future-oriented determination in their everyday activities, aided by a communal solidarity that resisted land colonization. Their daily experiences offer a useful example to the occupational justice movement, by sharing their stories of daily acts of *Sumud* as empirical evidence for belonging for becoming as an essential component of human occupations. It was shown that *Sumud* constitutes "the agency of everyday acts that prevent Israel's successful subordination of Palestinians" (ibid., 92). It places resisting the Israeli military occupation as "part of life for people focused on going forward and keeping their hope in a more just and human future alive" (ibid.).

The daily acts of *Sumud* analyzed in the stories of olive farmers represent an "unmistakable Palestinian determination," which is founded on "notable stubbornness" deriving from "a sense of accumulated Palestinian history" (Said, 1999, 147, 158). The everyday activities of *Sumud* of olive growers provide a conceptual window into creative and problem-solving means of actions; they offer insights to world solidarity and to communities resisting occupational injustices, by potentially inspiring these communities to act resistively in culturally specific ways. Daily acts of *Sumud* demonstrated by olive farmers embody a plurality of means of becoming and belonging, rooted in daily experiences that can be shared with the world. In that way, olive growing in Palestine offers a unique contribution to global communities by offering insights about everyday acts of resistance to ensure their occupational justice and well-being. Moreover, these collective ways of knowing and doing can be applied and tested in other contexts of injustice within which social scientists, helping professionals, and activists work.

Other Instances of Daily *Sumud* in the oPt

There are other everyday occupations done by other Palestinian groups as means of *Sumud* that demonstrate its omnipresence in everyday life here. The first instance I discuss here is not from my observations or from the literature, but from a powerful story about producing milk from cows during the first Intifada in the 1980s, based on a film I watched during one field visit and my reactions to it. The second example is about the daily occupation of preserving and sharing heritage vegetable and fruit seeds—the aims of a recent project that was named the Palestine Heirloom Seed Library (PHSL), founded by Vivien Sansour, whom I introduced earlier in this book.

The story of the cows of Beit Sahour is almost a utopian example of a daily act of *Sumud*. It has all the hallmarks and the characters of such a concept as discussed in this chapter. The story has been brought back to public awareness by a film codirected by a local man, Amer Shomali. I saw the film during my time in Beit Sahour, the town I used as a base during field work. *The Wanted 18* (Shomali and Cowan 2014) tells the true story of the local community, which sought to boycott Israeli produce in order to be self-sufficient and to produce their own milk. They found a friendly Israeli *kibbutz* that agreed to sell them eighteen cows so they could collectively rear them and produce milk for the people of the town. The film tells the story through interviews with women and men who participated in this activity. It also employs animation, reconstructions of events, and real footage from the period: the late 1980s at the peak of the first Intifada, when the town suffered curfews and closures as well as raids and violence. The community cleverly broke the conditions of curfew in order to milk the cows and deliver their milk to people's houses, guarding the cows in a place of hiding by sleeping with them in the stable. Eventually the Israeli authorities found out about the project and began to search for the herd. The townspeople then had to problem-solve and find other places to hide the cows, such as at the butcher's shop and in the butcher's home. Despite the creative and determined fight the town's people put up, they couldn't stand up to an Israeli force equipped with high technology and weaponry. Sadly, the town lost one of her sons, who was shot dead by the IDF during this episode, and the cows were all hunted down. This act of daily *Sumud* deeply troubled the Israeli forces, as one of the former generals interviewed in the film admitted. They did not want people elsewhere in the oPt to learn from such a story of creative challenge to the dominance of the military occupation over their lives.

As for why this act counts for an ideal instance of a daily *Sumud*, it demonstrates a mutual association between a specific human group, their context and the daily activities they wish and need to engage in. I start with the people involved. They were women and men who "were exceptional in not only coping with, but challenging great difficulties, and developing strategies to survive with" (Dabbagh 2015). As one of the interviewees said in the film: "The only thing we controlled was the air that we breathed." The military occupation and its practices "put it into your head that you are subhuman, you are not equal," as another interviewee said. However, still another one of the interviewees said: "It was very clear. Mentally we were superior to them." This mental attitude resembles Wade's small acts of resistance and Scott's story about the wise farting peasant discussed earlier. The people of Beit Sahour, despite the imposition of physical forms of violence and segregation such as the curfew, felt that they still had an agency to act to fulfill their sovereignty over their daily actions and lives. The second element in the story is the environment, both human and other-than-human. The human-made structures represented by the military occupation led to the experience of occupational apartheid systematically limiting their collective self-determination. It led to occupational apartheid through restrictions on the daily occupations of society: curfews and the closing down of schools, for example. An alternative and more liberating dimension of the context was expressed through the heritage and culture that created unique ways of believing and doing, and values of cooperation and solidarity—including cooperation with a sympathetic Israeli community. These values provided a motivator for the people to do the activity. The daily occupation of producing milk is the third element in this transaction. It was a necessary activity for survival, for maintaining and harnessing community roles and meanings, as well as having a collective function of claiming sovereignty over the participants' families, land, and daily doing.

That act of *Sumud* succeeded despite the sad ending caused by the Israeli forces. It was completed by the act of telling the story through the film to others. This initiative, as an example of an action and a value deeply rooted in the community, continues a tradition of this small town of Beit Sahour, a town with a history of resistive collective actions. This was a communal activity that originated from people at a grassroots level, and was not dictated by any outside force. This town had offered living examples of daily forms of *Sumud* in the past, such as infamous tax boycotts in the first Intifada (Qumsiyeh 2011). Other actions taken by this community included coordinating teaching committees and homeschooling during times of curfews and school and university closures. The role of women and people of all ages and backgrounds was distinctive to such actions in Beit Sahour. This collective occupation that was creatively done for belonging and self-rule was observed, by Berger (1979) and Scott (2012), as a marker of a peasant way of life. It has been shown as a means of doing and knowing described in the *Epistemologies of the South* (Santos 2014), and in some constructs conceptualized in occupational science that will be further discussed in the following chapter. One difference between the acts of *Sumud* done through olive farming and the example of producing milk in Beit Sahour is that, like the sit-ins and boycotts cited by Frank and Muriithi (2015) as historical examples of occupational reconstruction, the story of the cows was an organized daily occupation done for the purpose of civil disobedience (as well as sustenance), whereas the daily activities of olive farming were not intended as an organized act of civil disobedience.

The Palestine Heirloom Seed Library (PHSL)[5] is a local initiative established by Vivien Sansour. After a few years away, during which she studied and worked with farming communities in the Americas and in other regions of Palestine, Vivien returned home to find that the familiar smells and sights of local produce sold in her hometown had almost disappeared. She was shocked to see "markets flooded with a monoculture of alien species of vegetables and fruit." Reflecting on her project, Vivien explained in an interview with me: "The seed library team are operating as seed detectives, excavating elders' knowledge of the old varieties and the stories that go with them." The team visits the surrounding villages, meeting elders who collect the seeds of native fruits and vegetables. The library has been collecting and experimenting in planting heirloom varieties, including a disappearing white cucumber forgotten by the younger generations, and an old watermelon variety called *Jadu'i*. The library holds workshops in which local students and teachers learn and recreate knowledge that they gather from their parents and grandparents about native seeds and ways to collect, save, and grow them. The seed library aims to empower local communities to preserve Indigenous seeds, which are suited to local conditions and can grow organically with little artificial irrigation. It is hoped that this intergenerational and intercommunal project will help to overturn the pattern of turning local farmers into consumers dependent

Olive Growing for *Sumud*

on Israeli and global agribusiness companies. Such companies sell them seeds that are unsuitable for the local conditions, require scarce water resources and deadly chemicals to grow, and erase thousands of years of heritage.

Resembling the acts of *Sumud* of the olive growers who resist occupational apartheid, Vivien reflected on the resistive element of collecting seed: "The mere act of saving a seed becomes a subversive act that generates a sense of resurrection of the spirit of a people buried, and at the same time sprouting hope in the most essential of ways." The library collaborates with seed libraries elsewhere in the world, in order to share ideas and practices to further strengthen the food sovereignty of these communities. The story of the PHSL contains all the elements of the daily acts of resistance analyzed in this study; however this daily occupation, done for the purpose of resistance is, unlike olive growing, an organized and planned project whose main purpose is enabling and empowering those farmers who have already lost the occupation of seed collecting to revive this activity; whereas olive growing, as shown in this study, is not a planned project and has already been revived by families here since the 1970s.

In conclusion, olive growing as an everyday act of *Sumud* is a phenomenon rooted in the historic and daily realities of Palestinians. It relates to notions and practices of anti-colonial struggles globally and resembles other everyday activities of resistance studied elsewhere in the world. *Sumud* as daily resistance was translated into occupational science discourse as a principle of action representing the belonging for becoming dimension of daily activities. *Sumud* evolved throughout modern Palestinian history, emerging during the British Mandate in the early twentieth century, and since then evolved as a way of life that reflects the phrase: "To resist is to exist." Daily acts of *Sumud* carried out by olive farmers were shown to be informed by four values: They are adopted as essential acts for holding on to land and the survival of the community; they are selfless actions done by families who had to make sacrifices in the process; they are hopeful and future-oriented acts that aim at olive growers becoming more self-determined; and they are based on a specific sociopolitical, and occupational, consciousness of the dynamic of powers related to settler-colonialism and its aim to divorce people from their land and daily activities. Olive growers' daily acts of *Sumud* were analyzed as an empirical example of notions of resistive occupations and occupational reconstruction in occupational science. Finally, *Sumud* as a motivator for olive growing was compared to the relationship of doing for becoming and doing for belonging, as it expresses an ongoing collective attempt to emerge as a self-determined and sovereign community. It therefore offers a unique Palestinian contribution to the theory of the occupational nature of humans and the occupational justice movement in

A site of an uprooted olive grove. Photo taken by the author.

occupational science. In the next chapter, I further theorize the notion of Everyday Forms of Resistance—a form of synthesis of the three notions of *Sutra*, *'Awna*, and *Sumud*, which highlights a challenge to mainstream conceptualization of occupation, occupational justice, and their related terms such as doing, being, becoming and belonging, in the hope of contributing to a decolonized theory and practice that may offer some insights to activists, communities, and scholars who are interested in challenging structural injustices from the bottom up.

مقاومة يومية

CHAPTER 5

Everyday Forms of Resistance

It is not only the future of peasants which is now involved in
this continuity. The forces which in most parts of the world
are today eliminating or destroying the peasantry represent
the contradiction of most of the hopes once contained in the
principle of historical progress.

—John Berger 1979, xxvi

Following the introduction of the fourth participant family in this study, the
family of Nada and Abu Kamal, this chapter explores the final integrated theme of
Everyday Forms of Resistance. This theme was identified in the later stages of my
fieldwork when it was becoming clear that the three preceding themes of *Sutra-
'Awna-Sumud* share many aspects in common, practically and conceptually. I address this overarching principle of olive growing, along with some examples from
the field followed by insights into the multidimensional meanings (epistemological-
ontological-ethical-practical) of this principle of action for olive growing that
combines the other themes of this study.

The Family of Nada and Abu Kamal

To meet Nada, Abu Kamal, and their family, I drove to Al-Akhdar—a cultivated
wadi on the edges of the Beit Lahem region, which is "the only green space left in
Beit Lahem," Abu Nedal told me once, referring to the fact that a lot of Palestinian
land had been confiscated in this region. I drove through Beit Jala, the most western and highest of the trio of towns in the region, which include Beit Sahour in
the east, whose name means the house of night watch, where it is thought the

angels descended from heaven to deliver the news of the birth of Jesus to the shepherds who were staying up all night to guard their goats and sheep in the caves. To this day, shepherds are seen leading their herds in towns, villages, and on the edges of roads, looking for food for their herds on open grazing land. Beit Lahem is in the middle; its name, I was told by locals, means the house of bread, though I later discovered that it was named after the Canaanite god of the south hills; and Beit Jala, whose name means the house of the heights, is on the most western edge of the region. I passed the checkpoint with the Israeli military camp on my left, and into Area C, down a narrow and steep road, which continues into dirt roads at the bottom of the valley. Abu Deeb, the guard, greeted me with a walking stick in one hand, and made highly animated hand gestures with the other. The land Abu Deeb guarded, with the help of a dog tied to its kennel behind the gate, belonged to Abu Kamal's family, whom I was traveling to visit. Their land consisted of several terraces on both sides of the dirt road at the bottom of the valley. The terraces were mostly planted with olive trees, but there were also figs, grapes, apricots, and other fruit. In Abu Kamal's family land, there were herbs such as thyme and mint, and vegetables, such as pumpkins, growing among the trees. The wadi felt busier than normal, with families gathered around trees picking the olives and dropping them onto the colorful sheets placed on the ground under the trees. I saw donkeys resting patiently under trees waiting to help with transporting the yield. I saw and smelled smoke rising above the treetops from fires made to make lunch, tea, and coffee. I learned from locals that olive branches that have just been pruned are very good for burning, and the food and coffee cooked on them taste better because the fire gives a special aroma.

When I met Abu Kamal and Nada, Nada was in her thirties, a Palestinian who was born in a nearby Arab country. Abu Kamal was in his fifties and was born in a local refugee camp. They lived with their two daughters and son in a nearby town. Their eldest daughter, Heba, was in her early teens, followed by Reem and Sultan, both in primary school. Abu Kamal had an adult son, Kamal, and an adult daughter, Lana, from a previous marriage. Both lived abroad. Abu Kamal studied and lived in Eastern Europe, after which he returned to the camp, Al-Reyad, where tens of thousands of Palestinians live in crowded conditions resembling a shantytown. He left the camp when he married Nada and lived initially in a nearby town before they moved to this town, where they lived in a spacious apartment. Nada graduated from university and is now a housewife. She hoped to find a suitable job when her children grow older. Abu Kamal worked in a highly respected job nearby. Some of Abu Kamal's siblings and extended family remained in the camp, while others lived in nearby towns. His eldest brother was well-known for his community work, and together with Abu Kamal, bought some land recently and planted it with fruit and vegetables. One of those plots, I was told, is located in a nearby wadi described above. They bought them from land-owners originally from Beit Jala, who migrated to live in South America, joining thousands of others from that town who have been leaving since the late nine-teenth century. Abu Nedal from Dar El Shoke, who knew the family from when he lived in the camp, worked for the family to help rehabilitate and plant the land until he moved back to his village.

When I asked the couple what they considered the enablers to olive farming to be, their responses pointed to examples of witnessing, solidarity, and collabora-tion between locals and between locals and international groups.

> ABU KAMAL: What helps us is the solidarity of people, especially those who come from abroad to take part in the olive picking; more than anything it is a symbolic act: the person who comes from America or Scandinavia, they might have never picked an olive from a tree before, but they see how Palestinians live and work. A woman from Germany told me once, "What you are doing here is above the ability of any human," when I showed her the pictures of what the land was like before we worked on it, and considering the circumstances we live under, she was able to witness what we go through.

> NADA: When people began to see others on their land and that there is some movement and life in it, they feel encouraged and start planting and working their land again. Perseverance and persistence help.

Dayr Aban (real name)[1] was the village where Abu Kamal's family originated from. It was a small village of about 1,500 people who belonged to the same *hamoula*, or clan. It was situated on the western slopes of the southern hills not far from the coastal plains. The villagers planted fruit trees, such as olives and figs, on the hills, and had some fields on the fertile coastal plains, which they planted with grain and corn. The village was captured and destroyed by Zionist militias in the *Nakba* of 1948, and the villagers were expelled eastward and settled in a UN-funded refugee camp where most of their descendants and refugees from other destroyed villages still live. The village land is currently occupied by an Israeli Jew-ish settlement of Beit Shemesh situated within the Green Line. Since then, the family has lived without land, relying on UN aid in Al-Reyad camp. Camp resi-dents' lost villages, many of which are only a few kilometers away from the camp, still have strong meanings for them even for those younger generations who have never seen them. The population in the refugee camp is poor and suffers from high rates of unemployment. Many are politically active in movements that resist the military occupation, and many are now or have spent long periods in Israeli jails. Despite being in Area A, which is officially controlled by the PA, the camp is regularly invaded by IDF soldiers in night raids. Camp residents are often injured or killed during these raids. Education and culture, such as music and art, are highly regarded in the camp, where there are a few community centers for learning, performances, and other communal activities. However, people have no open green spaces to farm or to gather in as they did a generation or two ago in their original villages. Some schemes have been founded to tackle this, such as planting on the rooftops of homes in the camp. Abu Kamal and his family managed to move out of the camp and now belong to the professional urban classes, though they never forgot their origins and land, as they told me.

The wadi where the family grew olives bordered a highway, a checkpoint, and tunnel—all of which were constructed on private Palestinian land and were built to make it easy for settlers in nearby colonies to drive into Al-Quds. The family couldn't reach the capital unless a rare permit was granted. The rubble from constructing the highway was still visible on land and terraces on the slopes of the wadi when I last visited. During the rainy winter season, and due to poor drainage from the highway and tunnel, surges of water reached the wadi and damaged the crops. Aircraft were often heard in the sky above the wadi, and were thought to be flown by Israeli armed forces to take photographs of the wadi to ensure that no construction was taking place, as all building was banned in the wadi, located in Area C. Some structures belonging to a nearby restaurant have been destroyed several times in recent years. The family had some of their fencing and electricity wires destroyed. The IDF held the keys to the gate leading to the terraces owned by Abu Kamal's family, and could enter the land as they wished. When I visited the wadi in 2021, I noticed structures with a large Israeli flag hanging on their roof on the western slopes of the wadi, which belonged to a settler who had recently moved in with the protection of the army. He, I was told by locals, raised sheep and goats in the area and had even begun selling animals cheaply to Palestinian farmers to win their hearts.

When I asked the couple about what they thought the barriers to the activities of farming olives were, Abu Kamal replied: "The lack of infrastructure and the restriction imposed by the military occupation: we are forbidden from digging for water so we have to buy our own water despite the existence of underground sources of water." Nada added: "We had fences, gates and electricity poles being destroyed; more than once they [military] seized our diggers. On the other land we have not yet been able to plant trees as we heard that neighbours have been attacked."

In addition to the terraces in the wadi, Abu Kamal's siblings bought some land in another nearby area in order to plant it and save it from confiscation, as well as an investment for their children's future. They have been trying to fence it off and plant some olive trees, but until the winter of 2014/15, they were unsuccessful as the nearby colony's settlers attempted to stop some neighboring landowners from planting olives on their land, and the family were fearful for their safety. The fence they erected lately was destroyed by the IDF. There was no natural source of water on this land. The family managed to obtain some water tanks with the help of the local agricultural committee, but these were destroyed and removed by the IDF.

During the winter of 2015/16, the family, helped by volunteers, finally managed to plant two hundred or so olive saplings on their second plot of land. They hoped that the trees would remain unharmed, as they often heard of nearby groves that have been uprooted. In the spring the family hired a donkey and a plough to till their narrow, steep terraces in the wadi. Often tractors were unable to access such land due to the banning of infrastructure building. An international NGO managed to help with the opening of a wide dirt path to allow better access to people's land here. Early spring in the wadi was beautiful. The terraces were dotted with white daisies, yellow mustard flowers, poppies, and other wildflowers among the trees, and Nada and Abu Kamal often brought their children there on the weekends to picnic and spend some time in the fresh air.

When I asked them to tell me the story of their family's return to olive growing, Abu Kamal told me:

> It started in 1998 when we bought this land in the wadi and started planting other things in addition to olive. The land had an old house on it, and we began to host people and to encourage our children to connect with and love the land. In addition to olive there are other fruit trees such as fig, almond, peach, pear and cactus. So, we use it also for recreation, we go in the weekends to enjoy this very beautiful area.

When I asked about their motivation for working the land, Abu Kamal said:

> One of the most important factors is that it helps my emotional well-being, especially for those of us who otherwise during the week work in intellectual work; when I do some physical work in the land, it relaxes me a lot. Besides, it strengthens family relations, and our children's relation to the land, because today due to the military occupation and its policies, even since the British occupation, the aim was, and is today, to cause the Palestinian fallahin to lose connection with the land. For example, my father once told me that during the British rule the villagers planted some of their land with wheat and barley and other cereals, but the Brits used to import wheat from Australia and sell it almost for free to the people,

so the fallahin could not benefit from their yield. The British were hoping they would leave their land and look for work elsewhere. Then came the Zionist movement, and it controlled the land with agreement with the British, and the policy of controlling the land continues to this day. It is causing people to leave their land. For example, the villagers of Dar El Shoke had to look for work elsewhere as labourers in colonies and inside Israel. It is of course a thought-through strategy: restrictions such as cutting water resources is another example. Israel controls 80 percent[2] of the water resources in the West Bank, and these restrictions are imposed so the fallah loses income from unproductive yields, so they look for work elsewhere; so that's how our connection to land and olive growing developed for all of us, my wife and our children. My youngest son, his favourite place is the wadi: he plays here, breathes clean air; it remains one of the few open un-built areas in our locality for us, in which we can breathe fresh air.

On other factors that motivated them to cultivate the land, Abu Kamal said, "Our parents are originally fallahin and they breastfed us the milk of their attachment to the land and their stories about the land and working in it before the *Nakba*."

I asked them about their hopes for the future, and they expressed their own vision for a more just and self-determined future:

> ABU KAMAL: The ideal thing in this situation is our return to our original land. I want to build my house there, a house that will be a simple house and will fit with the nature that exists there. I would like to spend most of my time in that area, where I will practise the activity of planting and growing food on a daily basis.
>
> NADA: I imagine and dream of living in a village of our own, if *inshallah* we will return to Dayr Aban, each will take back their land.
>
> ABU KAMAL: So, ideally, we would return and live in historical Palestine, and co-exist with all the differences between the different groups of people. This is something we think about and which I feel will be the only solution to the problem we have here; co-existence is possible between people. You look at societies like in America, like Australia, like New Zealand: multicultural and multiracial; and they live together within a framework of modern and democratic states.

What Nada and Abu Kamal told me was a neat summary of the themes discussed in the previous chapters. They told me about a historical case of occupational apartheid that is continuing to this day. They demonstrated the notion that farming activities provided well-being through being in harmony with the natural environment, their community, and other activities they were involved in—a phenomenon termed Al-'afya that was shown to be a more inclusive and holistic notion than "occupational balance" described in Western literature (see chapter 2).

Additionally, Abu Kamal's awareness of their historical and current circumstances express an occupational consciousness of how settler-colonialism aimed to change people's occupations from self-sufficient farmers to wage-laborers dependent on opportunities to earn money provided by the outsiders, in particular Israeli employers. They recognize that through olive farming, they generate witnessing, solidarity, and collaboration, and inspire other people who might have been alienated from their land to come back to it and start cultivating it again. This collective type of mutual aid originates from an attachment to village, land, and family and is being sown in the new generations by encouraging them to love the land and olive growing, and as a result it strengthens family relationships and solidarity.

Nada and Abu Kamal's family story is also a clear illustration of the principles I have been hearing about throughout my decade-long fieldwork, which motivate people here to grow olives. This meaningful daily activity is done for the sustenance and dignity of the family and their community, by supplying them with olive products and respect (*Sutra*); it brings together people and expresses attachments to other human communities and land and trees (*'Awan*); and their final words expressed their insistence in perseverance and resistance, and hope and vision for a possible more self-determined and just future that pointed to another manifestation of *Sumud*.

Nada, Abu Kamal, and their family showed that *Sutra-'Awna-Sumud* are a manifestation of doing-being-becoming-belonging as concepts and practices that contribute to health, well-being, and community building and flourishing, and have been practiced for a long time in Palestine. Nada and Abu Kamal's story, like the other participant families' stories, demonstrated multidimensional and holistic alternatives more suitably applied to Global South communities living under conditions of structural injustices, such as settler-colonialism, patriarchy, capitalism, and climate change. Palestinian notions of *Sutra*, as doing and being; *'Awna* as doing for belonging; and *Sumud* as doing for belonging and becoming— compared to the depoliticized, ethnocentric and individualized doing-being-becoming-belonging as conceptualized in Western literature—lead to health, well-being, and community determination because they stem from a decolonial positionality. They fit better in Global South, and marginalized and colonized communities, because they illustrate an active opposition to the logics, systems, and violence of settler-colonialism. This positionality, consciousness, and form of living is termed here Everyday Forms of Resistance, and is articulated well by Abu Nedal in the next section.

Everyday Forms of Resistance

As I was mulling over the themes that have been highlighted to me by olive farmers as determinants of their daily actions related to growing olives, I asked Abu Nedal what he thought about how *Sutra-ʿAwna--Sumud* might be articulated in regard to olive growing. He told me:

> As for *Sutra*, *Allah* (God) is the *Sater*. The word *Sutra* comes from the same root as the word used to mean a protector. It also means dignity: if you grow olives you live in honour and dignity, and there is no need for you to rely on anyone. As the saying I told you about in the past goes, "whoever has a fig and an olive tree is rich." I also told you about how my father used to take a bag of figs, olive oil and bread to the orchard, and that was all he needed to eat during the day. Another meaning for *Sutra*, which we acquired because of colonialism and the Israeli military occupation, is that growing olive trees protects the land and protects you from your land being stolen. Also, it gives you an identity and self-confidence: people respect the one who is *mastour* [the adjective form of *Sutra*], and whoever has olive trees approaches people with a raised head and pride.
>
> *ʿAwna* is one of the most important moral values we associate with olive farming. *ʿAwna* means unity, solidarity, empathy. You are with me in good and in bad times. We collaborate and exchange expertise, we help each other and share our skills and tools for work, and all of that without exchange of pay. People need each other, and *ʿAwna* for me is a moral behaviour, a value and a cultural heritage passed from previous generations. We have less of *ʿAwna* today for many reasons, the most important of which is that Israel has destroyed the farming sector. As for *ʿAwna* as a universal concept, and its relationship to solidarity, I can give an example of university students from Italy who visited us. They advocate for you, support you, empathise with you, so solidarity is wider than *ʿAwna*. *ʿAwna* needs solidarity, it is part of it. When people come to support you, they make not only a physical effort, but they also express their moral support for the farmers. Even some Israelis are in solidarity with us. They translate this into action in the different forms of solidarity, and one of them is *ʿAwna* or volunteering to work with us. *ʿAwna* is based on humane and ethical principles, and on respecting human rights.
>
> Finally, *Sumud* is about if I don't have an olive tree, I don't have a living. *Sumud* in life is steadfastness against the military occupation.

I couldn't have asked for a better analysis and theorizing than this. As it has been throughout my fieldwork, Abu Nedal and others have shown that they not only taught me how they do the activity of olive farming, but they also instructed me as

Everyday Forms of Resistance

to why they do it from a moral-ethical perspective. They were able to shed light on the more abstract meanings of this activity, through expressing a unique way of seeing and experiencing their world and reality, which in academic terms is called ontology. Moreover, they showed me a special way of knowing and theorizing, which is often termed epistemology in intellectual circles. But before I address this complex set of ideas, I wanted to try to bring together the themes discussed so far to shed a more realistic light on how they are expressed in practice in the everyday lives of olive farmers.

Despite being presented so far in this book as distinct categories of meaning relating to the doing and conserving of the activity of farming olives, these three dimensions—*Sutra*, *'Awna*, and *Sumud*—share some features that coexist and relate to each other. In abstract thinking and for intellectual purposes we can separate them, but in the real world they were observed to be utilized together: farmers mix and choose what they need to focus on from each of those principles in order to get the task in hand done. The example of the daily activities of Um and Abu Weehab illustrate well this integration between these principles of action: they engage in olive-farming activities for their families' sustenance and well-being through picking olives and making oil (*Sutra*); by cooperating with other family members and locals and internationals (*'Awna*), who also support their engagement in resistive acts such as reclaiming land or going to the courts to challenge the occupational apartheid practiced against them; and to enable their and their community's becoming and self-determination (*Sumud*). This synthesis of the three themes is the topic of the following sections of this chapter. This synthesis is a further refinement of the intercultural translation conducted in this book, and resulted from analysis and interpretation of the findings, member checking, disseminating the findings, and ongoing study of the literature.

To enable the doing of olive growing for well-being, individuals and families need to collaborate, and this collaboration is based on a sociopolitical awareness, solidarity and coagency, and the need to resist occupational apartheid. These are common components of the three principles of olive growing observed in this study. *Sutra*, as a protective element of family and community, also expresses the associations between humans and other-than-human elements in the form of respect for, mutuality with, and love for trees, land, and animals. Similarly, *'Awna* has those environmental, social, and political features in the form of connectedness and solidarity at the level of family, village, locality, and globe, as well as the bond with the more-than-human that enables the continuation of this activity. This community element—including the natural environment and international groups—and the active awareness of oppression and the need to confront it, are key features of *Sumud*, and are common to the other two themes.

In this way *Sutra*, *'Awna*, and *Sumud* can be combined in a larger category of principles of action that illustrate a unique Palestinian moral and behavioral code. Everyday Forms of Resistance, in this sense, are an empirical example that can enrich, and provide alternative constructs, that lead to the refinement and further theorizing of human occupations. These alternatives are needed because the concepts related to human occupation have been limited in their application due to their epistemological and ontological origins in Global North fields of study. These concepts, which were discussed in this book in relation to the everyday lives of olive growers, are the notion of humans as occupational beings; doing-being-becoming-belonging; collective occupations; occupational apartheid; and occupational consciousness. Participant families taught me that for them to enable an occupation (olive-growing) done for individual and collective well-being (a collective occupation), they adopted an occupational consciousness (*Sutra-'Awna-Sumud*) based on their knowledge of inequalities and oppression regarding access to that occupation (occupational apartheid); more than mere recognition of such injustice, this occupational consciousness involves learning about, developing, and using problem-solving skills and creative daily responses to confront—indirectly or directly—attempts to restrict the activity.

Everyday Forms of Resistance as an Ontological and Epistemological Stance

The overarching association between *Sutra*, *'Awna*, and *Sumud* is not only a practical and moral means to allow the maintenance of olive farmers' way of life, but also an ontological and epistemological stance offered to us by the oPt olive-growing community. Everyday Forms of Resistance, as studied here, posed a challenge to knowledge founded on a conception of different identities as individual occupational beings with separate agencies, which was conceived within an epistemology of imperialism and might have led scholars to mostly ignore the risk of what has been termed "epistemicide" (Santos 2014). In contrast to such an "othering" interpretation of everyday realities by Eurocentric disciplines, olive farmers saw their realities as interconnected with their context. They conceived their families, land and trees and animals, local and global communities, not as binary features that can be separated, controlled, and quantified but instead perceived their daily realities as interlinked and in constant interaction with all those elements of their environment. This mutual connectedness led to their collective well-being and to their becoming (and dreams of becoming) more self-fulfilling and self-ruling.

This way of interpreting their world included collective meanings expressed through their daily lives, and interconnectedness between purposes they aimed to express in all spheres of their subjective experiences. Olive farmers were found to wish to engage in olive-growing activities for communal meanings, which encompassed the physical, emotional, social, cultural, spiritual, and political roles. These levels of meanings were not isolated when they spoke about, or engaged in actions related to, olive farming. They were observed to farm olives for multiple purposes and not isolate those when engaging in the doing of olive growing; they interpreted the need to do olive growing as combining self and community care goals, as well as for recreational and productive aims.

Everyday Forms of Resistance are not only ontological means of interpreting daily lives. They also expressed an epistemological position adopted by olive farmers. Everyday Forms of Resistance were enacted through olive growers' daily occupations as ways of knowing and producing new knowledge. They were means that led to the development of new forms of relationships, knowledge, and skills that empowered them to maintain their and their communities' well-being. In other words, olive-growing families were observed to enact *Sutra-'Awna-Sumud* as an occupational consciousness that enabled a helpful interpretation of their circumstances and contributed to the development of useful knowledge and skills: they learned about their history and heritage, their natural environment, and their local and global contexts in order to orchestrate and harmonize all these elements for the benefits of individuals and communities, including the natural environment. This unique collective occupational consciousness led them to be alert to the daily injustices they experienced; and at the same time, they adopted these principles as a means of doing (or intervening in the world), being (in the world), and knowing (about the world) to problem-solve and to challenge the systematic and systemic restrictions imposed on them, on their everyday activities and on the expression of their unique means of knowing and believing (values).

This practical, ethical, and ontological-epistemological position can be adopted in occupational science, occupational therapy, and in other social science fields and communities of praxis concerned with human and more-than-human well-being. I suggest that considering such means of interpreting the world, and acting on it, might inspire alternative ways to produce and apply knowledge in the aforementioned fields of study and practices.

CONCLUSION

Nada and Abu Kamal, and all the olive farmers I met, were very much aware that what they did in their lives in relation to farming olives does not have only practical implications to how their and their community's lives improved. They were aware how their Everyday Forms of Resistance provide them with hopes and dreams for a decolonized Palestine, and some practical solutions to how this might be done. Moreover, they realize how their Everyday Forms of Resistance led to an understanding of the ethical basis and implications of such solutions: The mutual aid Nada and Abu Kamal's family engaged in with other families from their camp, and the equality between groups in society they aspired to in a future decolonized Palestine were a cornerstone of their vision of the future. In addition to the behavioral and moral aspects Abu Nedal articulated when discussing *Sutra-ʿAwna-Sumud*, he also described to me the reality of the world (ontology) these notions emerged from, and how these Everyday Forms of Resistance are a cultural heritage, or a way of knowing (epistemology) that should be handed down to the next generations.

In this book I offer insights into how the daily lives of olive-growing communities, who are challenging settler-colonialism's impact on their daily lives, might help us begin to unpack work in Western disciplines concerned with humans' knowing, doing, being, becoming, and belonging. This unpacking is needed to correct historical injustices that ignored, or even actively denied, marginalized communities their voice in knowledge production, and in offering ways to combat daily injustices. This process of analyzing knowledge and praxis, and of acknowledging and correcting the denial to take part in producing knowledge and solutions, is often described by scholars and activists as "decolonization." Indigenous scholars have inspired us to engage in this discussion about centering voices, ways of living and

Conclusion

knowing that originate from peoples in the Global South. However, as discussed earlier, Tuck and Yang (2012) warn that decolonization should not be a tokenistic step. The decolonization of scholarship should be combined with steps taken to change individual and collective consciousness and circumstances, and the redistribution of power and resources. For example, these steps might include projects that aim to redistribute water, land, income, education, health, and well-being resources, and access to meaningful daily occupations. Decolonizing, according to Smith (2022) "has to open up possibilities for understanding and knowing the world differently and offering different solutions to problems caused by colonialism and the failure of power structures to address these historic conditions" (xiii).

The question, however, remains: How can readers from the Global South and North, and scholars and activists concerned with daily life of people, contribute to this process in the real world?

Smith and other decolonial scholars have begun answering such a question, and they all pointed to a first step that begins with decolonizing our own minds, and called for the praxis of reflexivity as a tool to position ourselves and raise our consciousness. This process of stepping back and considering our feelings, thoughts, and values, in relation to what we experience in the world, will eventually lead to taking correcting actions individually and collectively to abolish systems of oppression and build together a world in which all of us live well, meet our daily needs, and flourish.

As I learned from the daily lives of olive farmers and reflected on my own positionality as a Palestinian man who is placed in a liminal space between the Global South and North, and whose knowledge of my own community's history and heritage was kept away from me by the settler-colonial and apartheid system of Israeli education (see chapter 1), I began a process of decolonizing my own identity, knowledge, and practice. I attempted to "research back" (ibid.) and unlearn universal categories of knowledges and practices and started to realize the importance of how my everyday actions in academia, in the research field, and in my daily life, should be dedicated to resisting these systems and practices.

Researching back and unlearning was combined with intercultural translation, which aimed to center knowledge created by people whose ways of living have not been highlighted before in fields of study concerned with humans' everyday doing. In the foreword to the third edition of *Decolonizing Methodology: Research and Indigenous Peoples*, Linda Tuhiwai Smith (2022) wrote: "Knowledge and the power to define what counts as real knowledge lie at the epistemic core of colonialism. The challenge . . . is to simultaneously work with colonial and Indigenous concepts of knowledge, decentring one while centring the other" (xii). By performing the intercultural translations in this book, during which I compared and contrasted Everyday Forms of Resistance with Western-based concepts, and by centering the importance and utility of this Indigenous system of knowledge, I highlighted some means that have not been highlighted in scholarship in the past. This centering of *Sutra- 'Awna-Sumud* led to linkages being made between them and other means already discussed in the literature that have been highlighted in other Indigenous contexts, such as Ubuntu. This translation also highlighted that the Western way is not the only universal truth, and that there are diverse knowledges that need to be highlighted in order to change the firm belief in the idea of universality that has been inflicted on Global South communities and scholars, as a result of hundreds of years of coloniality and colonial thought.

A helpful insight about this process of decolonizing scholarship and praxis came from Walter Mignolo (2018) who introduced the term "pluriversal" after coming in contact with the Zapatistas' decolonial vision of a world "in which many worlds would coexist" (ix). To further explicate what this means to the ways of producing knowledge, Ramón Grosfogul (2011) explained:

> A decolonial epistemic perspective requires a broader canon of thought than simply the western canon (including the Left western canon) . . . a truly universal decolonial perspective cannot be based on an abstract universal (one particular that raises itself as universal global design), but would have to be the result of the critical dialogue between diverse critical epistemic/ethical/political projects towards a pluriversal as opposed to a universal world . . . decolonization of knowledge would require to take seriously the epistemic perspective/cosmologies/insights of critical thinkers from the Global South thinking from and with subalternized racial/ethnic/sexual spaces and bodies.

Mignolo and Grosfogul addressed the need to rearticulate universal categories of knowledge that have been taken for granted as applicable to all humans around the globe. Some scholars have even been questioning the category of "human." Smith (2022) questioned the binary of "human" vs. the "non-human," or "nature." The category of "human" was created during the European Renaissance period; she, like other decolonial thinkers, linked the creation of the notion of "human" to the core of the colonial powers who separated humans from nature, which led to forms of exploitation, extractions, and oppressions imposed on those colonized "others" who have been described as less human, and on natural resources, animals, lands, and plants—all of which are considered inferior to the human race (in its Judeo-Christian conceptualization) and therefore exploitable (ibid.).

What interests me in this book are categories, as conceptualized by Western scholars, that relate to people's daily actions, such as "occupation" and the separate types of occupations, for example, self-care, productivity, and recreation (see

Conclusion

chapter 2); health and well-being (chapter 2); independence and occupational balance (chapter 2); doing-being-becoming-belonging (chapters 3, 4, and 5)—all of which have been assumed as universal categories.

As shown throughout this book, *Sutra- 'Awna-Sumud*, as Everyday Forms of Resistance, are rooted in a way of understanding the world that is historical and contextual: it is a way of knowing that aims to resist systems of oppression including universalistic ideas about everyday life of colonized communities. It is a system of knowledge that doesn't necessarily separate between people and their natural environs. Moreover, *Sutra- 'Awna-Sumud*, as Everyday Forms of Resistance, have been shown here not only as demonstrating different forms of doing-being-becoming-belonging due to the different context they were observed in. These unique Palestinian forms of knowing, doing for being, doing for belonging, and doing for belonging and becoming, are better suited to lead to decolonial liberation than how they were conceptualized in the West, due to their anti-colonial ethical-ontological-epistemological stance. Scholars and activists concerned with people's daily actions, done as resistance to systemic injustices, might wish to consider this and other articulations from the Global South if they truly wish to decolonize the constructs, theories, and models of practice on which they have been basing their work.

Other Examples of Decolonization

In addition to examples of decolonization from my own experience and scholarship described above, I end this discussion by sharing examples from the fields of occupational therapy, occupational science, and sociology that illustrate small steps toward decolonizing these Western-centric fields of study and practices. These initiatives are not a complete list, but they help demonstrate how fields of study and practices concerned with humans' meaningful daily activity, and its relationship to individuals' health, well-being, and community building, can apply pluriversality in knowledge production, dissemination, and application to aid with the ongoing and collective process of decolonization. These are only hopeful beginnings, and we need to acknowledge that there is a long way before we can claim the project of decolonization to be complete.

Since the late 1970s, Brazilian occupational therapy scholars and practitioners have been developing knowledge and practices that are suitable and applicable to the Brazilian context, rather than—as occupational therapy practice elsewhere in the world has been—blindly copying and pasting knowledge from the Global North and mostly English-speaking scholars. What came to be termed "social occupational therapy" is a practice that advocates for "citizenship and rights" and acknowledges difference (Lopes and Malfitano 2021). Social occupational therapy addresses social problems such as inequality and poverty, endemic to Brazil but also other Global South and North contexts. Motivated by an ethical-political commitment, and inspired by scholars and activists who lived and worked in the Global South such as Paulo Freire and Boaventura de Sosa Santos, social occupational therapists in Brazil have developed theories, methods, and technologies addressing the needs of individuals and communities who lack access to, or are limited from accessing, social goods (Galheigo 2021). In the 1990s, and before the concept of occupational justice came to prominence in Western occupational therapy literature, Brazilian universities created partnerships with governmental and nongovernmental organizations to ensure that social occupational therapy is dedicated to promoting the citizenship of users of services whose social support networks have been broken down. Examples of such practices span different settings and populations, such as empowering the urban youth living in poverty to gain resources and technologies to enhance their daily living (Lopes 2021), or working with a student association in a school to empower students' daily activities related to education, leisure, sports, and cultural activities (Celegati Pan 2021).

By generating knowledge and practices suited to the specific context of the Brazilian state, in a collaborative way between concerned partners in the community, and by their ethical-political commitment to changing power dynamics and inequality in society, social occupational therapists have moved away from the Western hegemony in occupational therapy. However, the discussion about empowering citizenship under a nation-state and the alignment to human rights—as conceptualized by UN legislations—may still be limited in applicability to Indigenous populations and other Global South communities, such as refugees, the unhoused, and travelers' communities. These groups, and olive growers and their allies, view their world as one that exists outside the state and the globalized capitalist system—a system that the Israeli colonizing authority is entrenched in. Olive growers' view of reality is based on the instinct to mutually aid each other and on the abolishing of the binary between citizens and noncitizens, givers of support and receivers of support.

Decolonization, as conceptualized in this book, is a project that aims to counter universal ideas such as nation-states, human rights, and citizenship. Decolonization should aim to repatriate resources and power, and to overhaul systems of white supremacy. Some of these aims were articulated through efforts on both sides of the Atlantic Ocean since the 2020 "Black Lives Matter" uprising. Voices from occupational therapy practitioners and academics of color have been highlighting how systemic racism has been ignored in occupational therapy knowledge production and practices. In the United Kingdom, the Black and

Conclusion

Asian Minority Ethnic Occupational Therapy UK (BAMEOTUK),[1] a group of underrepresented occupational therapists from communities of color in the United Kingdom, has instigated discussions online and in-person of how to tackle these issues in the profession of occupational therapy. The group began a dialogue with the Royal College of Occupational Therapists (RCOT), the main body representing occupational therapists in the United Kingdom, to enhance their inclusive and antiracist practices and policies. As a result of this dialogue and pressure from occupational therapists of color in the United Kingdom, some changes were achieved, such as making space for more representations of people of color in decision-making positions in RCOT. However, some have questioned if this is enough, or even helpful, in changing the colonial foundations of the profession.

In the United States, the Disrupt OT movement has provided a needed safe space for Global South scholars and communities to raise important questions about the history of occupational therapy, its knowledge base and its practices, from anti-racist and anti-colonial perspectives. For example, an "Unconference" was organized in March 2024,[2] which aimed to amplify the voices of daily resistance around the globe, whether it be in response to war, natural disasters, or systemic injustices, including racism, ageism, ableism, sexism, homophobia, and transphobia.

These constructive conversations in the United Kingdom and the United States involving Global South and Global North practitioners and academics have paved the way to important publications that represent an emerging attempt to decolonize the field of occupational therapy. *Antiracist Occupational Therapy: Unsettling the Status Quo* (Ahmed-Landeryou 2024) introduces "antiracism as means and ends" in occupational therapy (Emery-Whittington, Leite Junior, and Ivlev 2024). It presents discussions from around the world by authors of color and their allies that center the need to abolish systemic racism in occupational therapy and Global North hegemony in producing knowledge and practices that do not apply to the majority of the world populations.

Occupational Therapy Disruptors: What Global OT Practice Can Teach Us about Innovation, Culture, and Community (Ivlev 2024) critiques occupational therapy's development, knowledge base, and practice that had been exclusive to white female practitioners when it first became a profession in the United States in 1917 (Black 2002). The profession of occupational therapy was developed by, and for, middle- to upper-class white people using a dominant Eurocentric worldview. Consequently, occupational therapy has not addressed racial identity or disparity in developing assessments and interventions, or in monitoring outcomes for people of color, for example (Grenier 2020). Ivlev's interviews with occupational therapy leaders situated mainly in the Global South, such as in Ghana and Palestine, amplify crucial voices, experiences, and communities that we all need to be listening carefully to. It reaffirms our belief that there is more than one way of doing occupational therapy.

The leading publication in occupational science, the *Journal of Occupational Science*, has been driving attempts to decolonize knowledge production and dissemination in this interdisciplinary field of study concerned with human doing and its relationship with health, well-being, and flourishing. The journal has been expanding to include publications in Spanish and Portuguese to reach communities beyond the English-speaking regions of the world, and instructs authors to include quotes from their research in their original language whatever the language is. The journal's Anti-Racism Pledge and its Policy on Territorial or Land Acknowledgement (Stanley et al. 2021) have begun some advocating for community-focused work, equality, diversity, and inclusion in knowledge and practices. In line with the *Journal of Occupational Science* "Pledge to Mobilize against Racism" (Stanley et al. 2021) and efforts to decolonize its publishing practices, the editorial board calls for diverse approaches to generating and presenting knowledge, including Indigenous and Global South methodologies. The editorial board of the journal asks all authors to ensure that their work addresses knowledge and scholarship produced by communities that are the focus of their research, and to include sources that reflect the range of scholarship production such as academies, community leaders, activists, and artists. The journal encourages a diversity of forms of publications such as photo essays, art installations, literary products, and oral histories. Another authorship practice that is required by the journal is describing authors' positionality in relation to the topic, community, occupations, and people described in the inquiry.

In sociology, the editorial board of the journal *Humanity and Society* was inspired by Indigenous scholars who aim to center their work, expertise, and knowledge in research about their communities already practiced in journals such as the *Australian Journal for Rural Health*, *Canadian Journal of Rural Medicine*, and the *Data Science Journal* (*Humanity and Society* 2024). These publications developed guidelines to promote inclusivity in authorship by and with Global South and marginalized communities, and established editorial practices to advance a more accurate analysis of data in research to center the voices of marginalized local communities (ibid.). The editorial board of *Humanity and Society* addresses the fact that sociology has contributed to the ongoing marginalization of Black, Indigenous, Asian, and Latinx communities in the United States and of non-European peoples around the world. Sociology has done so by an educational system designed for, and deeply implicated in, the control and subjugation of colonized peoples. Examples included scholarship legitimizing policies and ideologies that deny the experiences, expertise, and cosmologies of these groups. The board recognizes their own positionalities as settler scholars on stolen land (the journal is based in the United States).

Humanity and Society aims to address the "epistemic apartheid" in knowledge generating and presentation by encouraging authors to "engage deeply with historically marginalized and exploited communities." The journal board seeks "to centre work and voices that are often ignored, undervalued, and exploited within the academy" (ibid.). The journal instructs authors not to submit work "about them but without them." *Humanity and Society* will only agree to publish works that focus on marginalized communities that engage in scholarship that originate from those communities themselves. To ensure this engagement with communities' own sources, reviewers for the journal are asked to carefully inspect the literature engaged in, and references cited in, all papers submitted to the journal. The board believes that this will enable publishing work that is "deeply rooted in the experiences, knowledges, and understandings of those best situated to deeply address critically important sociological phenomena" (ibid.).

These are hopeful beginnings. However, the project of decolonizing fields of study and praxis concerned with humans' everyday activities needs to go further. For example, journals' editorial boards, like the *Journal of Occupational Science* and *Humanity and Society*, should explore ways to redistribute their power by opening up decision-making about publishing processes and policies, to include people from the communities themselves. As for the disciplines of sociology, and occupational therapy and occupational science, they should initiate a dialogue with the groups and societies who are the focus of their research and theorizing, about how they can become more inclusive and relevant to the communities they serve. Or even going a step further, this collective decolonizing process should include discussions about reparation and abolition.

Just like the Black Lives Matter movement's calls for defunding and abolishing the police, or the global refugee solidarity movement's call to give back powers and freedoms of movement to people and abolish borders, we perhaps need to begin a discussion about abolishing these fields of study, including occupational therapy, occupational science, and sociology. I suggest that these fields of study should reframe their justice-based and occupation-focused work as praxis that invites anybody who is interested in doing the work, or who is the focus of study and interventions, to take part in generating the knowledge and disseminating it. We cannot maintain a situation in which decision making is concentrated into the hands of a small circle of elite academics and practitioners, who are qualified by elite universities and regulated by exclusive regulatory bodies, all of which were part of a historical pattern of Eurocentric knowledge production and practices, and contributed to the repression of communities who did not belong to white middle-class elites. By not carrying the historical associations of exclusivity, the praxis of occupation and justice-based activism would welcome partners who might not otherwise participate in the project of studying how to make the world a safer and more inclusive place, in which individuals and communities are free to take part in meaningful and purposeful daily lives as they wish or need to. Replacing these elite disciplines and professions with occupation and justice-based activism should lead to making space for pluriversal ecologies of knowledges and praxis, and to centering communities, their stories, ways of life, and knowledge that have been marginalized for the last five hundred years and more.

What I presented in this book resulted from my own experiences, and many years of thinking, learning, and doing that reflect a specific positionality and sociohistorical and political context. This perspective is of course partial and located in a particular lived experience and context. Nonetheless, it adds a needed contribution to a collection of pluriversal Global South perspectives in the fields of occupational therapy, occupational science, sociology, and other disciplines and groups and social movements concerned with daily actions that contribute to wellness and sociopolitical change.

I invite readers to rethink, research back, and unlearn what might have been perceived as universal categories of knowledge and models of interventions. This is a call to reflect on our own positionalities and privileges in relation to the communities we interact and work with, to center their views on daily actions, wellness, and justice, and what all of these mean to them. Pluriversal Global South perspectives and knowledge about daily life and daily resistance should become paramount in scholarship. Incorporating values and praxis of daily resistance will hopefully lead to a more humane and inclusive knowledge, and eventually to a world in which there is a place for every perspective and practice that contributes to communities being able to live well—a way of life that should be celebrated and maintained for all of us.

POSTSCRIPT

Ongoing Daily Resistance

It was in the middle of the month of Ramadan in 2022. Baher was sitting under the shade of an olive tree and seemed quiet and occupied with his phone. Half a dozen Israeli and international activists were helping him weed his family's olive grove. We are in the area of Masafer Yatta in the southern hills of Al-Khalil. The name Masafer Yatta, I was told, refers to an ancient route that led traders and pilgrims from the Mediterranean to the Arabian Peninsula and beyond. Since the establishment of the state of Israel, borders have been erected, and people are not allowed to travel on this route anymore. Today, a few thousand people live here in small communities of farmers and shepherds. Some live in caves, others in houses made of zinc. The children in this area are often accompanied by activists and Israeli soldiers to protect them from settlers, who often attack them on their way to/from school. The residents and their allies are challenging, as I write this, a mass expulsion, which was recently approved by Israel's high court. This expulsion has been partially achieved since October 2023, as mentioned in chapter 1; communities of shepherds have been forced to leave their places of residence, and were expelled by violent settlers' militias supported by the Israeli authorities.

Baher was busy communicating via his phone to the outside world what was going on in his village and area. He writes about how IDF fighting units often invade his village and terrorize the residents in the middle of the night for training purposes. He was recently badly beaten by soldiers while he was documenting the destruction of structures a local farmer built on his land.[1]

Overlooking the grove is a hill dotted with natural caves, which locals use to store equipment or as stables for their animals, and some families use as their homes. Not far from there, I visited Ma'ayer El'abeed, one of the small communities Israel wants to expel from this area. Israel claims this area as a training zone for the military, and bans people from building any structures, farming the land, and grazing animals in an area that spans hundreds of kilometers. The roads that locals build, with the support of activists, are often destroyed; water wells vandalized; and animals killed or even confiscated by the IDF or the nearby settlers. "These are just few examples of the things that happen here on a daily basis to make the life of locals miserable so they give up and leave," I was told by Murad, one of the local activists in the area.

Here, the occupational apartheid is ongoing and even worsening. However, what is striking is the fightback and daily resistance the people of these hills are prepared to engage in to save their homes, livelihood, and their way of life. The *Sutra*, *'Awna*, and *Sumud* are alive and evolving here. Baher, Murad, and other local activists interact with international communities using the latest technologies that allow them to spread their and their communities' stories online, on social media platforms, and news outlets. People around the world are seeing daily life as it unfolds and through this they come together in solidarity, like the group I was with that day among the olive trees, who come here to practice all these values and the skills they learned from native land-based communities.

Leah is a member of All That's Left Collective (ATL),[2] a Jewish anti-(military) occupation group whom I joined on that day in Ramadan 2022. She told me that learning about the practice of *'Awna* was "a helpful model to think about how communities living outside of the frame of nation states think of their relationship to land as opposed to the settler-colonial model of control and exclusivism." Another activist saw his work with ATL as "a real communal support. It is radical care and resistance against imperialism of the country I came from." He was referring to the United States where he normally lives.

For Leah, these are communities who are protecting the land, maintaining their health and well-being, and fighting for their survival and freedom to determine their lives. Instead of romanticizing and orientalizing them, we ought to be inspired by them and humbled to learn about their practices, which two to three generations ago my ancestors still practiced in our small Galilean village of Tur'aan.

I have not been able to be back in the West Bank since that Ramadan in 2022, due to the latest war on Gaza. The updates I receive from farmers and shepherds are extremely worrying. The project of settler-colonialism and the attempt to ethnically cleanse parts of the West Bank have been accelerated while the world's attention is on Gaza. I am told that people don't distinguish anymore between the IDF and the armed settlers' militias, who are "helping Israel establish new borders and more annexation," as my friend Murad told me. Murad is a farmer, shepherd, scholar, and an activist from a village south of Beit Lahem, whom I met during my last visit in 2022, as part of my plan to extend my research to shepherding communities.

Postscript

As for the families whose stories are told in this book, I have been keeping in touch with them since the 7th of October, 2023, via online platforms, such as Signal, WhatsApp, and Zoom.

Yasino has not been able to go to school since the 7th of October, 2023, due to roadblocks and IDF and settlers' violence. School has responded to this by making it possible that he receives online lessons so he can learn at home. Yasin made a video with the help of his teachers and classmates to spread the word to the world and urge us all to advocate for the right to safety and the freedom to learn. The family minimizes being on the land due to the increase in settlers' violence in the area, but has not given up and still works the land.

In Al-Baydar, Um Weehab and Abu Weehab and their fellow villagers are concerned about new plans for building a colony on village land despite the World Heritage Site status the village gained and Israel's obligations not to build on land there. That has not stopped the family from working their fields and maintaining their groves.

In Um Nedal and Abu Nedal's village of Dar El Shoke, the military has been demolishing the houses of members of the extended family, claiming they have no permits to build. The family, however, continues to farm their land, and Abu Nedal continues to write about their situation on Facebook, so the world can witness what is going on in their village.

In the wadi where Nada and Abu Kamal's land is, settlers are stealing more land, water from wells, and other resources from local farmers and landowners.

Murad told me about the situation in his village during an online call in November 2023. He recounted how tons of ripe olives were left on the trees during the most recent olive harvest season, as farmers had been worried that they would be attacked by settlers or the IDF. They hear stories of farmers being killed, injured, and abducted by settlers on a daily basis. Murad is part of a campaign called Faz3a,[3] in which local activists urge international activists and volunteers to visit the West Bank to stay with local farmers and shepherds, and to accompany them to their fields and grazing areas, and to documents settlers' attacks and witness the deteriorating situation there.

About the daily resistance of the local communities in his area, Murad told me:

I hear this phrase "existence is resistance," I am telling you the existence of the Palestinians now is resistance. At this stage we need to just protect our heads, no one is able to reach the land, no one is able to take their sheep out, we just want to protect ourselves. So, I had to rethink this concept of "existence is resistance," and I found that existence is more than resistance, no resistance is resistance at this stage.

This "existence is resistance" is alive in the north of the Gaza Strip under the ongoing genocide. Yousef Sager (his real name)[4] and his family in Beit Lahia—a farming community famous for its strawberries (dubbed as "the red gold of Gaza")—have been leading a campaign to reclaim land, collect vegetables and fruit seeds, plant seedlings, and distribute them to the community. Yousef told me their story during an online meeting we set up after I had been following his updates closely on social media. The community has been growing vegetables since February 2024 in any space available in the rubble. Yousef started this venture when they decided to return to their home, during the temporary cessation of fire in November 2023, after they had been displaced several times. They found all their produce destroyed and decided to collect the seeds from the ruined vegetables, such as aubergines, which they could salvage from the destroyed fields. Seeing the lush fields of molokhiya (a staple food in Palestine harvested during the summer months) in the videos Yousef posts makes one think it is a normal peaceful corner of the world, and not a place where people live under constant threat of death, destruction, and displacement.

Yousef and his community embody the spirit of Everyday Forms of Resistance, the focus of this book, and they inspire us all to maintain the hope in the Palestinian values of *Sutra*, *'Awna*, and *Sumud*. When I asked Yousef to tell me what message he has for the world, he told me he wants people to remember "It's not health that should be the priority of people, but farming, which is the foundation of life." On October 21, 2024, Yousef was killed by a targeted drone attack, along with two of his friends who worked with him to supply vegetable seedlings to their community to allow them to feed themselves in the midst of the brutal attack on the people of Beit Lahia and other areas in the north of the Gaza Strip.

Since that day in October 2024, conditions deteriorated even further for farmers and all the people in the Gaza Strip and the West Bank. In Gaza, after a period of a cessation of fire in January 2025, which was broken by Israel in March 2025, more people were killed and displaced, and even aid was banned for weeks. In the West Bank, refugee camps were destroyed and emptied of their residents, and more people were killed by the army and gangs of settlers who continued to attack Palestinians in their fields and homes.[5] This has not stopped people from continuing their Everyday Forms of Resistance and farming their land. Yousef's family continues his legacy, and they post videos on social media of sowing, planting, and harvesting, despite the extreme conditions and danger under which they live. The Palestine Heirloom Seed Library continues to work with farmers in the West Bank and spread the word to the world on their everyday lives.[6]

Juman Simaan

June 2025

ACKNOWLEDGMENTS

Without the generosity and bravery of the olive farmers, their communities and allies quoted in this book, this study and book would not have been completed. *Shukran* and *Tadamon*.

I thank Vivien Sansour, Mahmoud Soliman, Ayed Arafah, and Ahmad Al-Bazz, and the JAI staff, who accompanied me throughout the process of the completion of the study and book.

Thank you to Gavin McGregor, my parents Suhela and Simon Simaan, and my siblings Janan, Rayan, and Younan, who supported me and put up with me in my moments of light and darkness.

Thank you to the reviewers of the drafts of the manuscript who provided valuable feedback and supported me through the revisions of this manuscript.

NOTES

CHAPTER 1. Studying Olive Growing in Palestine as an Everyday Form of Resistance

1. Western philosophers and occupational scientists conceptualize these terms as meaning what is considered right and fair within a society (often framed as what individuals deserve and protections afforded them), the spectrum of things people do (their activities including "what the doing does" at individual, communal, and environmental levels), and the rights and obligations members of a society have in relation to what they can and cannot do (with emphasis given to inclusion, equity, and health outcomes). For further critique of these concepts, see Simaan, Forthcoming.

2. The term "native" refers here to Palestinian communities and their descendants—Jewish, Muslim, and Christian (urban, rural, and seminomadic)—who resided in the land of historical Palestine and were the majority of the population and landowners and workers, before the *Nakba* of 1948—when mass forced displacement of Palestinians and mass Jewish immigration was in the process of causing great changes in demographics and land ownership in favor of settler groups. See Masalha 2012, 1–18; Said 1992, 3–15.

3. For the latest updates on this case, see ICJ 2024.

4. See UNOCHAoPt 2024; In July 2024, *The Lancet* reported that around 8 percent of the population of Gaza have lost their lives as a result of the Israeli onslaught, and this the authors claim is a conservative estimate. See Khatib, McKee, and Yusuf 2024, 237–38.

5. Political Zionism was founded by Theodor Herzl in late nineteenth-century Europe; the ideology and practices of political Zionism originated in German *volkisch* nationalism, key principles of which are notions of biological and racial purity, historical roots, and mythical attitudes to land and the connections between blood and soil; political Zionism sought a national home for European Jewish communities, which in addition to Palestine initially explored territories in South America and East Africa; later on the movement deployed religious Old Testament myths to justify its interest in Palestine as the "land of milk and honey" for the "chosen people" of the Bible. See Masalha 2012, 19–87.

6. The Council for European Palestinian Relations reported that the agricultural sector in the oPt formally employs 13.4 percent of the population and informally employs 90.0 percent of the population. See Cappellazzi 2012.

150   Notes to Pages 16–120

7. References in this book to the Israeli military occupation have their own meaning that is quite distinct from the concept of "occupation" as used in occupational therapy and occupational science.

8. "Historicist" truth refers to the historical priority scholars give to European civilization, which is considered superior and the first and only truth that everyone from all nations should adopt. See Anievas and Nişancioğlu 2015, 33–36.

9. The term "vernacular" refers to all forms of knowledge and praxis, which are informed by everyday needs, and the natural and environmental elements with which human groups interact. See Scott 2012, 34–30.

CHAPTER 2. Olive Growing for *Sutra*

1. The JAI has been my main gatekeeper to the community of olive farmers. See JAI, "Home," accessed November 28, 2024, https://www.jai-pal.org/en/.

2. For some Area C facts reported by the UN, see UNOCHAoPt 2011.

CHAPTER 3. Olive Growing for ʿAwna

1. In recent years there has been an increase in the number of extremist Jewish settlers who have adopted the Indigenous Palestinian farming and shepherding lifestyle and who have occupied Palestinian land to graze their animals, and who are supported and funded by the Israeli state. Kerem Navot, an Israeli organization, has recently published a report on this: see Kerem Navot 2022.

2. For more information on these women and lesbian, gay, bisexual, transgender, and queer (LGBTQ+) organizations, see Musawa, "Home," Accessed November 28, 2024, https://musawasyr.org/; Al-Qaws, "Home," accessed November 28, 2024, http://www.alqaws.org/siteEn/index/language/en; Aswat, "Instagram account," accessed November 28, 2024, https://www.instagram.com/aswatfreedoms/?hl=en.

3. For more information about this organization, see "Home," accessed November 28, 2024, https://www.taayush.org/.

4. The Land Institute, "Home," accessed November 28, 2024, https://landinstitute.org/.

5. A revised definition of "occupational apartheid" can be found in Kronenberg 2018.

CHAPTER 4. Olive Growing for *Sumud*

1. Since 1967, approximately 40 percent of adult Palestinian men in the oPt had been in Israeli prisons. For more information on this, see Addameer 2013.

2. For more on this agreement, see Waage 2011.

3. Al-Haq (The Right) is the first Palestinian human rights organization to be established in 1979. See Al-Haq, "Home," accessed November 28, 2024, https://www.alhaq.org/.

4. For more information on the Boycott, Divestment, and Sanctions movement, see BDS, "Home," accessed November 28, 2024, https://bdsmovement.net/.

5. For more information about the PHSL, see Peter Beaumont, 2016, "Palestinians Create New Seed Bank to Save Their Farming Heritage in the Holy Land's Hills," *The Guardian*, April 23, https://www.theguardian.com/world/2016/apr/23/palestinian-seed-bank-farming-heritage.

Notes to Pages 125–146

CHAPTER 5. Everyday Forms of Resistance

1. For the history of this village and others that were ethnically cleansed and destroyed by Zionist militias in 1948, see Khalidi 2006, 282–84.

2. See B'Tselem, "Water Crisis," last modified June 3, 2021, https://www.btselem.org/water.

CONCLUSION

1. See BAMEOT, "Home," accessed November 28, 2024, https://www.bameot.uk/.

2. See DisruptOT, "Home," accessed November 28, 2024, https://www.disruptot.org/.

POSTSCRIPT: Ongoing Daily Resistance

1. A recent film was made by a Palestinian-Israeli collective that shows the destruction of the area of Masafer Yatta by the Israeli Army and the alliance that developed between the Palestinian activist Basel and Israeli journalist Yuval: *No Other Land*, directed by Yuval Abraham, Basel Adra, and Hamdan Ballal (2024), https://www.imdb.com/title/tt30953759/.

2. All That's Left Collective, "Home," accessed November 28, 2024, https://allthatsleft collective.com/.

3. "Faz3a (فزعة, pronounced faz'a) is a colloquialism for reinforcement and directly coming to someone's aid at time of need, and is a long Palestinian tradition of coming to the rescue of communities en masse in the face of outside threats." See Defend Palestine, "Home," accessed November 28, 2024, https://www.defendpalestine.org/.

4. See Yousef Sager, "Instagram account," accessed November 28, 2024, https://www .instagram.com/yousef_sager99/.

5. For the latest reports on the situation in Gaza and the West Bank, see: UNOCHAoPt. 2025; British Red Cross, 2025, "Conflict Escalates in the Middle East," Accessed June 8, 2025, https://www.redcross.org.uk/about-us/what-we-do/international/israel-and-occupied -palestinian-territory.

6. See The Palestine Heirloom Seed Library, 2025, "Home," accessed June, 8, 2025, https:// phsl-website.webflow.io/.

BIBLIOGRAPHY

Abram, David. 1996. *The Spell of the Sensuous*. New York: Vintage Books.

Adalah. 2011. *The Inequality Report: The Palestinian Arab Community in Israel*, March. Accessed November 28, 2024, https://www.adalah.org/uploads/oldfiles/upfiles/2011/Adalah_The _Inequality_Report_March_2011.pdf.

Addameer. 2013. *General Briefing on Palestinian Political Prisoners in Israeli Prisons*. Ramallah, West Bank: Addameer, December 1. Accessed November 29, 2024. https://www.addameer.org /advocacy/briefings_papers/general-briefing-palestinian-political-prisoners-israeli-prisons-0.

Ahmed-Landeryou, Musharrat, ed. 2024. *Antiracist Occupational Therapy: Unsettling the Status Quo*. London: Jessica Kingsley Publishers.

Al-Batma, Nadia. 2012. *Falastin Al fusul Al arbaʾa: ʿAdat wataqalid wamawasem* [Palestine the Four Seasons: Customs, Traditions, and Seasons]. Jerusalem: Jerusalem Media and Communication Centre.

Alonso Bejarano, Carolina, Lucia López Juárez, Mirian A. Mijangos García, and Daniel M. Goldstein. 2019. *Decolonizing Ethnography: Undocumented Immigrants and New Directions in Social Science*. Durham, NC: Duke University Press.

Amnesty International. 2022. *Israel's Apartheid against Palestinians: A Cruel System of Domination and a Crime against Humanity*. London: Amnesty International, February 1. Accessed November 29, 2024. https://www.amnesty.org/en/latest/news/2022/02/israels-apartheid -against-palestinians-a-cruel-system-of-domination-and-a-crime-against-humanity/.

Anievas, Alexander, and Kerem Nişancioğlu. 2015. *How the West Came to Rule: The Geopolitical Origins of Capitalism*. London: Pluto Press.

Aoyama, Mami. 2012. "Indigenous Ainu Occupational Identities and the Natural Environment in Hokkaido." In *Politics of Occupation Centred Practice: Reflections on Occupational Engagement Across Cultures*, edited by Nick Pollard and Dikaios Sakellariou, 106–27. Chichester, U.K.: Wiley-Blackwell.

BAMEOTUK (Black, Asian, and Minoritised Ethnicities Occupational Therapists, United Kingdom). n.d. "Home." Accessed November 27, 2024. https://www.bameot.uk/.

Barber, Brian K., Carolyn Spellings, Clea McNeely, Paul D. Page, Rita Giacaman, Caira Arafat, Mahmoud Daher, et al. 2014. "Politics Drives Human Functioning, Dignity, and Quality

of Life." *Social Science & Medicine* 122: 90–102. http://doi.org/10.1016/j.socscimed.2014
.09.055.

Barghouti, Mourid. 2000. *I Saw Ramallah*. Translated by Ahdaf Soueif. Cairo: American
University in Cairo Press.

Bayoumi, Moustafa, and Andrew Rubin, eds. 2001. *The Edward Said Reader*. London: Granta
Books.

Benvenisti, Meron. 2000. *Sacred Landscape: The Buried History of the Holy Land since 1948*.
Berkeley: University of California Press.

Berger, John. 1979. *Pig Earth*. London: Bloomsbury.

Berger, John. 2007. *Hold Everything Dear: Dispatches on Survival and Resistance*. London: Verso.

Black, Roxie M. 2002. "Occupational Therapy's Dance with Diversity." *American Journal of
Occupational Therapy* 56, no. 2: 140–48. https://doi.org/10.5014/ajot.56.2.140.

Braun, Virginia, and Victoria Clarke. 2006. "Using Thematic Analysis in Psychology."
Qualitative Research in Psychology 3, no. 2: 77–101.

B'Tselem. 2021. *A Regime of Jewish Supremacy from the Jordan River to the Mediterranean Sea:
This Is Apartheid*. Jerusalem: B'Tselem, January 12. Accessed November 29, 2024.
https://www.btselem.org/publications/fulltext/202101_this_is_apartheid.

B'Tselem. 2024. *Forcible Transfer of Isolated Palestinian Communities and Families in Area C
under Cover of Gaza Fighting*. B'Tselem, October 30. Accessed November 29, 2024.
https://www.btselem.org/settler_violence/20231019_forcible_transfer_of_isolated
_communities_and_families_in_area_c_under_the_cover_of_gaza_fighting.

Cabell, Rebecca. 2012. *Rooting Occupation in Nature and Community: The Lived Experience of
Community Based Ecological Farmers*. Master's thesis, Dalhousie University, Nova Scotia,
Canada. http://dalspace.library.dal.ca/handle/10222/15379.

Cappellazzi, Marcello. 2012. *Agriculture in Palestine: A Post-Oslo Analysis*. Brussels: European
Palestinian Council for Political Relations (EUPAC). Accessed November 29, 2024.
https://web.archive.org/web/20150904044734/http://thecepr.org/images/stories/pdf
/memo%20agriculture.pdf.

Celegati Pan, Lívia. 2021. "Social Occupational Therapy in School: Experiences with a Student
Association." In *Social Occupational Therapy: Theoretical and Practical Designs*, edited by
Roseli Esquerdo Lopes and Ana Paula Serrata Malfitano, 177–81. Philadelphia: Elsevier.

Clouston, Teena. 2014. "Whose Occupational Balance Is It Anyway? The Challenge of
Neoliberal Capitalism and Work-Life Imbalance." *British Journal of Occupational Therapy*
77 (10): 507–15.

CSDH (Commission on Social Determinants of Health). 2008. *Health Equity through Action
on the Social Determinants of Health*. Geneva: WHO.

Dabbagh, Selma. 2015. "Beit Sahour's First Intifada Heroes Celebrated in Intelligent, Funny
Film." *The Electronic Intifada*, April 16. https://electronicintifada.net/content/beit-sahours
-first-intifada-heroes-celebrated-intelligent-funny-film/14434.

Dar Al-Mashriq. 1986. *Al Munjid fi 'lughah wa e 'alaam* [*Al-Munjid Arabic-Arabic Dictionary*].
Beirut: Dar Al-Mashriq.

Davies, Angela Y. 2016. *Freedom Is a Constant Struggle: Ferguson, Palestine, and the Foundations of a Movement*. Chicago: Haymarket Books.

de Certeau, Michel. 1988. *The Practice of Everyday Life*. Translated by Steven Rendall. Berkeley:
University of California Press.

Bibliography

Dickie, Virginia, Malcolm P. Cutchin, and Ruth Humphry. 2006. "Occupation as Transactional Experience: A Critique of Individualism in Occupational Science." *Journal of Occupational Science* 13: 83–93. https://doi.org/10.1080/14427591.2006.9686573.

DisruptOT. 2024. "Home." Accessed November 30, 2024. https://www.disruptot.org/.

Durocher, Evelyne. 2017. "Occupational Justice: A Fine Balance for Occupational Therapists." In *Occupational Therapies without Borders: Integrating Justice with Practice*, edited by Dikaios Sakellariou and Nick Pollard, 8–18. Edinburgh: Elsevier.

Durocher, Evelyne, Barbara E. Gibson, and Susan Rappolt. 2014a. "Occupational Justice: A Conceptual Review." *Journal of Occupational Science* 21 (4): 418–30. https://doi.org/10.1080/14427591.2013.775692.

Durocher, Evelyne, Barbara E. Gibson, and Susan Rappolt. 2014b. "Occupational Justice: Future Directions." *Journal of Occupational Science* 21 (4): 431–42. https://doi.org/10.1080/14427591.2013.775693.

Emery Whittington, Isla, Jamie Daniel Leite Junior, and Sheela Ivlev. 2024. "Antiracism as Means and End." In *Antiracism Occupational Therapy: Unsettling the Status Quo*, edited by Musharrat J. Ahmed-Landeryou, 119–36. London: Jessica Kingsley Publishers.

Farias, Lisette, and Debbie Laliberte Rudman. 2016. "A Critical Interpretive Synthesis of the Uptake of Critical Perspectives in Occupational Science." *Journal of Occupational Science* 23 (1): 33–50. https://doi.org/10.1080/14427591.2014.989893.

Federici, Silvia. 2014. *Caliban and the Witch: Women, the Body and Primitive Accumulation*. 2nd ed. Brooklyn: Autonomedia.

Frank, Gelya. 1996. "Crafts Production and Resistance to Domination in the Late 20th Century." *Journal of Occupational Science: Australia* 3 (2): 56–64. https://doi.org/10.1080/14427591.1996.9686408.

Frank, Gelya. 2011. "The Transactional Relationship between Occupation and Place: Indigenous Cultures in the American Southwest." *Journal of Occupational Science* 18 (1): 3–20. https://doi.org/10.1080/14427591.2011.562874.

Frank, Gelya. 2012. "The 2010 Ruth Zemke Lecture in Occupational Science: Occupational Therapy/Occupational Science/Occupational Justice: Moral Commitments and Global Assemblages." *Journal of Occupational Science* 19 (1): 25–35. https://doi.org/10.1080/14427591.2011.607792.

Frank, Gelya, and Bernard A. K. Muriithi. 2015. "Theorising Social Transformation in Occupational Science: The American Civil Rights Movement and South African Struggle Against Apartheid as 'Occupational Reconstructions.'" *South African Journal of Occupational Therapy* 45 (1): 11–19.

Galheigo, Sandra Maria. 2021. "Social Occupational Therapy in Brazil: A Historical Synthesis of the Constitution of a Field of Knowledge and Practice." In *Social Occupational Therapy: Theoretical and Practical Designs*, edited by Roseli Esquerdo Lopes and Ana Paula Malfitano, 11–21. Philadelphia: Elsevier.

Galvaan, Roshan. 2010. *A Critical Ethnography of Young Adolescents' Occupational Choices in a Community in Post-Apartheid South Africa*. PhD diss., University of Cape Town.

Ghanim, As'ad, and Muhanad Mustafa. 2009. *Al Felestiniun fi Esrael: Siyasat al Aqaliya al Asliya fi e' Dwlla al Ethniya* [The Palestinians in Israel: Policies for the Native Minority in an Ethnic State]. Madar, the Palestinian Centre for Israeli Studies, April.

Giacaman, Rita, Rana Khatib, Luay Shabaneh, Asad Ramlawi, Belgacem Sabri, Guido Sabatinelli, Marwan Khawaja, et al. 2009. "Health Status and Health Services in the Occupied Palestinian Territory." *The Lancet* 373: 837–49.

Grenier, Marie-Lyne. 2020. "Cultural Competency and the Reproduction of White Supremacy in Occupational Therapy Education." *Health Education Journal* 79 (6): 633–44. https://doi.org/10.1177/0017896920902515.

Grillo, Trina. 1995. "Anti-Essentialism and Intersectionality: Tools to Dismantle the Master's House." *Berkeley Women's Law Journal* 10: 16–30.

Grosfogul, Ramón. 2011. "Decolonizing Post-Colonial Studies and Paradigms of Political-Economy: Transmodernity, Decolonial Thinking, and Global Coloniality." *Transmodernity* 1 (1). https://doi.org/10.5070/T411000004.

Guajardo Córdoba, Alejandro. 2020. "About New Forms of Colonization in Occupational Therapy: Reflections on the Idea of Occupational Justice from a Critical-Political Philosophy Perspective." *Cadernos Brasileiros de Terapia Ocupacional* 28 (4). https://doi.org/10.4322/2526-8910.ctoARF2175.

Hitch, David, Genevieve Pépin, and Karen Stagnitti. 2014a. "In the Footsteps of Wilcock, Part One: The Evolution of Doing, Being, Becoming, and Belonging." *Occupational Therapy in Health Care* 28 (3): 231–46. https://doi.org/10.3109/07380577.2014.898114.

Hitch, David, Genevieve Pépin, and Karen Stagnitti. 2014b. "In the Footsteps of Wilcock, Part Two: The Evolution of Doing, Being, Becoming, and Belonging." *Occupational Therapy in Health Care* 28 (3): 247–63. https://doi.org/10.3109/07380577.2014.898115.

Hopkirk, Jane, and Linda H. Wilson. 2014. "A Call to Wellness—Whitiwhitia i te Ora: Exploring Māori and Occupational Therapy Perspectives on Health." *Occupational Therapy International*. https://doi.org/10.1002/oti.1373.

Human Rights Watch. 2021. *A Threshold Crossed: Israeli Authorities and the Crimes of Apartheid and Persecution*, April 27. Accessed November 28, 2024. https://www.hrw.org/report/2021/04/27/threshold-crossed/israeli-authorities-and-crimes-apartheid-and-persecution.

Humanity and Society. "Home." Accessed November 28, 2024. https://journals.sagepub.com/overview-metric/HAS.

ICJ (International Court of Justice). 2004. *Legal Consequences of the Construction of a Wall in the Occupied Palestinian Territory*, July 9. Accessed November 28, 2024. https://www.icj-cij.org/case/131.

ICJ. 2024. *Application of the Convention on the Prevention and Punishment of the Crime of Genocide in the Gaza Strip* (South Africa v. Israel). The Hague: ICJ, October 9. Accessed November 28, 2024. https://www.icj-cij.org/case/192.

Ivlev, Sheela. 2024. *Occupational Therapy Disruptors: What Global OT Practice Can Teach Us about Innovation, Culture, and Community*. London: Jessica Kingsley Publishers.

Iwama, Michael K. 2006. *The Kawa Model: Culturally Relevant Occupational Therapy*. Philadelphia: Elsevier.

Kantartzis, Sarah. 2017. "Exploring Occupation beyond the Individual: Family and Collective Occupation." In *Occupational Therapies without Borders: Integrating Justice with Practice*, edited by Dikaios Sakellariou and Nick Pollard, 19–28. Edinburgh: Elsevier.

Kantartzis, Sarah, and Mathew Molineux. 2012. "Understanding the Discursive Development of Occupation: Historico-Political Perspectives." In *Occupational Science: Society, Inclusion, Participation*, edited by Gail E. Whiteford and Clare Hocking, 38–53. Chichester, U.K.: Wiley-Blackwell.

Bibliography   157

Kerem Navot. 2013. *Israeli Settler Agriculture as a Means of Land Takeover in the West Bank*.
    Jerusalem: Kerem Navot, August. Accessed November 28, 2024. https://www.keremnavot
    .org/_files/ugd/cdb1a7_370bb4f21ceb47adb3ac7556c02b8972.pdf.
Kerem Navot. 2022. *The Wild West: Grazing, Seizing and Looting by Israeli Settlers in the West
    Bank*. Jerusalem: Kerem Navot, May. Accessed November 29, 2024. https://www
    .keremnavot.org/_files/ugd/a76eb4_9d3dee006d0e4decac505bf432bbd56e.pdf.
Khalidi, Rashid. 2021. *The Hundred Years' War on Palestine: A History of Settler Colonialism
    and Resistance 1917–2017*. London: Profile Books.
Khalidi, Walid, ed. 2006. *All That Remains: The Palestinian Villages Occupied and Depopulated
    by Israel in 1948*. Washington, DC: Institute for Palestine Studies, 282–84.
Khalidi, Walid. 2010. *Before Their Diaspora: A Photographic History of the Palestinians
    1876–1948*. Washington, DC: Institute for Palestine Studies.
Khatib, Rasha, Martin McKee, and Salim Yusuf. 2024. "Counting the Dead in Gaza: Difficult
    but Essential." *The Lancet* 404 (10449): 237–38. https://www.thelancet.com/journals
    /lancet/article/PIIS0140-6736(24)01169-3/fulltext.
Kimmerling, Baruch. 2003. *Politicide: Ariel Sharon's War against the Palestinians*. London:
    Verso.
Kramer-Roy, Debbie. 2011. "Occupational Injustice in Pakistani Families with Disabled
    Children in the UK: A PAR Study." In *Occupational Therapies without Borders: Towards an
    Ecology of Occupation-Based Practice*, vol. 2, edited by Frank Kronenberg, Nick Pollard, and
    Dikaios Sakellariou, 385–92. Edinburgh: Elsevier.
Kremnitze, Mordechai, and Lina Saba-Habesch. 2015. "House Demolitions." *Laws* 4: 216–28.
    https://doi.org/10.3390/laws4020216.
Kronenberg, Frank. 2018. *Everyday Enactments of Humanity Affirmations in Post-1994
    Apartheid South Africa: A Phronetic Case Study of Being Human as Occupation and Health*.
    PhD diss., University of Cape Town. Accessed November 28, 2024. file:///C:/Users/
    juman/Downloads/thesis_hsf_2018_kronenberg_franciscus_c_w.pdf.
Kronenberg, Frank, and Nick Pollard. 2005. "Overcoming Occupational Apartheid: A
    Preliminary Exploration of the Political Nature of Occupational Therapy." In *Occupational
    Therapy without Borders: Learning from the Spirit of Survivors*, edited by Frank Kronenberg,
    Salvador S. Algado, and Nick Pollard, 58–86. Edinburgh: Elsevier.
Kronenberg, Frank, Nick Pollard, and Dikaios Sakellariou, eds. 2011. *Occupational Therapies
    without Borders: Towards an Ecology of Occupation-Based Practice*, vol. 2. Edinburgh: Elsevier.
Kronenberg, Frank, Salvador Simó Algado, and Nick Pollard, eds. 2005. *Occupational Therapy
    without Borders: Learning from the Spirit of Survivors*. Edinburgh: Elsevier.
Laliberte Rudman, Debbie. 2014. "Embracing and Enacting an 'Occupational Imagination':
    Occupational Science as Transformative." *Journal of Occupational Science* 24 (4): 373–88.
    https://doi.org/10.1080/14427591.2014.8888970.
Lopes, Roseli E. 2021. "Citizenship, Rights, and Social Occupational Therapy." In *Social
    Occupational Therapy: Theoretical and Practical Designs*, edited by Roseli E. Lopes and
    Ana P. Malfitano, 1–10. Philadelphia: Elsevier.
Lopes, Roseli E., and Ana P. Malfitano, eds. 2021. *Social Occupational Therapy: Theoretical and
    Practical Designs*. Philadelphia: Elsevier.
Manor, Keren. 2017. "Israeli Authorities Uproot Olive Trees to Build Settler-Only Road." *+972
    Magazine*, January 16. https://972mag.com/photos-israeli-authorities-uproot-olive-trees-to
    -build-settler-only-road/124285/.

Marmot, Michael. 2005. "Social Determinants of Health Inequalities." *The Lancet* 365 (9464): 1099–104. http://www.thelancet.com/journals/lancet/article/PIIS0140-6736(05)71146-6 /abstract.

Masalha, Nur. 2012. *The Palestine Nakba: Decolonising History, Narrating the Subaltern, Reclaiming Memory*. London: Zed Books.

Masalha, Nur. 2013. *The Zionist Bible: Biblical Precedent, Colonialism and the Erasure of Memory*. Durham, NC: Acumen.

Masalha, Nur. 2018. *Palestine: A Four Thousand Years History*. London: Zed Books.

Maslow, Abraham H. 1970. *Motivation and Personality*. 2nd ed. New York: Harper and Row.

Massad, Joseph A. 2016. *Islam in Liberalism*. Chicago: University of Chicago Press.

Mattingly, Cheryl. 1998. *Healing Dramas and Clinical Plots: The Narrative Structure of Experience*. Cambridge, U.K.: Cambridge University Press.

McGareth, Margaret, and Helen McGonagle. 2016. "Exploring 'Wicked Problems' from an Occupational Perspective: The Case of Turf Cutting in Rural Ireland." *Journal of Occupational Science* 23 (3): 308–20. 10.1080/14427591.2016.1169437.

McNeely, Clea, Brian K. Barber, Carolyn Spellings, Rita Giacaman, Cairo Arafat, Mahmoud Daher, Eyad El Sarraj, et al. 2014. "Human Insecurity, Chronic Economic Constraints and Health in the Occupied Palestinian Territory." *Global Public Health* 9 (5): 495–515. https://doi.org/10.1080/17441692.2014.903427.

McNeill, Hinematau N. 2016. "Māori and the Natural Environment from an Occupational Justice Perspective." *Journal of Occupational Science* 23 (3): 308–20. https://doi.org/10.1080 /14427591.2016.1245158.

Mignolo, Walter D. 2018. "On Pluriversality and Multipolarity." In *Constructing the Pluriverse: The Geopolitics of Knowledge*, edited by Bernd Reiter, ix–xiv. Durham, NC: Duke University Press.

Nashef, Khaled. 2002. "Tawfik Canaan: His Life and Works." *Jerusalem Quarterly File* 16. https://www.palestine-studies.org/sites/default/files/jq-articles/16_canaan_2_0.pdf.

Norgaard, Kari Marie. 2019. *Salmon and Acorns Feed Our People: Colonialism, Nature and Social Action*. New Brunswick, NJ: Rutgers University Press.

Núñez Valderrama, Cristian M., Sofia S. Hernández, and Alejandro H. Alarcón. 2022. "Collective Occupations and Nature: Impacts of the Coloniality of Nature on Rural and Fishing Communities in Chile." *Journal of Occupational Science* 29 (2): 252–62. https://doi .org/10.1080/14427591.2021.1880264.

Oxfam. 2010. *The Road to Olive Farming: Challenges to Developing the Economy of Olive Oil in the West Bank*, October 15. Accessed November 28, 2024, https://policy-practice.oxfam.org /resources/the-road-to-olive-farming-challenge-to-developing-the-economy-of-olive-oil-in -t-115032/.

Pappe, Ilan. 2006. *The Ethnic Cleansing of Palestine*. Oxford, U.K.: Oneworld.

Pappe, Ilan. 2017. *The Biggest Prison on Earth: A History of the Occupied Territories*. Oxford, U.K.: Oneworld.

Pierce, Doris. 2012. "The 2011 Ruth Zemke Lecture in Occupational Science: Promise." *Journal of Occupational Science* 19 (4): 298–311. https://doi.org/10.1080/14427591.2012.667778.

Pollard, Nick, Dikaios Sakellariou, and Frank Kronenberg. 2008a. "Occupational Apartheid." In *A Political Practice of Occupational Therapy*, edited by Nick Pollard, Dikaios Sakellariou, and Frank Kronenberg, 55–67. Edinburgh: Elsevier.

Bibliography

Pollard, Nick, Dikaios Sakellariou, and Frank Kronenberg, eds. 2008b. *A Political Practice of Occupational Therapy*. Edinburgh: Elsevier.

Puar, Jasbir. n.d. *Treatment without Checkpoints*. Anemones. MT Collective, 17–22.

Qumsiyeh, Mazin B. 2004. *Sharing the Land of Canaan: Human Rights and the Israeli-Palestinian Struggle*. London: Pluto Press.

Qumsiyeh, Mazin B. 2011. *Popular Resistance in Palestine: A History of Hope and Empowerment*. London: Pluto Press.

Ra'ad, Basem L. 2010. *Hidden Histories: Palestine and the Eastern Mediterranean*. London: Pluto Press.

Ramugondo, Elelwani L. 2012. "Intergenerational Play within Family: The Case for Occupational Consciousness." *Journal of Occupational Science* 19 (4): 326–40. https://doi.org/10.1080/14427591.2012.729206.

Ramugondo, Elelwani L. 2015. "Occupational Consciousness." *Journal of Occupational Science* 22 (4): 488–501. https://doi.org/10.1080/14427591.2015.1042516.

Ramugondo, Elelwani L., and Frank Kronenberg. 2015. "Explaining Collective Occupations from a Human Relations Perspective: Bridging the Individual-Collective Dichotomy." *Journal of Occupational Science* 22 (1): 3–16. https://doi.org/10.1080/14427591.2013.781920.

Rasras, Khader. 2005. "A Human Rights Approach to Psychotherapy." *The International Journal of Narrative Therapy and Community Work* 3 (4): 57–60. https://dulwichcentre.com.au/wp-content/uploads/2014/03/palestinian-perspectives-on-trauma-and-torture.pdf.

Rijke, Alexandra, and Toine van Teeffelen. 2014. "To Exist Is to Resist: Sumud, Heroism, and the Everyday." *Jerusalem Quarterly* 59: 86–99. https://www.palestine-studies.org/sites/default/files/jq-articles/To_Exist_to_Resist_JQ_59_0.pdf.

Rosenfeld, Maya. 2004. *Confronting the Occupation: Work, Education, and Political Activism of Palestinian Families in a Refugee Camp*. Stanford, CA: Stanford University Press.

Said, Edward W. 1992. *The Question of Palestine*. 2nd ed. New York: Vintage Books.

Said, Edward W. 1995. *Peace and Its Discontents: Gaza-Jericho 1993–1995*. New York: Vintage Books.

Said, Edward W. 1999. *After the Last Sky: Palestinian Lives*. 2nd ed. New York: Columbia University Press.

Said, Edward W. 2000. *Reflections on Exile: And Other Literary and Cultural Essays*. London: Granta.

Said, Edward W. 2003. *Orientalism*. 3rd ed. London: Penguin.

Sakellariou, Dikaios, and Nick Pollard, eds. 2017. *Occupational Therapies without Borders: Integrating Justice with Practice*. 2nd ed. Amsterdam: Elsevier.

Sansour, Vivien, and Alaa Tartir. 2014. Palestinian Farmers: A Last Stronghold of Resistance. *Al Shabka Policy Brief*, July 1. Accessed November 28, 2024. https://al-shabaka.org/briefs/palestinian-farmers-a-last-stronghold-of-resistance/.

Santos, Boaventura De Susa. 2014. *Epistemologies of the South: Justice against Epistemicide*. New York: Routledge.

Sayigh, Rosemary. 1979. *Palestinians: From Peasants to Evolutionaries*. London: Zed Press.

Scott, James C. 1976. *The Moral Economy of the Peasant: Rebellion and Subsistence in Southeast Asia*. New Haven, CT: Yale University Press.

Scott, James C. 1985. *Weapons of the Weak: Everyday Forms of Peasant Resistance*. New Haven, CT: Yale University Press.

Scott, James C. 2012. *Two Cheers for Anarchism*. Princeton, NJ: Princeton University Press.

Seger, Karen. 1981. *Portrait of a Palestinian Village: The Photographs of Hilma Granqvist*. London: Third World Centre for Research.

Sehwail, Mahmud. 2005. "Responding to Continuing Traumatic Events." *The International Journal of Narrative Therapy and Community Work* 3 & 4: 54–56. https://dulwichcentre .com.au/wp-content/uploads/2014/03/palestinian-perspectives-on-trauma-and-torture. pdf.

Sheehi, Lara, and Stephen Sheehi. 2024. *Psychoanalysis under Occupation: Practicing Resistance in Palestine*. New York: Routledge.

Shehadeh, Raja. 1982. *The Third Way: A Journal of Life in the West Bank*. London: Quartet Books.

Shetty, Raviraj, and Shoba Nayar. 2024. "Understanding the Person-Occupation Enmeshment through Exploring the Erosion of Tribal Occupations in India." *Journal of Occupational Science* 31 (1): 88–101. https://doi.org/10.1080/14427591.2023.2231960.

Shomali, Amer, and Paul Cowan. 2014. *The Wanted 18*. National Film Board of Canada (NFB), Kino Lorber.

Simaan, Juman. 2017. "Olive Growing in Palestine: A Decolonial Ethnographic Study of Daily Forms of Resistance." *Journal of Occupational Science* 24 (4): 510–23. http://dx.doi.org/10 .1080/14427591.2017.1378119.

Simaan, Juman. 2018. *Olive Growing in Palestine: An Everyday Form of Resistance*. Unpublished doctoral thesis, Canterbury Christ Church University, Canterbury, U.K.

Simaan, Juman. Forthcoming. "Every-Day Forms of Resistance among Olive Growing and Shepherding Communities in Palestine." In *Handbook of Social Justice in the Global South*, edited by Nikhil Deb, Manjusha Nair, and Glenn W. Muschert. Cheltenham, U.K.: Edward Elgar.

Simaan, Juman, and Vivien Sansour. 2016. "Tales of Agri-Resistance." *Stir to Action*, Autumn. Accessed November 30, 2024. https://www.resilience.org/stories/2017-01-04/tales-of-agri -resistance/.

Smith, Linda Tuhiwai. 2022. *Decolonizing Methodology: Research and Indigenous Peoples*. 3rd ed. London: Bloomsbury.

Spade, Dean. 2020. *Mutual Aid: Building Solidarity during the Crisis (and the Next)*. London: Verso.

Spivak, Gayatri Chakravorty. 1993. *Outside the Teaching Machine*. New York: Routledge.

Stanley, Mandy, Sandra Rogers, Susan Forwell, Clare Hocking, Shoba Nayar, Debbie Laliberte Rudman, Birgit Prodinger, et al. 2021. "A Pledge to Mobilize against Racism—Translated." *Journal of Occupational Science* 28 (3): 388–97. https://doi.org/10.1080/14427591.2021 .1921562.

Thibeault, Rachel. 2002. "Fostering Healing through Occupation: The Case of the Canadian Inuit." *Journal of Occupational Science* 9 (3): 153–58. https://doi.org/10.1080/14427591.2002 .9686503.

Thompson, Thompson L. 2000. *The Bible in History: How Writers Create a Past*. London: Pimlico.

Tuck, Eve, and K. Wayne Yang. 2012. "Decolonisation Is Not a Metaphor." *Decolonization: Indigeneity, Education & Society* 1 (1): 1–40.

UNHRC (United Nations Human Rights Council). 2013. *Report of the Independent International Fact-Finding Mission to Investigate the Implications of the Israeli Settlements on the*

Civil, Political, Economic, Social and Cultural Rights of the Palestinian People throughout the Occupied Palestinian Territory, including East Jerusalem. Geneva: UNHRC, February 7. Accessed November 28, 2024. https://digitallibrary.un.org/record/745109?v=pdf.

UNOCHAoPt (United Nation's Office for the Coordination of Humanitarian Affairs in the Occupied Palestinian Territories). 2011. *Humanitarian Fact Sheets on Area C of the West Bank.* New York: United Nations, July. Accessed November 29, 2024. https://www.un.org/unispal/document/auto-insert-207046/.

UNOCHAoPt. 2012. *Olive Harvest Factsheet.* New York: United Nations, October 16. Accessed November 28, 2024. https://www.ochaopt.org/content/olive-harvest-factsheet-october-2012.

UNOCHAoPt. 2024. *Reported Impact Snapshot, Gaza Strip.* New York: United Nations, September 11. Accessed November 28, 2024. https://www.ochaopt.org/content/reported-impact-snapshot-gaza-strip-11-september-2024.

UNOCHAoPt. 2025. *Humanitarian Situation Update, Gaza Strip.* New York: United Nations, June 2025. Accessed June 8, 2025, https://www.ochaopt.org/content/humanitarian-situation-update-294-gaza-strip.

Waage, Hilde Henriksen. 2011. "The Winner Takes All: The 1949 Island of Rhodes Armistice Negotiations Revisited." *Middle East Journal* 65 (2): 279–304. https://www.prio.org/publications/4874.

Wade, Allan. 1997. "Small Acts of Living: Everyday Resistance to Violence and Other Forms of Oppression." *Contemporary Family Therapy* 19 (1): 23–40.

Whalley Hammell, Karen. 2004. "Dimensions of Meaning in the Occupations of Daily Life." *Canadian Journal of Occupational Therapy* 71: 296–305. https://doi.org/10.1177/000841740407100509.

Whalley Hammell, Karen. 2009. "Self-Care, Productivity, and Leisure, or Dimensions of Occupational Experience? Rethinking Occupational 'Categories.'" *Canadian Journal of Occupational Therapy* 76 (2): 107–14. https://doi.org/10.1177/000841740907600208.

Whalley Hammell, Karen. 2014. "Belonging, Occupation, and Human Well-Being: An Exploration." *Canadian Journal of Occupational Therapy* 81 (1): 39–50. https://doi.org/10.1177/000841741352089.

Whalley Hammell, Karen. 2015. "Respecting Global Wisdom: Enhancing the Cultural Relevance of Occupational Therapy's Theoretical Base." *British Journal of Occupational Therapy* 78 (11): 718–21. https://doi.org/10.1177/0308022614564170.

Whalley Hammell, K., and M. K. Iwama. 2012. "Well-Being and Occupational Rights: An Imperative for Critical Occupational Therapy." *Scandinavian Journal of Occupational Therapy* 19: 385–94. https://doi.org/10.3109/11038128.2011.611821.

Whiteford, Gail E., and Clare Hocking, eds. 2012. *Occupational Science: Society, Inclusion, Participation.* Chichester, U.K.: Wiley-Blackwell.

Wicks, Alison, and Maggie Jamieson. 2014. "New Ways for Occupational Scientists to Tackle 'Wicked Problems' Impacting Population Health." *Journal of Occupational Science* 21 (1): 81–85. https://doi.org/10.1080/14427591.2014.878208.

Wilcock, Ann A. 1998. "Occupation for Health." *British Journal of Occupational Therapy* 61 (8): 340–45.

Wilcock, Ann A. 2006. *An Occupational Perspective of Health.* 2nd ed. Thorofare, N.J.: Slack.

Wilcock, Ann A., and Clare Hocking. 2015. *An Occupational Perspective of Health.* 3rd ed. Thorofare, NJ: Slack.

Wilcock, Ann A., and Elizabeth Townsend. 2000. "Occupational Justice: Occupational Terminology Interactive Dialogue." *Journal of Occupational Science* 7: 84–86. https://doi .org/10.1080/14427591.2000.9686470.

Winstanley, Asa. 2013. "The Old Will Die and the Young Will Forget—Did Ben-Gurion Say It?" *The Electronic Intifada*, August 11. Accessed November 30, 2024. https:// electronicintifada.net/blogs/asa-winstanley/old-will-die-and-young-will-forget-did-ben -gurion-say-it.

Wolfe, Patrick. 2006. "Settler Colonialism and the Elimination of the Native." *Journal of Genocide Research* 8 (4): 387–409.

Yerxa, Elizabeth J., Florence Clark, Gelya Frank, Jennifer Jackson, Diane Parham, Doris Pierce. 1989. "An Introduction to Occupational Science, a Foundation for Occupational Therapy in the 21st Century." In *Occupational Science: The Foundation for New Models of Practice*, edited by Anne Johnson and Elizabeth J. Yerxa, 1–17. New York: Haworth Press.

Yish Din. 2024. *Summary of the 2023 Olive Harvest Season*. Tel-Aviv: Yish Din, February 1. Accessed November 30, 2024. https://www.yesh din.org/en/summary-of-the-2023-olive -harvest-season/.

Zureik, Elia. 1977. "Toward a Sociology of the Palestinians." *Journal of Palestine Studies* 6 (4): 3–16.

Zureik, Elia. 2016. *Israel's Colonial Project in Palestine: Brutal Pursuit*. New York: Routledge.

INDEX

Note: Page numbers in italics refer to illustrations and captions.

'abaya (Bedouin gown), 3

Abu ʿAttallah family (Um Yasin, Abu ʿAttallah, Yasin), 32, 33, 36–39, 73; in Al-Raha, 33, 36, 38–39; daily life and farming of, 37, 40–44; *Sutra* and, 35–36, 42–43, 45, 97, 108

Abu Kamal family (Nada, Abu Kamal, Heba, Reem, Sultan), 34, 125–29; Al-Akhdar wadi farmed by, 123–24; *'Awna* and, 67–70, 81; Everyday Forms of Resistance by, 123, 129, 134

Abu Nedal family (Um Nedal, Abu Nedal, Nedal, Nahed), 34; daily life and farming of, 44, 92–96, 99, 106–7; in Dar El Shoke, 92, 94; Everyday Forms of Resistance and, 97, 130–33; occupational harmony and, 51–52; *Sumud* and, 97, 99, 107–8; *Sutra-ʿAwna-Sumud* synthesis and, 130–33

Abu Samir, 87–88

Abu Weehab family (Um Weehab, Abu Weehab, Weehab), 100, 109, 131; in Al-Baydar, 34, 61–62; *'Awna* and, 32, 60–68, 71, 75, 81; daily life of, 61–66

academia: decolonization of, 19, 134–42; eurocentrism in, 8–9, 16, 19, 22–23, 27, 29, 45, 53, 58, 69, 87, 110, 129, 132; Global North and, 138–41; Global South and, 137–40. *See also* scholarship, scholars; *and individual fields of study*

activism, activists, 7, 84, 135, 141–44; decolonial, 134–35; international, 2, 83–87, 104, 108, 125;

local Palestinian, 80, 93, 106, 143–45; PHSL as, 120–21; political, 12, 56, 80, 93, 106–7; social justice, 137, 142; student, 138; women's, 93, 103, 112, 119. *See also* resistance; solidarity

Adra, Basel, 151n1 (postscript)

agribusiness, 78, 110, 116, 121. *See also* agriculture and farming

agri-resistance, 78, 120. *See also* resistance; Sansour, Vivien

agriculture and farming, 7, 9, 25, 94–97, 100, 103–8, 126–32; *Al-ʿafya* and, 17, 49–50; Al-Batma on, 10, 61, 72; committees for, 80, 96, 103, 107, 127; heritage and traditions of, 72, 78, 109, 120; irrigation for, 38, 41, 45, 62, 73, 80, 120; knowledge of, 25, 72, 120; as main occupation, 42, 44, 48; occupation's impact on, 5, 11–12, 16, 19–21, 30–31, 38–39, 45, 58, 60, 63–66, 80, 87–89, 109–10, 114–16, 119, 121, 123, 143–45; practices of, 31, 40–42, 46, 61, 66, 71, 73, 75, 85, 87, 93, 100, 114, 143. *See also* animals and livestock; land; olive growing; olive trees; peasants

Ahmed-Landeryou, Musharrat, 139

Al-ʿafya (Palestinian concept of well-being), 17, 32, 49–51, 53, 58, 129

Al-Akhdar (wadi), 123

Al-Batma, Nadia, 10, 61, 72

Al-Baydar (village), 61–62, 68; land confiscation in, 64–66; UNESCO World Heritage Site application for, 63, 66–67, 80, 145

Al-Haq (The Right; human rights organization), 98, 150n3 (chap. 4)

Al-Khalil (Hebron), 2, 7, 36, 143

Allah (God), 36, 50, 130

All That's Left Collective (ATL; Jewish anti-occupation group), 144

Alonso Bejarano, Carolina, 19

Al-Qaws (LGBTQ+ organization), 78, 150n2 (chap. 3)

Al-Quds (Jerusalem), 2–3, 36, 62, 92, 96, 126

Al-Raha (wadi), 33, 36–39

Al-Reyad (refugee camp), 124–25

Amir (teacher and farmer), 104–5

'Amer (Bedouin man), 3

Amnesty International, 13

ancestors, 5–6; 'Awna and bond with, 71, 73–75; traditions and land passed down from, 73–74, 94, 108, 144

Anievas, Alexander, 23

animals and livestock, 10, 21, 61, 68, 71–72, 76, 131, 143–44

anticolonialism, 19, 57, 101, 121, 137. See also decolonization; settler-colonialism

apartheid: Israeli, 7, 9, 13, 135; South African, 13, 88–89, 103, 109–10, 112, 114–15. See also occupational apartheid; segregation

Area A, 12, 125

Area B, 13

Area C, 13, 39, 68, 124, 126

Aswat (Palestinian feminist queer movement), 78

Australia, 13, 127, 128

'Awna (عونة) (Palestinian concept of collaboration or belonging), 68–90, 61, 131, 144, 146; Abu Kamal family and, 67–70, 81, 129; Abu Weehab family and, 32, 60–68, 71, 75, 81, 131; as bond with more-than-human, 60, 71–73, 89; as doing for belonging, 32, 60, 68–71, 89, 117, 129; Everyday Forms of Resistance and, 32, 59, 97, 121, 123, 129–32, 136, 144, 146; global community and, 83–87, 131; intergenerational and intercommunal collaboration and, 73–75, 131; interfamilial (hamoula) connectedness and, 75–79; local and national belonging and, 79–82, 131; meanings of, 61, 68, 130; occupational apartheid confronted by, 60, 87–89; Sutra-'Awna-Sumud synthesis and, 32, 59, 89, 97, 121, 123, 129–32, 136. See also belonging; collaboration; solidarity

Ba'al (Canaanite god), 71–72

Balfour Declaration (1917), 30

BAMEOTUK (Black, Asian, and Minoritised Ethnicities Occupational Therapists, United Kingdom), 139

Barber, Brian K., 17

Barghouti, Mourid, 5

barrier gates, 21, 59

BDS (Boycott, Divestment, Sanctions) movement, 103

becoming (dimension of occupation): 'Awna and, 74; Everyday Forms of Resistance and, 129, 131–32; olive growing and, 131; Sumud as doing for, 32, 91, 97, 115–17, 121. See also doing-being-becoming-belonging; self-determination

Bedouins, 3, 4, 15, 76, 103

bees and honey, 4, 149n5

Beit Jala (town), 123, 125

Beit Lahem (Bethlehem), 1–3, 6, 75, 76, 123; Abu 'Attallah family and, 36–39, 41; Abu Nedal family and, 52, 92–93, 95

Beit Lahia (Gaza), 146

Beit Sahour, 2, 118–20, 123

beliefs, 16, 25, 86, 101, 133; communal acts and, 16, 119; Indigenous, 71, 119; land-based, 25, 71–72

belonging (dimension of occupation): 'Awna as doing for, 32, 60, 68–71, 89, 129, 131; to community, 68–71, 74–82, 109, 117; decolonial perspective on, 70–71, 137; doing-being-becoming-belonging, 22, 31, 129, 132, 137; Everyday Forms of Resistance and, 129, 131–32; to family, 68–69, 75–79; to global community, 83–87, 111, 131; to land and nature, 50–51, 69, 71–73, 107, 109, 129, 131; occupational therapy and science views on, 69–70; Sumud as doing for, 32, 91, 97, 115–17, 121. See also 'Awna; coagency; hamoula; solidarity

Ben-Gurion, David, 74

Benvenisti, Meron, 25

Berger, John, 26, 35, 120, 123

Bible, 1, 108, 149n5

Bilal (olive farmer), 71, 74, 81, 97–98

Black Lives Matter movement, 138, 141

borders: Green Line, 12, 53, 63, 89, 93–95, 102, 125; Israeli-Jordanian, 2; Masafer Yatta and, 143. See also segregation wall

boycotts, 103, 112, 118; as resistance, 102, 115, 120

Brazil, 137–38

Index

British Mandate in Palestine, 79, 102, 121, 127; administration during, 11–12, 38; land laws from, 65, 104

B'Tselem (Israeli human rights organization), 13

bypass roads, 92, 126

Cabell, Rebecca, 113

Canaan, Tawfik, 75

Canaanites, 62, 71–72, 76

capitalism, 7, 15, 103, 110; critique of, 26–27, 111; globalized, 74, 79, 101, 116; institutionalization and, 24–25; resistance to, 18, 22, 129. *See also* neoliberalism

CCTV cameras, 36

Celegati Pan, Lívia, 138

checkpoints, 1–2, 100, 106; farmers and, 3–4, 15, 20, 31, 38–39, 61, 63, 84, 87, 89, 145. *See also* movement restrictions; permits; segregation wall

children and youth: Abu Kamal's, 124, 127; Abu Nedal's, 92–93, 107; Abu Weehab's, 62, 64, 106, 109; Abu Yasin's, 62, 106–7, 109, 120, 124, 127; Bedouin (Nour), 3; future of, 43, 64, 66, 74, 97, 100, 108–9, 113, 117, 121, 127, 145; land connection of, 73, 107, 109, 127; Palestinian, 38, 62, 78, 81, 106–7, 109, 111, 120, 124, 127, 145; political activism of, 106–7; protection of, 62, 143; South African Black, 109–10; street, 88; teaching of, 48, 120. *See also* education

Chile, 113

Christianity, Christians, 11, 71, 81; in Palestine, 11, 81, 149n2. *See also* religion and religious beliefs

citizenship, 5, 6, 8–9, 137, 138

civil administration, Israeli, 12, 20, 39, 105

civil disobedience, 12, 119–20. *See also* resistance

civil rights, 78, 114

climate crisis, 7, 27, 74, 113, 129

Clouston, Teena, 50

coagency (Zureik), 74, 82, 112; 'Awna and, 32, 74, 82–83, 89

collaboration: 'Awna as, 32, 60–61, 68, 131; in decolonization, 135, 138; between global communities, 83, 86; intercommunal, 73–82; local, 79–82, 125; in olive growing, 68, 130–31; research on, 7. See also 'Awna; international collaboration and solidarity; solidarity

collective occupations: 'Awna as, 82; defined, 15, 82; examples of, 15, 82, 111–13, 118–20; Everyday Forms of Resistance as, 132; in Greece, 82–83;

resistance through, 15, 111–13, 118–20; theory of, 82. *See also* Occupation

Commission on Social Determinants of Health (CSDH), 17

confiscation of land, 4, 20–21, 38, 41, 45, 58, 63–66, 68, 80, 89, 94–95, 98, 104, 106–7, 116, 123, 126, 128

consciousness: collective, 102, 119, 135; decolonial, 135; historical, 55, 109; occupational, 56, 109–11, 129, 132–33. *See also* sociopolitical awareness

construction work, 3, 51, 93, 95

Cowan, Paul, 118

crafts: olive wood, 10; production as resistance, 47, 112

Cutchin, Malcolm P., 47, 53–54

Dabbagh, Selma, 119

dabke (folk dance), 61

Dal 'awna (song genre), 61

Damir (farmer), 83, 108, 113–14

Dar El Shoke (village), 63, 94; Abu Nedal family in, 34, 92, 94; agricultural committee in, 80, 96; military demolition in, 145; olive growing in, 87, 95–96

Davies, Angela Y., 77, 104

Dayr Aban (village), 125, 128

Dead Sea, 2

de Certeau, Michel, 25

decolonization, 19, 133, 135; of academia and scholarship, 9, 19–22, 134–42; defined, 19, 134–35, 138; Everyday Forms of Resistance and, 129, 132; of occupational therapy and science, 33, 70, 111, 121, 137–42; of Palestine, 22, 134; praxis of, 19, 135, 137–38, 141–42; of sociology, 33, 137, 140–41. *See also* anticolonialism; Epistemologies of the South; postcolonialism

democracy, 65, 116, 128

development, concept of, 116

Dewey, John, 54, 114, 116

Dheisha (refugee camp), 80

diabetes, 37

dibis (grape molasses), 42

Dickie, Virginia, 47, 53–54

dignity, 26, 28, 30, 130; 'Awna and, 69; Everyday Forms of Resistance and, 26, 129; fragmented, 58; olive growing and, 44, 56, 58, 93. See also *Sutra*

disability, 8, 31, 47, 69, 111, 117

displacement, 11, 103, 143; of Palestinians during *Nakba*, 5, 11–12, 55–56, 79, 94, 125, 149n2; threat of, 20, 143. *See also* ethnic cleansing; *Nakba*; refugees, Palestinian

Disrupt OT movement, 139

doing-being-becoming-belonging (occupational science theory): *'Awna* and, 69–71; critique of, 22, 129, 137; Everyday Forms of Resistance as manifestation of, 129, 132; *Sutra* and, 45–46, 58; *Sumud* as doing for, 32, 91, 97, 115–17, 121. *See also* becoming; belonging; Occupation; Wilcock, Ann A.

donkeys, 1, 72, 100, 106, 124, 127

Durocher, Evelyne, 88

economy and economic conditions: global, 15, 24, 27, 101, 116; in Palestine, 17, 20–21, 38, 40, 44, 55, 64, 78, 85, 93, 96, 106, 112, 114, 116, 125. *See also* capitalism; livelihood; poverty

education, 6, 8, 103, 109, 138; decolonizing, 135, 140; denial of, 145; of farmers' children, 107, 109, 120, 124, 145; in oPt, 17, 56, 93, 103, 109, 119–20, 124, 126, 135; in refugee camps, 56, 80, 126; value of, 62, 80, 126; Western system of, 6, 8, 135. *See also* children and youth

Egypt, 12

el'giri (following neighbors' example), 66

Emery-Whittington, Isla, 139

epistemicide (Santos), 27, 132. *See also* injustice: cognitive

Epistemologies of the South (Santos), 15, 18, 22, 26–31, 116, 120, 135; Everyday Forms of Resistance and, 132, 134, 136. *See also* decolonization; epistemology

epistemology: decolonial, 19, 132–37; Eurocentric, 22–23, 25, 129, 132; Everyday Forms of Resistance and, 132–34; of imperialism, 22–23, 28–29, 132; Indigenous, 136; olive growers', 7, 131–33; Western, 27, 116, 132. *See also* Epistemologies of the South

eshail (star), 73

ethnic cleansing, 63, 118–19, 125, 144; during *Nakba*, 12, 55; settler-colonialism and, 12–14. *See also* displacement; genocide; *Nakba*

ethnography, 6, 19–22; decolonial, 9, 19, 135

Eurocentrism, 9, 19, 29, 45, 53, 58, 87, 129, 132, 136; in academia, 8, 22–23, 27, 69, 110, 141; challenges to, 70, 116, 137; in development notions, 116; in occupational theory and science, 8, 16, 46, 139. *See also* decolonization; Western thought

Europe: colonialism of, 13–14, 19, 23–25, 27–28, 74, 136; Jewish communities from, 30, 149n5; settlers from, 39, 89. *See also* Eurocentrism

Everyday Forms of Resistance (يومية مقاومة) (*Sutra-'Awna-Sumud* synthesis), 32, 123–33, 146; Abu Kamal family and, 123, 129, 134; Abu Nedal on, 130; *Al-'afya* and, 129; as defined and conceptualized, 5, 7, 32, 122–23, 129, 131–32, 134, 136, 146; as ontological and epistemological stance, 132–34; Scott on, 15–16, 26, 101, 120. See also *'Awna*; resistance; *Sumud*; *Sutra*

exile, 57, 102. *See also* displacement

extractivist imperialism, 24, 27

Fako'a hills, 1

fallahin (rural land-based peasants), 5, 15, 72, 76, 79, 89, 94, 98, 106, 127–28

family, families, 7, 33–34. *See also* children and youth; *hamoula*; kinship; *and names of specific participant families, e.g., Abu 'Attallah family*

Fayyad, Salam, 103

Faz3a (فزعة) (call for aid), 145, 151n3

Federici, Silvia, 77

Fertile Crescent, 11

Filastin (Palestine), 11

food sovereignty, 5–6, 51, 121

Frank, Gelya, 16, 19, 47, 54, 112, 116

freedom, freedoms, 26–27, 29–30, 144; of movement, 20, 141; religious, 20; from restriction, 4, 141. *See also* self-determination; sovereignty

Galvaan, Roshan, 111

g'areeb (stranger), 79

Gaza Strip, 10, 13, 144; genocide in, 13, 146, 149n4; history of, 11–12; Israel invades, 13, 36, 144, 146; *Sumud* in, 103, 146

genocide, 13, 14, 146, 149n4. *See also* ethnic cleansing

Germany, 125, 149n5

Ghanim, As'ad, 15

Giacaman, Rita, 17

Giddens, Anthony, 55

Global North, 138–41. *See also* Eurocentrism; Europe; Western thought

Global South, 6, 9, 15, 18, 22, 27, 32, 86, 111, 132, 134–42; communities in, 7–9, 33, 50, 55, 69–70, 113, 116, 129; intercultural translation with, 28, 135; knowledge from, 7–8, 28, 129; practitioners

from, 139. *See also* decolonization; Epistemologies of the South
gleaning (*tasyeef*), 66–67, 81
goats, 1, 124, 126
Golan Heights, 12
"Good Living," 18
Granqvist, Hilma, 75
grassroots organizing, 12, 103; in agricultural committees, 80, 96, 107, 127; PHSL, 48, 74, 118, 120–21; popular resistance and, 104, 120; *Ta'ayush*, 84. *See also* activism, activists; Intifadas; JAI; NGOs
Greece, 54, 82–83
Green Line (1949 Armistice Border), 12, 53, 63, 89, 93–95, 102, 125
Grenier, Marie-Lyne, 139
Grillo, Trina, 77
Grosfogul, Ramón, 136
Guajardo Córdoba, Alejandro, 18

hamoula (clan), 79–80, 94, 125; *'Awna* and, 75–79. *See also* family, families; kinship
Hanna (Christian farmer), 81
harvest, olive: *'Awna* during, 75; description of, 7, 9, 41–42, 46, 61, 66–67, 75, 104, 124; restrictions on, 21, 87, 145; seasonal timing of, 40, 73
health and well-being, 16, 18, 47; decolonial approaches to, 137, 142; Everyday Forms of Resistance and, 129, 131–32; Global South perspectives on, 50, 117; Indigenous perspectives on, 50–51, 54, 72; mental health and, 17, 44, 49, 111; military occupation's impact on, 5, 8–9, 17, 31, 46, 51, 54, 88; occupational balance and, 48–51, 53, 58, 129; occupational justice and, 17–18, 31, 88; olive growing's promotion of, 31–32, 35, 42–51, 58, 88–89, 128–29, 131–33, 144; *Sutra* and, 32, 35–36, 43–51, 58. See also *Al-'afya*
Hebrew language, 6, 8, 25, 84, 87
heritage, 6, 109, 135; Bedouin, 3; Canaanite, 62, 76; cultural, 70, 97, 108, 119–21, 130, 134; erasure of, 25, 74, 121; of land and farming, 70, 97, 120, 129; Palestinian, 6, 62, 70, 74, 88, 97, 117, 120, 129; PHSL and, 118, 120–21; premonotheistic, 71; Roman, 61; seeds as, 48, 74, 78; threats to, 74, 109, 121; UNESCO and, 63, 66–67, 80, 145. *See also* fallahin; Palestinian culture; tradition and traditional practices
Herzl, Theodor, 149n5
Heyam (Abu Nedal's wife), 92

high modern rationality (Santos), 24
Hilal (activist), 84–85
historicist truth, 23, 150n8
Hocking, Clare, 70
honey, 4, 149n5
honor killings, 78
hope: *'Awna* and, 74; for decolonized Palestine, 134; for future, 43, 47, 97, 99, 108, 113, 117, 121, 128–29, 146; PHSL and, 121; *Sumud* and, 99, 108, 113, 117, 121
Hopkirk, Jane, 50
hospitality, 68, 83
human rights: abuses of, 12; concept of, 30, 86, 116, 130, 138; ICJ, 12, 15; organizations for, 13, 21, 78, 98, 150n3 (chap. 4); Palestine and, 30; UNHRC and, 15, 20–21. *See also* occupational justice; social justice
Human Rights Watch, 13
Humanity and Society (journal), 140–41
Humphry, Ruth, 47, 53–54

ICJ (International Court of Justice), 12, 15
IDF (Israeli Defense Forces): Abu 'Attallah family and, 37; Abu Nedal family and, 94–95; Abu Samir and, 87; Abu Weehab family and, 63; acts against farmers and land, 12, 20–21, 38–39, 63, 84, 87–89, 94–95, 103, 105–6, 108, 112, 118–19, 126–27, 143–45; Area B and, 13; Area C and, 39; civil administration of, 39; collaborates with settlers, 105, 144; destruction by, 13, 38, 94–95, 103, 105–6, 108, 118–19, 126–27, 143–45; night raids by, 126; "unworked land" policy of, 89, 107. *See also* military occupation (Israeli)
imperialism: epistemology of, 22–23, 28–29, 132; extractivist, 24, 27. *See also* colonialism; settler-colonialism
India, 14, 51, 101, 112, 113
Indigenous communities. *See names of specific identifications, e.g., Palestinians*
infrapolitics (Scott), 26
infrastructure: agricultural, 20, 38, 63, 72, 89, 106, 126–27; destruction of, 13, 126; lack of, 12, 63, 126. *See also* roads
inheritance: of land, 73, 94; of traditions and values, 50, 73–74, 98, 108–9, 120, 130
injustice: cognitive (Santos), 27–28, 31–33; occupational, 7, 9, 17–18, 31, 51, 88, 111, 117–18, 121, 132. *See also* epistemicide; occupational apartheid
institutional neurosis (Scott), 24

institutionalization, 24
intercultural translation, 9, 22, 28, 35, 111, 131, 135.
    See also decolonization; Epistemologies
    of the South
international collaboration and solidarity: *'Awna*
    and, 61, 68, 83–87, 125, 131; critique of, 84–85;
    examples of, 2, 38, 63, 80, 83–87, 104–5, 108, 125,
    127, 130, 143–44; importance of, 83, 85; *Sumud*
    and, 104. *See also* activism, activists;
    collaboration; NGOs; solidarity
international law, 12, 20–21
Intifadas: First (1987–93), 12, 51, 93, 103, 112,
    118–20; Second (early 2000s), 12, 83, 104
Inuit communities, 49, 51
invasions (military), 11; of Gaza, 13, 36, 144, 146; of
    OPT (1967), 11–12, 45; of West Bank, 12, 45
Ireland, turf-cutting in, 47, 49, 73, 113
irrigation, 38, 41, 45, 62, 73, 80, 120
Islam and Muslims, 11, 28, 36, 71, 149n2
Israeli Defense Forces. *See* IDF
Israeli settlements and settlers, 1, 13, 20; Abu Kamal
    family and, 126–28, 145; Abu Nedal family and,
    92, 94–96; Abu Weehab family and, 63; All
    That's Left Collective confronting, 144;
    characteristics of, 13, 20, 89, 94; expansion of
    and encroachment by, 2, 12–13, 20–21, *33*, 38, 89,
    92, 94–95, 103, 107, 145; Masafer Yatta and,
    143–45; number of, 13, 20; *Ta'ayush* monitoring
    of, 84; violence by, 3, 9, 20–21, 38–39, 84, 94,
    103–5, 127, 143–45. *See also* settler-colonialism
Israel, State of, 30, 40; All That's Left Collective
    and, 144; citizenship of, 5–6, 8–9; civil
    administration of, 12, 20, 39, 65, 105;
    co-existence with, 128; courts and laws of, 63,
    65–67, 89, 107; economy of, 116; educational
    system of, 6, 135; establishment and
    recognition of, 6, 11–12, 14, 80, 143, 149n2;
    genocide accusation against, 13, 146, 149n4;
    international law and, 12, 20–21; *Ta'ayush* and,
    84; "unworked land" policy of, 89, 107. *See also*
    ethnic cleansing; IDF; Israeli settlements and
    settlers; land: confiscation of; military
    occupation (Israeli); violence: Israeli military
    and settler; water: control of; Zionism
Ivlev, Sheela, 139
Iwama, Michael K., 69, 72

Jadu'i (variety of watermelon), 120
JAI (Joint Advocacy Initiative), 36, 84–85, 150n1
    (chap. 2); farmers and, 41, 84, 104–5

Jewish people and communities: All That's Left
    Collective, 144; in Europe, 30, 149n5; Judaism
    and, 11, 71, 136; in Palestine (historic), 11, 149n2;
    Ta'ayush, 84. *See also* Israeli settlements and
    settlers; Israel, State of; Zionism
jihad (effort to confront oppression), 43, 108
Jolene (French artist), 2–3
Jordan: administration of West Bank by, 11–12, 38,
    63, 94, 104; border with West Bank, 2; refugee
    camps in, 102
Jordan Rift Valley, 11
Jordan Valley, 1
Journal of Occupational Science, 140
Judaism, 11, 71, 136

K18 (olive variety), 40
Kamal (Abu Kamal's son), 124
Kantartzis, Sarah, 54, 82
Karuk people, 51
Kerem Navot (Israeli NGO), 21, 150n1 (chap. 3)
Khalidi, Rashid, 11
Khalidi, Walid, 11
Kherbe (area), 39
kibbutzes, 118
Kimmerling, Baruch, 14
kinship, 75–76, 79. *See also* family, families;
    hamoula
knowledge, vernacular, 24–25
koushan el taboo (Turkish land registration), 39, 65
Kramer-Roy, Debbie, 117
Kremnitze, Mordechai, 97
Kronenberg, Frank, 7, 15, 32, 82, 88–89

Laliberte Rudman, Debbie, 16, 18–19
Lana (Abu Kamal's daughter), 124
land and property, 4, 6, 9, 45, 64–66, 88, 89, 100;
    access to, 13, 15, 20, 31, 38, 63, 84, 87–88, 106,
    126–27, 132, 145; ancestral, 54, 67, 72, 79, 94,
    125, 128; *'Awna* and connection to, 60–61,
    68–69, 71–74, 89, 131; confiscation of, 20–21,
    38, 41, 58, 63, 68, 80, 94–95, 98, 104, 106–7,
    116, 123, 126, 128; cultivation and working of,
    24, 31, 37, 39–40, 42–43, 45, 52, 55, 71, 73, 85,
    93, 95, 97, 105, 107–8, 113, 125, 127–28, 130, 143;
    defense and protection of, 42–43, 80, 84,
    97–98, 104, 107–8, 113–15, 121, 130–31,
    144–46; laws regarding, 20, 39, 41, 104, 107;
    Nakba and, 5, 12, 56, 128, 149n2; ownership of,
    37–39, 41, 61, 63–66, 93–94, 104, 107, 125,
    149n2; reclamation of, 22, 84, 100, 106, 115,

146; rights to, 63, 80, 84, 86, 98, 102, 106; Said on, 12, 22, 29–30, 55, 57–58; settler-colonialism and, 12–15, 19–20, 25, 38, 45, 54, 56, 58, 70, 74, 78, 97, 109–10, 116, 121, 128–30, 132; *Sumud* and connection to, 91–92, 95, 97–98, 100, 102, 104, 107–10, 115–17, 119, 121, 130; *Sutra* and connection to, 36, 43, 45, 50, 55, 58, 89, 130; symbolism of, 97–98, 128; Zionism and, 14, 25, 128, 149n5

Land Institute, The, 84

language, languages: Arabic, 6, 8, 35–36, 60–61, 71, 76, 91–92, 108, 123; English, 8, 16, 22, 54, 83, 137–38, 140; Hebrew, 6, 8, 25, 84, 87; Portuguese, 140; Spanish, 140; Turkish, 39

law and laws: British Mandate, 65, 104; English, 65; international, 12, 20–21; Israeli, 65–66, 89, 107; Ottoman, 39, 41, 65, 94, 104, 107. *See also* Human rights; ICJ

Leah (activist), 144

Lebanon, 55, 102

liminality, 6, 9, 22, 56–57, 58, 135

livelihood: *'Awna* and, 74; craft-making as, 112; farming as, 6, 41, 44–45, 56, 58, 80, 93, 96, 106, 108, 125, 128–30, 133, 144; fishing as, 113; forestry as, 113; from land, 4, 6, 24, 41, 44–45, 56, 58, 74, 80, 93, 96, 106, 108, 125, 128–30, 133, 144; milk production fas, 118–19; *Sutra* for, 36, 44–45, 56, 58, 130. *See also* sustenance; work

logic of elimination (Wolfe), 14

Ma 'ale Adumim (Israeli colony), 2

malban (grape delicacy), 42

Māori communities, 50, 72

marginalized communities, 7, 32–33, 86, 129; *'Awna* and, 59; decolonial ethnography and, 19; Epistemologies of the South and, 27; occupational justice for, 18, 70, 111; resistance by, 15, 19, 25, 27, 59, 82, 101, 111, 132, 134–37, 140–42. See also *fallahin*; Palestinians; refugees, Palestinian

Marmot, Michael, 17

marriage, marriages, 37–38, 76, 92–93

Marxism, 27, 56, 109

Masalha, Nur, 11, 12, 14, 71, 109, 149n5

Masafer Yatta, 143, 151n1 (postscript)

Maslow, Abraham H., 115–16

mastour (protected, dignified), 130. See also *Sutra*

McGareth, Margaret, 73

McGonagle, Helen, 73

McNeill, Hinematau N., 72

media: dominant narrative in, 6, 83, 86; social, 81, 97, 144–46; Western, 6

Mediterranean Sea, 11, 13, 61, 143

memory, 12, 17, 73, 99, 129; historical, 55; *Nakba* and, 56;

mental health, 17, 44, 47, 49, 111. *See also* health and well-being; trauma

methodology: decolonial ethnography as, 9, 19–22, 135; Epistemologies of the South and, 22, 27–30, 120, 135; ethnography, 6, 9, 19; intercultural translation, 9, 22, 28, 35, 60, 111, 131, 135; participant observation, 6–7; qualitative and quantitative, 56; reflexivity in, 135; research questions, 30–31

Mignolo, Walter D., 28–29, 136

military occupation (Israeli), 9, 11–13, 113; *'Awna* against, 60, 64, 87–89; civil administration of, 12, 20, 39, 65, 105; curfews under, 51, 118–20; Everyday Forms of Resistance against, 5, 97, 100, 119, 121, 130; house demolitions under, 13, 103, 145;; night raids, 126; settler-colonialism and, 5, 7, 14, 16, 19–20, 30, 74, 88–89, 91, 97, 100, 106, 109–10, 116, 119, 121, 128–30, 132, 141, 143–44; *Sumud* against, 32, 91, 97, 100, 102–3, 106–7, 109–10, 117, 119, 121, 130; *Sutra* against, 45, 130. *See also* IDF; Intifadas; movement restrictions; permits; settler-colonialism; violence: Israeli military and settler

milk production, as resistance, 118–20

mines, warning of, 1

minority groups: Christian, 81; ethnic, 27, 56, 81, 101, 111, 139; Palestinian in Israel, 6, 56, 102; religious, 111; sexual, 31, 111, 136

Molokhiya (staple food), 146

Molineux, Mathew, 54

Moneer (JAI coordinator), 2, 36

moral economy (Scott), 26

morality: *'Awna* as, 61, 130; Everyday Forms of Resistance and, 123, 131–32, 134; of family, 76, 78–79; of peasant, 24–26; rural, 25; *Sutra* and *Sumud* and, 130

more-than-human communities: *'Awna* and bond with, 60–61, 68, 71–73, 89, 131; *Sutra* and *Sumud* and, 131. *See also* animals and livestock; land and property; nature; olive trees

movement restrictions, 1–2, 100, 106; farmers and, 3–4, 15, 20, 31, 38–39, 61, 63, 84, 87, 89, 145. *See also* checkpoints; permits; roads; segregation wall

mukhtars (village chiefs), 79

Murad (activist), 144–45

Muriithi, Bernard A. K., 114–15, 120

Musawa (Palestinian women's rights organization), 78

Mustafa, Muhanad, 15

mutual aid: 'Awna as, 61, 68, 78, 129; Everyday Forms of Resistance and, 7, 129, 134. See also collaboration; solidarity

Nakba (1948 catastrophe), 5, 12, 63, 125, 149n2; fallahin and, 15, 56, 79, 125, 128; memory of, 12, 17, 56, 128

naming, names, 6, 25, 34, 76

narration and narratives, 6: of decolonization, 135; dominant, 83, 86, 110; of occupation, 114; Palestinian, 30, 55, 57, 83, 86, 98–99, 110, 117, 135; personal, 8, 98; of resistance, 98–99, 114, 117–19; of self-determination, 110; of victimhood, 29

national belonging, 79–82, 102, 117

nationalism, 14, 102, 149n5; critique of, 23, 86, 101–2

nation-state: critique of, 24, 27, 30, 101, 117, 138, 144; Palestinian aspiration for, 102–3. See also Israel, State of

native, natives, as term, 9, 149n2. See also fallahin; Palestinians

nature, 1, 25; harmony with, 51, 68–69, 70, 71–73, 89, 128; as non-human, 136; as other, 23–24. See also animals and livestock; extractivist imperialism

nebali (olive variety), 40

neoliberalism, 7, 103, 116; critique of, 38, 50–51, 80, 103. See also capitalism

New Testament, 1, 108

New Zealand, 13, 72, 128

NGOs (non-governmental organizations): international, 21, 63, 80, 83–87, 104–5, 108, 125, 127, 138, 143–44; Israeli, 21, 63, 84, 143–44; Palestinian, 21, 78, 80, 96, 98, 103, 107, 118, 120–21, 127, 145, 150n3 (chap. 4). See also activism, activists; grassroots organizing; solidarity; and names of individual NGOs

No Other Land (2024 film), 151n1 (postscript)

Norgaard, Kari Marie, 51, 113

North Africa, 62

Núñez Valderrama, Cristian M., 113

Occupation (occupational science concept): 'Awna and, 59–60, 68–71, 82, 87–89; critical perspectives on, 16, 19, 47, 53–55, 69–70, 111, 113–15, 137–42; decolonizing, 33, 70, 111, 121, 137–42; Everyday Forms of Resistance and, 129, 131–33; Indigenous conceptualizations of, 47, 50–51, 54, 72; meaningful, 8, 31, 99, 119, 129, 135, 137, 142; meanings of, 5, 9, 16, 46–47, 49, 54, 150n7; purpose of, 45–46, 49, 58, 114, 132–33; resistive, 45, 55, 89, 91, 97, 100, 111–15, 121, 129, 131–32; Sumud and, 91, 97, 99–100, 107, 111, 113–15, 117–19, 121; Sutra and, 35–36, 43, 45–46, 48–49, 53, 58; transactional nature of, 53–54, 57–58; "wicked problems" and, 113. See also doing-being-becoming-belonging; and various "occupational" entries below

occupational apartheid, 7, 32, 39, 60, 63–64, 97, 107, 110, 119, 121, 128, 143–44; 'Awna vs., 60, 87–89; defined, 7, 88; Everyday Forms of Resistance against, 129, 131–32; Sumud against, 97, 107, 110, 119, 121; Sutra against, 89. See also apartheid; military occupation (Israeli); segregation

occupational balance: Al-'afya and, 49–51, 129; defined, 48–49; occupational imbalance and, 48, 51–53; olive growing and, 48–51, 53, 58; Sutra and, 48–51, 53, 58. See also health and well-being

occupational consciousness, 56, 109, 129; Everyday Forms of Resistance and, 129, 132–33; of olive growers, 109–11, 121, 129, 132–33; Sutra-'Awna-Sumud as, 132

occupational domain (Dickie, Cutchin, Humphry), 53

occupational justice: Brazilian social occupational therapy and, 138; concept of, 5, 9, 17–18, 31; decolonizing of, 33, 70, 111, 121, 137–42; defined, 17; engagement with, 5, 9, 31, 33, 111, 121, 137, 142; Global South and, 18; Good Living and, 18; Palestinian contribution to, 58, 89, 121; "wicked problems" and, 113. See also human rights; social justice

occupational reconstructions (Frank and Muriithi), 114–15, 120–21

occupational science, 69–70, 111, 121, 137–42; critical turn in, 16, 19, 47, 53–54; decolonizing of, 33, 70; defined, 16; engagement with, 7, 9, 19, 33, 59, 133; Eurocentrism in, 16, 46, 139; journals of, 140; Sumud in, 91, 113–15; Sutra in, 35–36, 45–46, 48–49, 53, 58; transactional perspective in, 53–54, 57; "wicked problems" in, 113. See also doing-being-becoming-belonging; Occupation; and other "occupational" entries

Index

occupational therapy, 137–39; critical, 16, 19, 47; decolonizing of, 33; Eurocentrism in, 8, 16. *See also* Occupation; occupational science

October 7, 2023, events, 13, 143, 145

Old Testament, 149n5

olive culture, 5–11, 52, 58, 60, 64, 66, 89, 96–98, 100, 107–8, 114–16, 126–34; as daily activity, 31, 35, 40–45, 55, 88, 91, 95, 99–100, 104, 107, 123, 137, 142; economic aspects of, 21, 40, 44, 64, 93, 96, 106, 114; Israeli occupation and, 7, 11–12, 16, 19–21, 30–31, 38–39, 45, 63–66, 80, 87–89, 94–97, 103–7, 109–10, 119, 121, 123, 143–45; intergenerational aspect of, 73, 107; meanings of, 5, 9–10, 32, 36, 43–46, 49–50, 71–73, 89, 98, 113; resistance through, 4–5, 7, 9, 22, 32, 43, 45, 55, 64, 66, 68–71, 73–74, 78, 80, 84–89, 91, 95, 97–121, 123, 143–46; tasks involved in, 7, 9, 31, 40–42, 46, 61, 66, 71, 73, 75, 85, 87, 93, 95–96, 104–7, 143. *See also* agriculture and farming; fallahin; harvest, olive; land and property; *and "olive" entries below*

olive oil, 5, 9, 44; economic value of, 21, 40, 42, 67, 96; *jefet*, 42; pressing, 7, 31, 40, 42; uses of, 42–44, 61. *See also* olive culture; olives

olives: eating and pickling of, 9, 40, 43; gleaning of, 66–67, 81; varieties of, 40. *See also* harvest, olive; olive culture; olive oil; olive trees

olive trees, 45; ancient terraces for, *90*, 62, 80; byproducts of, 10, 44; destruction of, 2, 12, 21, 45, 84, 95, 103–5, 108, 115, 127; care for, 9, 41, 44–45, 64, 71, 93, 95, 98, 100, 106–7, 114, 130; cultivars of, 40; planting of, 7, 9, 21, 31, 41, 45, 64, 73, 84–85, 96–97, 100, 103–7, 114, 127–28, 130; *rumi*, 75; symbolism of, 5, 10, 43, 45, 64, 96–97, 102, 130; uprooting of, 25, 95, 103–4, 108, 115, *122*, 127. *See also* olive culture; olives

ontology: decolonial, 133–34, 137; Everyday Forms of Resistance as, 123, 131–34; of imperialism, 29; of olive growers, 131–33; Western, 27, 132

OPT. *See* Occupied Palestinian Territories

oral history, 140

Orientalism, 14, 57. *See also* other, othering; Said, Edward W.

Oslo Accords (1993), *10*, 12, 103

other, othering: decolonial critique of, 132, 136; epistemology of imperialism and, 23, 57; resistance to, 57, 86. *See also* Orientalism

Ottoman Empire and Turks: land laws and registration of, 39, 41, 65, 104, 107; Palestine and, 11, 78–79

PA (Palestinian National Authority), 12, 74, 84, 103, 107, 110, 116; farmers and, 38, 96

Palaestina Prima, 11

Palestine, history of, 5, 6, *10*, 15, 56, 62, 83; ancient, 61–62, 71, 75–76, 78; British Mandate in, 38, 65, 79, 102, 104, 121, 127; Oslo Accords and, 12, 103; Ottoman Empire and, 39, 41, 65, 79, 104, 107; post-1948 in, 12–13, 56, 102; Roman rule in, 11, 61, 75, 108; *Sumud* in, 102–4, 121; Zionism in, 14, 25, 128, 149n5. *See also* Intifadas; Military occupation (Israeli); *Nakba*; settler-colonialism

Palestinian Authority. *See* PA

"Palestinian condition," 55

Palestinian culture: *'Awna* in, 61, 68; family in, 75–79; food in, 40, 42, 61, 93, 96, 124, 146; hospitality in, 68, 83; music, poetry, and dance in, 61, 102; olive tree in, 5, 10, 43, 45, 64, 96–97, 102, 130; preservation of, 47, 73, 117, 119; *Sumud* in, 91–92, 98, 102, 117; *Sutra* in, 35–36; traditional life in, 72, 109. *See also* fallahin; heritage; tradition and traditional practices

Palestinian National Authority. *See* PA

Palestinians, 14, 17, 129–31, 145; *Al- 'afya* concept of, 32, 49–51, 53; *'Awna* concept of, 32, 59–90, 97, 117, 119, 121, 123, 125, 136, 144, 146; familism among, 76, 78–79; as minority in Israel, 6, 56, 102; Jewish, 11, 149n2; "othering" of, 23, 29–30, 57, 83, 86; traditional lifeways of, 72, 109. *See also* Bedouins; Christianity, Christians; fallahin; Islam and Muslims; Palestine, history of; Palestinian culture; peasants; refugees, Palestinian; women, Palestinian

Pappe, Ilan, 26

patriarchy: critique of, 15, 18, 22, 27, 47, 77–78, 111–12, 129; Palestinian women and, 77–78, 112. *See also* women

peace: graffiti for, 2; Oslo and, 12, 103

peasants, 25–26, 55, 77, 84, 99, 101, 117, 120, 123. *See also* fallahin

permits, 3–4, 15, 39, 145: for access to groves and land, 66, 95, 126; for travel and work, 92, 95, 126

perseverance. *See Sumud*

photography, as documentation and surveillance, 2, 65–66, 126, 143

PHSL (Palestine Heirloom Seed Library), 48, 74, 118, 120–21, 150n5

pine trees, 26, 61

pluriversality (Mignolo), 29, 135–37, 142. *See also* decolonization; Epistemologies of the South

poetry, Palestinian, 61, 102

politicide (Kimmerling), 14. *See also* genocide; settler-colonialism

Pollard, Nick, 89

positionality, 5–6, 8–9, 22, 129, 142; of Global South scholars, 18–19, 27, 135–41; of journal editorial boards, 141; of researchers, 19, 135, 140–41

postcolonialism: critique of, 19, 109–10; studies, 19, 57, 81, 109; theories, 16, 19, 109. *See also* decolonization

poverty, 67, 85, 86, 125, 138

power: colonial, 14, 23–25, 27–29, 86, 135–36; dynamics of, 18, 56, 86, 109, 132, 138, 141; of elite, 24, 103, 139, 141–42; of oppressors, 101, 104; redistribution of, 135, 138, 141; of state, 24, 30, 76, 84, 101–4, 117, 138, 144

praxis, 6, 135; decolonial, 19, 135, 137–38, 141–42; Epistemologies of the South and, 27–28, 134–35, 137, 141–42; Everyday Forms of Resistance as, 5, 123, 131–34; of olive growers, 7, 19, 25, 131–34; vernacular, 25

press, olive, 7, 9, 31, 40, 42, 44

prisons, prisoners (Palestinian), 12, 93

protection: *'Awna* for, 62, 74, 81; of children, 62, 143; of land, 4, 42–43, 45, 64–66, 80, 84, 88–89, 97–98, 104, 107–8, 113–15, 121, 130–31, 144–46; *Sutra* for, 32, 35–36, 42, 44–45, 48, 58, 130–31

Puar, Jasbir, 7

public health, 16–17

pumpkins, 124

qareeb (kin), 79

Qumsiyeh, Mazin B., 12, 15, 45, 83, 94, 108; on popular resistance, 101, 104, 112, 120

Race and racism: anti-racism and, 139–40; critique of, 13, 23, 86, 88, 100–101, 111, 135, 139–40; racial exclusivity and, 14; racial identity and, 139; segregation based on, 13, 88, 109–10, 112. *See also* apartheid; ethnic cleansing; other, othering

Ramadan, 143–44

Ramugondo, Elelwani L., 109–10

RCOT (Royal College of Occupational Therapists), 139

reciprocity, 18, 69

reflexivity, 135

refugee camps, 126; Al-Reyad, 124–25; conditions in, 55, 67, 79–80, 93–94, 102; Dheisha, 80; education in, 56; music and art in, 126; origins of, 12, 55, 79, 94, 102, 125; *Sumud* in, 102. *See also* refugees, Palestinian

refugees, Palestinian, 55, 56, 80, 102, 104, 134; displacement of, 12, 79, 94, 125, 138, 141; *Nakba* and, 5, 12. See also *Nakba*; refugee camps

religion and religious beliefs, 11, 71, 78, 81; Bedouin, 3; Islamic, 36; in Palestinian life, 17, 73; religious freedom and, 20; religious identity and, 30. *See also* Christianity, Christians; Islam and Muslims; Judaism; spirituality

resistance: agri-resistance, 78, 120; bees as, 4; civil disobedience, 12, 119–20; cows of Beit Sahour as, 118–20; honey of, 1, 4; land reclamation as, 22, 64, 66, 84, 100, 106, 115, 146; milk production as, 118–20; nonviolent, 113; olive growing as, 4–5, 7, 9, 22, 32, 42–45, 55, 58, 60, 64, 66–71, 73–74, 78, 80, 84–91, 95, 97–121, 123, 128–34, 143–46; Ongoing Daily Resistance, 143–46; seed saving as, 120–21; "small acts of living," 100; tax boycotts as, 120. *See also* activism, activists; decolonization; Everyday Forms of Resistance; Intifadas; *Sumud*

revenge, code of, 78

Rijke, Alexandra, 98, 102–3, 117

Road 60 (Israeli settler road), 3

roads: access to, 1, 3, 63, 92, 100, 106, 124, 127, 144–45; bypass, 92, 126; construction of, 21, 89, 94, 126; dirt, 37, 87, 124, 127; Israeli-only, 4, 21, 89, 94; patrol, 1. *See also* movement restrictions

Rosenfeld, Maya, 56, 80

roujouleya (manhood), 79

"roundabout of death" (Al-Raha), 38

rumi (Roman) trees, 75

sacrifice, *Sumud* and, 108, 121

Sager, Yousef, 146

Said, Edward W., 19, 55, 86, 116–17; on epistemology of imperialism, 22–23, 28; on "new universality," 22; on Palestine and Palestinians, 30, 55, 57–58, 83; on *Sumud*, 57, 91, 99–101; on "worldliness," 29–30, 86

Sakellariou, Dikaios, 89

Salem (construction worker), 3–4

samada (Arabic root for Sumud), 92

samidin (steadfast ones), 98. *See also* Sumud

Sansour, Vivien, 77–78, 97, 110, 116, 118; PHSL and, 118, 120–21

Santos, Boaventura de Sousa, 24, 138; on epistemicide, 27, 132; on Epistemologies of the

Index

173

South, 27–32, 116, 120, 132; on sociology of emergence, 29

sarha (walking in field to gather food), 77

sater (protector), 36, 130. See also *Sutra*

Sayigh, Rosemary, 6, 55–56, 75–78, 79, 80, 84

scholarship, scholars: Arab, 55; Brazilian, 137–38; decolonial, 18–19, 22, 29, 31, 111, 121, 134–42; Indigenous, 134, 140; Israeli, 14, 55–56; Native American, 22; Zionist, 25. *See also* academia; *and names of specific scholars*

Scott, James C.: on everyday resistance, 26, 100–2, 120; on vernacular knowledge, 24–26, 150n9

seeds and seed libraries, 48, 74, 78, 118, 120–21, 146

segregation, 12, 46, 88, 109–12; ethnic and racial, 6–7, 11, 13, 15, 20; gender, 77; land, 15, 20, 45–46, 58, 80, 116. *See also* apartheid; occupational apartheid; movement restrictions; segregation wall

segregation wall, 2, *4*; Abu Nedal family and, 92; Al-Baydar and, 63, 67; construction and legality of, 12, 21, 63, 67, 89, 103; graffiti on, 2, 102; impact of, 4, 12, 21, 63, 67, 89, 92, 103. *See also* apartheid; movement restrictions; segregation

seha (Arabic for health), 49

self-care, 16, 46, 133, 136

self-confidence, 25, 44, 130

self-determination, 32, 43, 58, 101–2, 104, 108–13, 119, 121; *'Awna* and, 74; collective, 91, 97, 116–17, 129, 131–34; denial of, 6, 12, 14, 20; Everyday Forms of Resistance and, 5, 26, 89, 91, 97, 115–17, 121, 129, 131–34; hope for, 97, 100, 108, 117, 128–29, 146; individual, 6, 14, 24, 26; Maslow on, 115–16; *Sumud* for, 91, 97, 100–101, 115–17; *Sutra* for, 58. *See also* freedom, freedoms; sovereignty

self-reliance, 44, 45; of fallahi, 15, 56; promotion of, 84, 103

settler-colonialism, 5, 7, 9, 13–15, 30, 45, 70, 74, 97, 101, 109–13, 116, 121, 128–32; *'Awna* against, 60, 82, 87; critique of, 19–20, 22, 25, 38, 54–58, 78, 82, 86–89, 116, 132, 134, 141, 144; Indigenous communities and, 20, 25, 38, 54, 56, 78, 88–89; nature of, 19, 55, 57, 144; Zionism as, 25, 149n5. *See also* colonialism; Israeli settlements and settlers; military occupation (Israeli); resistance

settlers, Israeli. *See* Israeli settlements and settlers

Shakir (IDF commander), 105

shame, 51–52

shantytowns, 109, 124

Shehadeh, Raja, 98–99, 103

Sheehi, Lara, 113

Sheehi, Stephen, 113

sheep and shepherds, 1, 7, 41, 126; daily life of, 4, 106, 124, 143–45, 150n1 (chap. 3)

Shetty, Raviraj, 113

Shomali, Amer, 118

Sinai Peninsula, 12

sit-ins, 114–15, 120

slavery, 72

Smith, Linda Tuhiwai, 135–36

soap, olive-based, 10, 40, 44

social conditions, 55, 83, 86, 135–42; in Palestine, 5–7, 11–21, 30–31, 38–39, 45, 51, 56–60, 63–66, 74, 79–82, 87–89, 91–123, 126–34, 141–46; global, 23–24, 27–30, 101, 111, 116, 132. *See also* military occupation (Israeli); settler-colonialism

social justice, 5, 18, 19, 31, 33, 85, 111; cognitive justice as, 27–28; concept of, 9, 17–18; decolonization and, 134–35, 137, 141–42; Epistemologies of the South and, 27–28. *See also* human rights; occupational justice

social media, 81, 97, 144–46

social movements: anti-apartheid, 103, 114; Black Lives Matter, 138, 141; civil rights, 114; decolonial, 135, 137–38, 141–42; Epistemologies of the South and, 27; refugee solidarity and, 141; women's, 93, 103, 112, 119. *See also* activism, activists

social occupational therapy (Brazilian), 137–38

social support: *'Awna* as, 61, 68–69, 73–87; importance of, 17, 69; networks of, 138; *Sutra* as, 44. *See also* collaboration; solidarity

sociology, 140–41; decolonizing, 33, 137; of Palestinians, 56. *See also* scholarship, scholars

sociopolitical awareness, 109–11, 121; *'Awna* and, 131; Everyday Forms of Resistance and, 129, 131–32; of olive growers, 107, 129; *Sumud* and, 91, 107; *Sutra* and, 131. *See also* occupational consciousness

Sokot (Jewish holiday), 1

solidarity, 68–69, 75–76, 112, 117, 119, 125, 129–31; *'Awna* as, 32, 61, 73–87; with Bedouins, 3; between communities, 18, 57, 73–87, 134, 138, 142, 144; family, 37–38, 40, 42, 75–79; global, 18, 83–87, 104, 110, 118, 130–32, 134, 138–44; of *hamoula*, 79; of Israeli activists, 84, 143–44; local and national, 79–82, 102; mutual aid as, 7, 78, 134; olive growing and, 38, 42, 61, 73–87, 143–44; *Sumud* and, 104; *Sutra* and, 130–31;

solidarity (*cont.*)

   village, 79–82, 102. *See also* coagency; collaboration; international collaboration and solidarity; mutual aid

Soor (village), 37

South Africa, 13; apartheid in, 88–89, 103, 112, 114–15; Black communities in, 109–10; collective occupations in, 15, 82; Ubuntu in, 69, 82, 110, 116, 136

South America, 15, 81, 125; occupational therapy in, 88, 111, 137–38

Southeast Asia, 15, 25–26

sovereignty, 5–6, 30, 51, 119, 121. *See also* freedom; freedoms; self-determination

Spanish language, 140

spirituality, 49–50, 71–73; *'Awna* and, 71, 73; *Al-'afya* and, 49; of land connection, 45, 50; Māori, 72; olive growing and, 5, 10, 36, 43–47, 58, 89, 98, 113, 128–33; premonotheistic and pagan, 71, 78; *Sumud* and, 98; *Sutra* and, 36, 44–45, 58. *See also* religion and religious beliefs

standardization, 24–25

steadfastness. See *Sumud*

strawberries, 146

stress, 17

Sultan (Abu Kamal's son), 124

Sumud (صمود) (Palestinian concept of steadfastness and resistance), 32, 91–122, 144, 146; Abu Nedal family and, 91–97, 99, 107–8; agri-resistance as, 78, 120; as belonging for becoming, 91, 97, 115–17, 121; characteristics of, 107–11, 121; cows of Beit Sahour as, 118–20; daily acts of, 78, 91, 97–100, 102, 104–8, 111–15, 117–21; defined, 91–92, 98–100; Everyday Forms of Resistance and, 97, 121, 123, 129–32, 136, 146; historical development of, 102–4, 121; hope and, 99, 108, 113, 117, 121; individual and collective, 97; Intifadas and, 103; olive growing as, 91, 95, 97, 99–100, 104, 107–8, 114–15, 121, 130; Said on, 55, 57, 91, 99–101, 116–17; seed saving as, 120–21; Shehadeh on, 98–99, 103; *Sutra-'Awna-Sumud* synthesis and, 59, 89, 97, 121, 123, 129–32, 136. *See also* becoming; resistance

suri (olive variety), 40

survival, 32, 55, 58, 121; *'Awna* for, 69; Everyday Forms of Resistance for, 5, 26, 111, 129; olive growing for, 35–36, 43–45, 68, 81, 89, 96–98, 107–8, 128–31, 133, 144; of peasants, 24, 26; *Sumud* for, 91–92, 97–98, 107–8, 144; *Sutra*

for, 35–36, 43–45, 130. *See also* livelihood; sustenance

sustenance: *'Awna* for, 74, 78; olive growing for, 5, 32, 35–36, 43–45, 55, 58, 96, 129–31; *Sumud* for, 98; *Sutra* for, 32, 35–36, 43–45, 55, 58, 130. *See also* livelihood; survival

Sutra (سترة) (Palestinian concept of doing for well-being), 32, 35–59, 144, 146; Abu 'Attallah family and, 32, 35–43, 45, 97, 108, 129; *Al-'afya* and, 49–51, 53, 58; defined, 35–36, 43–44, 58, 130; as doing for well-being, 35, 43–44, 48–51, 89, 129; Everyday Forms of Resistance and, 123, 129–32, 136; meanings of (protection, dignity, sustenance), 36, 43–45, 130; nonbinary human-environment relationship in, 53–58; occupational balance and, 48–51, 53; *Sutra-'Awna-Sumud* synthesis, 32, 58–59, 89, 97, 123, 129–32, 136. *See also* doing and being; health and well-being; protection; sustenance

symbolism: of bees, 4; of land, 97–98, 128; of olive tree, 5, 10, 43–45, 64, 96–97, 102, 130

Ta'ayush (coexistence organization), 84

tanzim (organization), 97

Tartir, Alaa, 110, 116

tasyeef (gleaning), 66–67, 81

tax boycotts, 120

Teeffelen, Toine van, 98, 102–3, 117

Tourism and tourist attractions, 21

trade unions, 103, 112

tradition and traditional practices, 75–76, 79; *'Awna* as, 61, 68–69, 73–87; *dabke*, 61; *Faz3a*, 145; food preparation, 40, 42, 61, 93, 124, 146; gleaning, 66–67, 81; healing, 10, 49; hospitality, 68, 83; maternal roles of, 76–77; medicine, 10, 44, 46; mutual aid, 7, 68, 78, 129, 134; oral history, 140; of peasants, 25–26, 55, 120; renewal of, 109; seed saving, 48, 74, 78, 118, 120–21, 146; *Sumud* as, 91–92, 98, 102, 117; *Sutra* as, 35–36; threats to, 74–75, 109, 121; vernacular knowledge, 24–25; ways of living, 72, 109, 111, 134, 142, 144. *See also* agriculture and farming; fallahin; heritage; land and property; olive culture

transactional relationship (occupation-place-person), 54–55, 57–58

trauma, 17; from violence, 39, 98, 100, 143, 145. See also *Nakba*

trees: almond, 3, 96, 105, 127; apple, 39–41, 64, 105; destruction of, 12, 21, 45, 84, 95, 103–5, 108, 115,

Index

122, 126–27, 146; fig, 96, 124–25, 130; fruit, 3, 37, 41, 48, 61, 64, 67, 73, 96, 105, 107, 120, 124–25, 127, 130, 146; love for, 71, 131; pine, 26, 61; pruning of, 9, 37, 41–42, 44, 71, 75, 124. *See also* more-than-human communities; *and "olive" entries*

Tuck, Eve, 22, 135

Turʿan (village), 6, 144

turf-cutting (Ireland), 47, 49, 73, 113

Turkey, Turks. *See* Ottoman Empire and Turks

Turkish Taboo registration (land), 39, 65

Ubuntu (African ethic), 69, 82, 110, 116, 136

UN (United Nations), *10*, 13, 15, 20–21, 39, 63, 66–67, 80, 106, 125, 138. *See also* UNESCO; UNHRC; UNOCHAOPt

"Unconference," 139

unemployment, 17, 46, 125

UNESCO (UN Educational, Scientific and Cultural Organization), 63, 66–67, 80, 145

UNHRC (UN Human Rights Commission), 15, 20–21

uniformity, utopian image of (Scott), 24

United Kingdom, 5–6, 8–9, 139

United Nations. *See* UN; *and acronyms of* UN *agencies*

United States: activists from, 144; civil rights movement in, 114; decolonizing and Disrupt OT movement in, 139; Indigenous communities in, 18–19, 47, 51, 54, 111, 113; settler-colonialism in, 13, 15; settlers from, 39; sit-ins in, 115

universality and universalism, 135–37, 142; critique of, 18, 22, 28, 70, 116, 138; pluriversality vs., 29, 86; Said's "new," 22, 29–30

universities, 8, 120; students of, 52, 120, 124, 130, 138. *See also* academia; education; scholarship; scholars

UNOCHAOPt (UN Office for the Coordination of Humanitarian Affairs in the oPt), *10*, 21

uprooted olive groves, *122*, 25, 95, 103–4, 108, 115, 127

vegetables: cucumbers, 120; Molokhiya, 146; pumpkins, 124; growing of, 1, 38, 42, 48, 62, 93, 95–96, 107, 146

vernacular knowledge and practices, 24–25

victimhood, 29, 56

violence, 9, 112, 132; against animals, 144; domestic abuse, 100; ethnic cleansing as, 12–13, 26, 55, 94, 144; gender-based, 78; Intifadas and, 12, 51, 93,

103, 118–20; Israeli military and settler, 3, 11–13, 20–21, 38–40, 45–46, 52, 63–64, 84–85, 87–88, 94–95, 98, 100, 103–6, 108, 118–19, 126–27, 129, 143–45; *Nakba* as, 5, 12, 56; settler-colonialism as, 5, 7, 9, 13–14, 16, 19–20, 22, 25, 30, 38, 45, 54–58, 70, 74, 78, 82, 86–89, 97, 101, 109–11, 113, 116, 119, 121, 128–30; structural, 87, 129; war and, 11–13, 36, 46, 92, 102, 139, 144. *See also* resistance

volunteers, 38, 84, 127, 130, 143–44; international, 2, 63, 80, 83–87, 104–5, 108, 125; JAI, 36, 41, 104–5; local, 40, 80–81, 96, 107

Wade, Allan, 100, 119

wadis (valleys), 42, 61, 67, 92; Al-Akhdar, 123–24, 126–27; Alnar, 2; Al-Raha, 33, 36–39; Dayr Aban, 125, 128

war: 1967, 11–12, 45; daily life impacted by, 46, 92; on Gaza (2014; 2023–), 13, 36, 144, 146; Lebanese civil, 102; resistance in, 92, 102, 139. *See also* military occupation (Israeli); *Nakba*; violence

water, 38, 62, 80, 120–21; control of, 13, 20, 89, 96, 106, 125–28, 135, 144; irrigation, 41, 45, 62, 73; rain-, 41, 71–72, 106; springs, 73, 87, 94; wells, 106, 144

wealth, 5

West Bank, *10*, 11–12, 103; Abu Kamal family in, 123–24, 126–27; Abu Nedal family in, 92, 95–96; Abu Weehab family in, 62, 64, 66; agricultural situation in, 21, 38, 63, 80, 89, 94–96, 103–7, 109–10, 116, 121, 123–24, 126–27; displacement from, 13, 143; fieldwork in, 1–2, 6, 9, 21, 31, 46–47, 51, 53, 70, 74, 77, 90, 102, 106, 121, 144; history of, 38, 45, 63, 94, 103–4; Jordanian administration of, 2, 38, 63, 94, 104; water resources in, 13, 128. *See also* checkpoints; Green Line; Israeli settlements and settlers; land and property; military occupation (Israeli); olive culture; oPt; PA; roads; segregation wall; *and specific West Bank locations*

Western thought, 14, 27–29, 53–55, 58, 69–70, 115–16, 132, 134–42; critique of, 6, 8–9, 16, 19, 22–30, 45–47, 50, 85–87, 89, 101, 110, 120, 129; dualism in, 23, 58; epistemology of imperialism (Said) and, 22–23; Global South influenced by, 6, 8, 24–25, 85, 101, 110; individualism in, 6, 8–9, 19, 46–47, 58, 91, 129; on well-being, 16, 48–49, 129. *See also* Europe; Eurocentrism; Global North; Occupation

Whalley Hammell, Karen, 46–47, 49; on
belonging, 69–70, 73, 82
wheat, 42, 127
Wilcock, Ann A., 45–46, 69–70, 115
Wilson, Linda H., 50
Wolfe, Patrick, 13–14
women, 76–77, 112; Bedouin, 3; Black, 29;
Brazilian, 138; education of, 62; honor killings
of, 78; Indigenous, 47; LGBTQ+, 78;
marginalized, 27, 101; peasant, 26; social roles
of, 76–78, 103, 118–19, 124; South African, 112.
See also women, Palestinian
women, Palestinian, 76–77, 103, 112, 118, 124;
activism of, 93, 103, 119; craft production by, 47;
education of, 62; honor killings of, 78
work, workers, 6, 16, 48, 62, 93, 95, 106, 113;
construction, 3, 51, 93, 95; domestic, 76–77, 111;
embroidery, 112; engineering, 62; factory, 24,
66; migrant, 112; office, 24; paid, 46, 50, 85;

printing, 38; professional, 80, 110, 124, 126;
rebellions of, 101; rights of, 106; teaching, 104,
109, 120, 145; trade unions and, 103, 112; wages
and, 4, 15, 56, 85, 93, 106, 129. *See also*
agriculture and farming; fallahin; Occupation;
olive culture; peasants
work-life balance, 50. *See also* health and
well-being; occupational balance

Yish Din (Israeli human rights organization), 21

za 'tar (wild thyme), 61, 96
Zapatistas, 136
Zayyad, Tawfiq, 102
Zionism, 14, 25, 128, 149n5; militias and, 63, 94,
125; myths of, 14. *See also* settler-colonialism;
Israel, State of
Zureik, Elia, 56–57, 81–82, 86
Zurayk, Constantine, 12

www.ingramcontent.com/pod-product-compliance
Lightning Source LLC
Chambersburg PA
CBHW020935230426
43666CB00008B/1683